ECONOMICS OF THE OCEANS

D0145374

It is an unfortunate truth that our oceans offer valuable resources that are too often used unsustainably. Time and again this is due to the failure of international law to provide a framework for adequate governance. *Economics of the Oceans* examines this issue and provides a comprehensive study of ocean uses from the perspectives of law and economics.

Themes covered in the book include ocean governance, the economics of oceanic resource exploitation, offshore oil, coral reefs, shipwrecks and maritime piracy. Analytical techniques such as basic game theory, environmental economics of the commons, and cost–benefit analysis are employed to illuminate the topics.

This book will also be of interest to students of environmental economics and natural resource management.

Paul Hallwood is Professor of Economics at the University of Connecticut, USA.

ECONOMICS OF THE OCEANS

Rights, rents and resources

Paul Hallwood

Routledge
Taylor & Francis Group

LONDON AND NEW YORK

First published 2014
by Routledge
2 Park Square, Milton Park, Abingdon, Oxon OX14 4RN

and by Routledge
711 Third Avenue, New York, NY 10017

Routledge is an imprint of the Taylor & Francis Group, an informa business

© 2014 Paul Hallwood

The right of Paul Hallwood to be identified as author of this work has been
asserted by him in accordance with the Copyright, Designs and Patent Act
1988.

British Library Cataloguing in Publication Data

A catalogue record for this book is available from the British Library

Library of Congress Cataloging-in-Publication Data

A catalog record for this book has been requested

ISBN: 978-0-415-63909-5 (hbk)
ISBN: 978-0-415-63911-8 (pbk)
ISBN: 978-0-203-08361-1 (ebk)

Typeset in ApexBembo
by Apex CoVantage, LLC

Printed and bound in the United States of America by
Edwards Brothers Malloy on sustainably sourced paper.

This book is dedicated to my wife Barbara and my three children, Sarah, Alexander and Philip.

On the surface of the blue-green planet people have fought over the green bits for ages. However, because they didn't seem worth fighting over, they hardly bothered with the blue bits. Strange as it might seem, the green bits are mainly well tended, while the blue bits are in awful disrepair. Why is this? Let's see if we can find out.

—Lyme, Connecticut, June 30th, 2013

CONTENTS

PART VIII
Pollution   **215**

PART IX
Minerals   **231**

ILLUSTRATIONS

Figures

Tables

Boxes

PREFACE

Economics of the Oceans uses the discipline of economics to examine various issues relating to the use of ocean resources. I examine whether "Law of the Sea" treaty obligations, ratified by many countries and coming into force in 1994, are proving effective in improving the use of ocean resources. Sadly, there is not much evidence so far that enlightened cooperative interest is carrying the day. Over-fishing and severely depleted fish stocks are a worldwide phenomenon. International relations specialists describe an anarchic world where countries agree only to those international laws they want to acknowledge. Over-exploitation of many ocean resources is a good illustration of this anarchy. Even in the exclusive economic zones, where national writ could be made to be effective, so often it is not.

As there is more to the oceans than fish, a little more than one-half of this book is about non-fishery issues such as the economics of maritime piracy, the law and economics of historic shipwrecks, the setting of maritime boundaries, marine pollution, whaling, the nature of international public law as it relates to the oceans, and the recovery of offshore oil from the continental shelf and metals from the deep ocean.

I examine, specifically, what the objectives are of the nation-states both internally and between themselves. What constraints do they face? How can either the objectives or the constraints be modified to create a superior legal and economic environment governing use of ocean resources?

The "rents" of the subtitle ("*Rights, rents and resources*") are the economic rents – akin to "profits" – that could be garnered from well-managed ocean living and non-living resources.

One of the paradoxes I find is that the large energy corporations in the business of offshore oil, with plenty of money to spend on lobbyists, are well regulated and share significant amounts of the economic rents they make with their respective governments. The much smaller fishing concerns and individuals are the ones who often run amok with resulting over-fishing and low or non-existent economic rents.

The "rights" addressed in the subtitle are the rights to access ocean resources. At one extreme is the right of open-access to common pool ocean resources, especially fisheries. At the other is the existence of property rights, as with individual fishing quotas, licensed offshore oil lease blocks, and deep sea tenured mining leases. The issue of "rights" also addresses the question of who can share in the bounty of the ocean and what economic rent it can provide with careful exploitation.

In the early days, when the *Law of the Sea* was being negotiated, developing countries pressed the concept of the "common heritage of mankind", under which all countries would share in the oceans' bounty. As it turned out, ocean boundaries, the exclusive economic zones, were agreed and coastal states get to keep the economic rents, assuming that there are any of course. The *common heritage* doctrine does though apply in one area – an area that perhaps one day could become extremely profitable – and that is deep sea mining beyond any exclusive economic zone. One of the responsibilities of the International Seabed Authority is to design a fiscal system for the sharing of economic rents with commercial ventures and to pass them on to UN members. So far progress is slow and is bound to be controversial.

If I was to pick just one of the many issues that excite me I would have to choose the question broached in Chapter 13: "Why do countries sign treaties even though they know the agreements will be ineffective in practice?" Many of the chapters contribute to answering this puzzle, and I do come up with suggestions.

PART I

Introduction

1

OCEAN RESOURCES, OCEAN GOVERNANCE

Economics of the Oceans: Rights, rents and resources studies the economic uses of ocean resources, rights to exploit them, and the division of surpluses (or economic rents) between the users and the "owners" of ocean space. But who owns the oceans? The answer is that within agreed exclusive economic zones coastal states have sovereign rights where national laws apply; beyond, lies the two-thirds of the oceans called the "high seas", where loose and often ineffective international public law applies.

Until the end of the Second World War the oceans were *tabula rasa*. What international law did exist – for example, over the width of the territorial sea, freedom to fish, and freedom of navigation – was customary international law, itself a voluntary regime that independent countries could choose to obey or not. Much of this book is about the need for and progress of attempts to bring ocean resources under effective international law that promotes the rational economic use of ocean resources. As we will see, this progress is limited.

Economic theory is used to assess existing regimes governing the use of these resources. Two broad questions are investigated: are existing governance regimes economically rational in making best use of ocean resources? And, how are economic rents – approximately the profits – distributed between producers such as the fishing industry or offshore oil companies on the one side, and the sovereign owners of the submerged lands on the other?

In this book simple game theory is used to analyze governance regime formation and operation.[1] Environmental economics is used to analyze issues arising from the oceans as a commons. Theories of industrial organization are used in the analysis of some ocean industries; a "law and economics" framework is used to analyze laws governing the recovery of economic values from historic shipwrecks. Benefit–cost analysis is used in the analysis of issues such as the drawing of marine boundaries ("lines in the sea") and the formation of joint development zones. Theories drawn from auction theory will be used in the analysis of offshore lease block sales and economic rent sharing. Standard fisheries economics is used to analyze fisheries regimes, and spatial economics is applied to assess the design of marine protected areas. Policing the oceans against maritime pirates is discussed in a public goods framework in which free riding and under-enforcement is a problem.

1 Resources

Ocean resources are diverse. There are economically and ecologically valuable fisheries as well as marine mammals (whales, seals, dolphins and walrus) and sea birds. Coastal and estuarine wetlands are vital as fish hatcheries. Offshore oil deposits are at the present time the most valuable ocean resource measured by dollar value of annual production. Some other mineral resources are polymetallic nodules widely scattered across the bed of the oceans. Wind farms for the generation of electricity are often situated on the continental shelf. Of course, the surface of the ocean is used by shipping. As in some places pirates attack ships, international cooperation against piracy at sea has been organized. The ocean beds also carry submarine cables and pipelines that are also organized under legal rules. Of special interest are historic shipwrecks, often surprisingly well-preserved "time capsules" of history. Then there is the matter of the use of the oceans as a dump for pollution – by ship and from land by point sources such as sewerage plants, and non-point sources such as agricultural nitrogen runoff.

2 Regulating use of the oceans

Overuse of ocean resources – especially over-fishing, the hunting of marine mammals, and pollution – is at the forefront of concerns for managing the global commons for sustainability and the long-run benefit of mankind.

A first step in the management of ocean resources was the enclosure of the oceans, which in modern times began with President Truman claiming the USA's continental shelf and water column above it for the exclusive use of the USA. This set off a wave in the 1950s and later years of other coastal nations making claims to their own continental shelves. These claims were formalized in the *Law of the Sea*, which was ratified and came into force in 1994. Today, about one-third of the oceans are "nationalized", being contained in exclusive economic zones (EEZs). The other two-thirds are "high seas", but the most valuable ocean resources – fish and minerals – are today included in the EEZs (deep-sea polymetallic nodules are an exception) and are at least open to management under national jurisdiction. Management of high seas resources has to be through international agreement.

Management institutions include marine parks (or "marine protected areas") often centered over coral reefs and other high biological value ocean substrata. There is quite well-developed international regulation of pollution from ships on the high seas. Some countries have well-developed effective systems of fisheries regulation in their own waters. The USA largely does not, and is flirting with destroying some of its fisheries; similarly, with the European Union, where 88 percent of fish stocks are over-fished, fishing quotas are often ignored, and fishing fleets are far too large, operating only with government subsidies.[2] International management of fisheries on the high seas exists, but is largely ineffective due to problems with fishing by non-signatories, non-agreement to critical treaty clauses by some signatories, and wastefully large fish by-catches – fish caught but thrown back, usually dead.

While effective management of ocean resources aimed at sustainability is desirable, development of effective management institutions is proving to be difficult. A major problem is that restricting use imposes costs on some people while creating benefits for others. This is the issue of dividing economic rents. If there are to be fewer fishermen some will have to leave the industry, while those that stay on will benefit as fish stocks recover. Moreover, even if agreement within a fishery can be reached there is also the issue of sharing benefits between fishers and governments – the effective owners of submerged lands within the EEZs. Should, for example, the right to access a fishery be paid for, as is the case with access to offshore oil exploration? On the high seas, agreement over exploitation of living ocean resources is proving just as hard to reach; national self-interest in sharing the oceans' bounty is to the fore.

Another problem is impatience – if only fishing effort was to be reduced for just a few years many fish stocks would recover, but fishers are just too impatient to wait for what would be easier fishing days from recovered fish stocks.

As it is, worldwide over exploitation of fisheries is rife, with, on best estimates, for prime fish stocks such as cod and tuna, the oceans today supporting stocks of only 10 percent or less of what they supported shortly after World War II.

3   Ocean governance

There are four different high seas governance regimes – all of them examples of international public law:

1   Freedom of the high seas – *res communis* (something that belongs to a group of people and cannot be preempted by anyone) – effectively open access for navigation and fishing. This is customary international law – discussed in Section 4. The source of this is usually stated by legal scholars, such as Hugo Grotius in his book *The Freedom of the High Seas* (1604). He is taken as asserting that the high

seas could not be occupied and that marine resources could not be exhausted.[3] However, from the early nineteenth century *res communis* became qualified by specific international arrangements. The British banned the trans-Atlantic slave trade in 1807, so interfering with navigation, and was supported in this by Portugal and Spain. *The International Convention for the Protection of Submarine Cables* (1884) adopted the law of first possession of the sea bed, providing for both civil and criminal penalties; and the *Fur Seal Arbitration* of 1893 was based on "reasonable use" of marine resources.

2 Enclosure of ocean space by coastal states – as far out as 200 miles, or the width of the continental shelf to 350 miles. This allows coastal state governance in their exclusive economic zones (EEZs). Here they have sovereign rights. Enclosure has narrowed the geographic scope of the high seas for legal purposes, but international disputes over exactly where the "lines in the sea" should be drawn arise from time to time – for example in 2013 in the East China Sea between China and Japan over the islands known as Diaoyu in China and Senkakun in Japan.

3 Management of the high seas under the *common heritage of mankind* doctrine, whereby governance is through an international organization such as the United Nations and benefits are shared between countries. Prior to the signing of the *United Nations Convention on the Law of the Sea* in 1982, many developing countries and landlocked countries favored the *common heritage* concept, as it was thought to allow them larger shares of the oceans' bounty. However, this regime exists for only one high seas resource – polymetallic nodules under the 1994 *Agreement Relating to the Implementation of Part XI* of UNCLOS – see Chapter 23.

4 Governance in the "common interest of the international community" (Vicuna, 1999, p. 10) – a concept that incorporates the idea of "regulated high seas freedoms" and "reasonable use". Common interest trumps individual interest. At issue is how to implement governance in the name of "common interest" when there are so many cross-currents. Countries often have different ideas of what constitutes the common interest: should the objective be maximum sustainable yield from existing but depleted fish stocks, or should the objective be to allow fish stocks to re-attain those historical levels? Should the "common interest" be defined in terms of fisheries management or more broadly as environmental or ecosystem management? Reaching agreement is difficult when potential solutions create losers (e.g. countries that must restrain their fishing or whaling efforts) as well as winners, and also when impatience is a problem. Agreements may not be reached if policing of high seas is too costly. And international agreements may be ineffective if they run counter to national laws.[4]

4 What is "international public law"?

Any governance arrangement for managing ocean resources has to be set in a legal framework. What is the nature of this arrangement as it now stands in international public law?

By definition, international public law (IPL) governs legal relationships between states and it is created by states. There are two main forms of IPL: customary and treaty. Customary international law is "standard practice" between states and is not written down so as to bear signatures. Treaty law is written down and countries choose whether to sign and ratify it. IPL is weaker than national law as sovereign states can refuse to abide by laws they don't like. Many legal scholars question whether international public law in fact changes state behavior at all; states merely choose to abide by IPLs that allow continuation of existing behaviors.

We distinguish between international public law that results from pursuit of self-interest – "utility maximization" (or "utilitarianism") that really doesn't affect state behavior – and IPL based on moral obligation. We offer the view that the development of shared social norms among states – such as those of human rights or environmentalism – creates moral obligations, changes objectives ("change utility payoffs"), and thereby leads to new international laws. Thus, utility payoffs are endogenous, as they are influenced by new social norms.

International law and utilitarianism

Goldsmith and Posner (1999) and Gould (2011) reject the notion of *jus cogens*: "obligations that are absolute, unconditional, exceptionless, and (perhaps) not dependent upon consent" (Gould, 2011, p. 255).[5] These and some other authors mentioned below prefer the explanation of "positivism" – behavior that can be explained as resulting from rational utility maximizing decision-making not beholden to moral obligations. Guzman (2009) and Goldsmith and Posner (1999) view the development of international law as growing out of the resolution of a series of prisoners' dilemma games where both parties are made better off by reaching an agreement to constrain a damaging behavior.[6] This theory of international public law applies standard rational-choice assumptions common in economics: the theory is utilitarian.

While noting the near absence of enforcement mechanisms to encourage compliance with international public law, Guzman (2009) offers an explanation as to why IPL can be effective in constraining behavior. According to him, the disciplining device is "reputation for compliance" – failing to comply with IPL may cause a state to lose reputation for being a good "global citizen"; but a state's reputation for complying with international law in one area has value in dealing with other states in other areas of IPL. Guzman also recognizes roles for fear of retaliation (if you don't comply we won't either), and for reciprocity (if you comply we will too). A strong reputation for fair dealing is likely to negate the former and promote the latter. Brewster (2009) elaborates, pointing out that a good reputation for compliance is used by other states to predict future behavior. A state's word is valuable because by gaining the trust of other states they are more likely to want to cooperate in the resolution of other prisoners' dilemma problems. Moreover, collective good reputations (and presumed wishes to maintain them) are transaction cost-reducing devices, especially reducing costs of policing and even enforcement.

The above authors therefore argue that international public law – customary and treaty – exists because countries that adhere to it see themselves as benefiting from it; not adhering would make them worse off in a utilitarian sense. Similarly, Koskenniemi (2011) points to the "mystery of [international] legal obligation" and the search by scholars to develop a unified theory of it. Like the preceding authors he too largely rejects the idea that international public law is based upon moral obligation, and he endorses the idea that binding international law is a voluntary and self-interested choice on a state's part.

International public law and moral obligation

Brunnee and Troope (2011) note that if states simply make international laws that suit themselves, and do not have to agree to laws that do not suit them, then, to a large extent, international public law does not influence behavior, and it has no independent effect. With Goldsmith and Posner (1999) in mind, they write that "some have gone so far as to suggest that the concept of international legal obligation is theoretically uninteresting and practically irrelevant" (p. 307). However, at a deeper level than utilitarianism, Brunnee and Troope (2011) argue that the making of IPL is really based on shared social norms and that these norms are not exogenous to the social, economic and security interests reflected in international law. Rather, social norms develop over time and in turn influence the development of international law.

Furthermore, "influential norms will not emerge in the absence of processes that allow for the active participation of relevant social actors. Social actors in the global domain include states, of course, but [our] interactional framework acknowledges the importance of robust participation by intergovernmental organizations, civil society organizations, other collective entities, and individuals" (Brunnee and Troope, 2011, p. 309). Or, as Thomson (2009) puts it: "For international law scholars who focus on the normative characteristics of law, states feel an internalized obligation to comply with international rules, which exert an independent 'compliance pull'. . . . The norm-based perspective is generally optimistic: compliance is the default behavior" (p. 307). Indeed, Young (1989) points out that compliance in the development of international rules, for example the *Convention for the Conservation of Antarctic Marine Living Resources* (coming into force in 1982), is most likely when states are unclear as to the specific material benefits they might each expect, but recognize a greater good – environmental protection in this case.

In the context of international law governing the ocean, new norms are required if cooperation is to create something more akin to binding commitments, rather than mere promises to "cooperate" in some undefined and therefore non-obligatory way, as is the case with the *United Nations Convention on the Law of the Sea* (1982, coming into force in 1994). An avenue here that could create new norms is that of a greater understanding of ocean ecosystems – more particularly, their fragility and what fifty or so years of industrial fishing has done to them. The importance of marine science and pressure groups such as Greenpeace is in originating and spreading knowledge on the poor state of the oceans that has in fact worsened under the system of non-binding "cooperation".

Of course, there is no certainty that more widespread realization that ocean ecosystems are being denuded and economic returns lowered will lead to the acceptance of a new social norm such that "nations should come together responsibly to manage ocean resources". But it could happen. Indeed, as Kydd (2009) points out, the utilitarian state-level maximizing models discussed above have no room for national politics, yet it is at the level of national politics that new social norms expressed by states in international *fora* are first expressed. Or, as Brewster (2009) has put it, the "reputation" that Guzman (2009) refers to is that of upholding international law, but this is not necessarily the same thing as a reputation for being a good "global citizen". Indeed, one can venture that all states that have ratified the *United Nations Convention on the Law of the Sea* would argue that they abide by its letter, but the fact that the *Convention* has not led to sustainable use of ocean resources is quite another matter. Exactly how many States Parties have created a reputation for being a good "global citizen" in this sense is very much an open question.

Customary international law

Customary international law derives from general and consistent practice of a group of states – such as claims for a three-mile territorial sea or freedom of navigation and of fishing on the high seas – over an extended period of time. It is defined as the "customary practice of states followed from a sense of legal obligation".[7] National laws are not just "followed as a sense of legal obligation"; rather, they are enacted and enforced by a central authority – "the government". But there is no "central authority" to enact and enforce customary international laws. At issue is where customary international law comes from.[8] Conventional wisdom is that CIL is followed as a matter of moral obligation; a given code in CIL is established once enough countries act in accordance with it. Against this, as already mentioned, Goldsmith and Posner (1999) argue that CIL develops out of countries following their own self-interests. A practice may be international – such as recognition of claims to a territorial sea – because of a coincidence of interests.[9] Or, a powerful state may coerce weaker states into adopting a common practice: the British blockade of the slave trade off West Africa in the early nineteenth century comes to mind. Or, a CIL may develop as a solution to a repeated prisoners' dilemma game where the payoffs from cooperation are seen by all players as being greater than "going it alone". The creation of the *Fur Seal Treaty* (1911) is an example of this (see Barrett, 2003). Finally, common state practices may arise as a matter of coordination – we are both better off if we don't drop nuclear bombs on each other.

What is interesting in this typology is that the making and keeping of international public law has always been a difficult matter with individual countries (those who are not coerced) choosing whether or not to follow laws that are followed by other countries. This is true of both CIL and treaty law. This said, customary international law does exist and is embodied in the opinions of courts such as the International Court of Justice, in diplomatic practices between states, in international organizations between states, and in the domestic laws of states. The ICJ can also search for commonalities in the laws of "civilized states", and these can become a source of IPL.

Treaties

Treaties create international law when states agree to be bound by them. The *Vienna Convention on the Law of Treaties* (VCLT) (Article 2 (1)(a)) defines a treaty as "an international agreement concluded between states in written form and governed by international law, whether embodied in a single instrument or in two or more related instruments and whatever its particular designation". A state must consent to a treaty (by a signature, ratification or accession) – otherwise, it is not bound by it. Article 18 of the *Vienna Convention* states that in the interim period after signing, but before entry into force, a state has an "obligation not to defeat the object and purpose of a treaty". After entry into force, Article 26 applies, as to general good faith conduct. The concept is *Pacta sunt servanda*: every treaty in force is binding upon the parties to it and must be performed by them in good faith. A treaty may be terminated or suspended by the other signatories if a state breaches the treaty in question. The "grim strategy" is that a breach by one signatory triggers all signatories to renounce that treaty. However, a breach need not be an automatic trigger.

Multilateral treaties are usually negotiated with the aim of encouraging as many states as possible to sign on, in which case compromise is inevitable. One form of compromise is the "reservation" – "a unilateral statement . . . made by a state when signing, ratifying, accepting, approving or acceding to a treaty, whereby it purports to exclude or modify the legal affect of certain provisions of the treaty in their application to that state" (VCLT, Article 2 (1)(d)). For example a state may be a member of a regional fishing council organized under the *United Nations Convention on the Law of the Sea*, yet take a reservation not to be bound by fishing quotas. However, Article 19 of the VCLT states that a reservation is not allowed if it conflicts with the purpose of a treaty. This raises the following question: when does a reservation against a fishing quota defeat the purpose of high seas fisheries management under the *Convention*? If several signatories take reservations a treaty is said to be "fragmented". Thus, while the practice of reservations may encourage more states to sign a treaty, they are likely to weaken it, defeat its purpose, and place greater burdens on signatories not taking reservations.

Disputes settlement

Disputes over international public law may be resolved (if at all) through direct negotiation – usually through diplomatic channels – or through the setting up of a joint commission. A neutral third party could be engaged to mediate – to make suggestions on how to resolve a dispute. More formal is conciliation through a commission that conducts its own investigations leading to its own suggestions for resolution. The most formal process is an arbitration commission – the members and rules of which have to be agreed by the states in dispute – that makes binding recommendations resolving a dispute. When a resolution is between private parties the prevailing party may enforce the arbitration award through the courts of the other party. The ICJ is used to judge inter-state disputes and the countries involved have to agree to go before the court.

An international legal system?

An interesting interpretation of international public law is offered by Benvenisti (2008). Like some other authors, he argues that the idea of IPL as an enforceable legal system is open to challenge, especially in the US. In the USA a view is offered of IPL as merely a mixture of solitary treaties with no laws agreed or treaty inter- pretation being allowed outside of those treaties. Even the VCLT is interpreted by the USA and many other countries as a document aimed only at clarifying treaty obligations. In the US view, state sovereignty reigns supreme.

Against this is the doctrine of international public law as a legal system. "Within this system there is space for judges to use the rhetoric of law, to create legal prin- ciples using the traditional lawyers' tools of interpretation, deduction and inference to justify specific rules they articulate. This legal discourse empowers primarily judges . . . to proclaim what is legal. The vision of international law as a legal system rather than a mix of discrete treaties allows them to interpret, deduct, draw inferences and resolve conflicts not only by resorting to the specific treaties at hand but also by relying on the basic principles of the system and its underlying norms" (Benvenisti, 2008, p. 4). In other words, under this doctrine judges could make IPL. However, this is not the case

5 The chapters

In at least one case, judges with the scope to develop laws relating to the use of ocean resources have made a success of it. The case in point is that of the US law of salvage that was originally developed to return lost- (or about to be lost-)at-sea cargoes to the stream of commerce. In the early days there was no question of recovering archaeological values from shipwrecks because the technology for doing so did not exist. However, these technologies do now exist, and admiralty court judges, in rewarding "treasure hunters" with a share of recovered treasure cargoes, take into account the care that had been taken in also recovering archaeological values. A poor job will be met with a low salvage reward, and in especially bad cases a judge may refuse to award property rights to an offending salvage company to dive over other wrecks.

Much of the rest of this book catalogues the struggle to match international public law with efficient management of the oceans. Thus, Chapters 3 and 4 examine maritime piracy, finding, among other things, that efficient enforcement against it is bedeviled by free rider problems as countries try to avoid some portion of policing, arrest, trial or imprisonment costs. The argument is that international enforcement efforts against maritime piracy are sub-optimal.

Chapters 5, 6 and 7 discuss the subject of enclosure of the oceans – "drawing lines in the sea" – and the creation of Exclusive Economic Zones. Three important things to note are that within the EEZs sovereign rights exist so that the power of the sovereign can be brought to bear to promote efficient economic use of the oceans – the case of offshore oil is a notable example; that when countries are in dispute drawing boundaries is by no means straightforward – about one-half of marine boundaries have yet to be drawn, in particular in the Far East; and that beyond the EEZs is the high seas where international law applies.

Fisheries economics is the subject of Chapters 8 and 9, where the tendency for over-fishing and the difficulty of introducing economically efficient (rent-maximizing) management or property rights systems are both explained.

Chapters 10 to 14 examine problems of fisheries regime formation in both international and high seas contexts. This is where customary and treaty law applies and their weaknesses for developing systems of efficient high seas living resource management are exposed. While there are rare successes, most fisheries are over-fished. In a few cases, a preponderant actor – a leading nation – has taken over and imposed solutions aimed at efficient management, but the scope for this is limited and was, anyway, a desperation measure.

High seas whaling is examined in Chapter 15. While deadlock on the International Whaling Commission is lamented by some commentators – there is a ban on commercial whaling, but the take of whales for "scientific" purposes is about 2,000 whales each year – it is suggested that this might approximate an optimal solution by default. The limited take to some extent satisfies the use value of whales – for those that will eat their meat – as well as the non-use values of whales, as the limited catch means that whale stocks are slowly recovering such that option, existence and bequest values are also being satisfied.

Chapters 16 to 18 examine some zonal management instruments used to improve the economic and ecological productivity of ocean resources. The Great Barrier Reef Marine Park is held up as an exemplar of efficient management zoning. Protection of coastal wetlands – important for many fish species at some point of their life cycles – is also examined in the context of zonal management.

The last five chapters of the book turn attention away from living marine resources. Thus, Chapter 19 examines the problem of non-point source pollution, in particular fertilizer runoff. In extreme circumstances this creates coastal "dead zones" with destruction of fisheries and ecosystems. Efforts to deal with the dead zone problem have met with limited success because of its intractability, since modern farming is largely based on large fertilizer input. On the other hand, international efforts as expressed in international law to reduce oil pollution from ships have met with a good deal of success. The reasons for this are discussed in Chapter 20.

Chapters 21 and 22 discuss some important features of the offshore oil industry, pointing out that it is really quite well regulated and that governments share economic rents with the oil companies. Finally, Chapter 23 examines deep sea mining for polymetallic nodules and other minerals. Governing international law is based on the *common heritage of mankind* doctrine, with the result that access to the seabed for mining purposes is regulated by an international organization, the International Seabed Authority; in principle, economic rents are to be shared between the mining companies and, through the UN, by mankind as a whole.

Notes

1 For a review of advanced game theory methods used by fisheries economists see Bailey, Sumaila and Lindroos (2010). While these add theoretical niceties, the basic lessons of a simpler approach remain intact: namely, that effective policing is needed to prevent cheating on agreements, and that uninhibited behavior by non-signatories can destroy the beneficial effects of changes in behavior by signatories (Pintassilgo, 2003). It is precisely because of the rule of law with effective policing power over all citizens that the "green bits" of the planet are quite well managed; while it is the absence of a policing power to enforce rules over all agents that is the bane of the "blue bits".

2 Commission of the European Communities, "Reform of the Common Fisheries Policy", Green Paper, Brussels, 22.04.2009 COM(2009)163 final.

3 Sources of international law derive from political and legal theories – such as those offered by Grotius. Whether Grotius in fact claimed non-depletability is questioned by Vicuna (1999, p. 5). He quotes Grotius to the effect that some marine resources are depletable, so undermining the very source upon which customary international law of open access stands. Vicuna also points to nineteenth-century authorities that pointed to the growing scarcity of some marine resources.

4 Such as with UNESCO's *Convention on the Protection of the Underwater Cultural Heritage*, which runs counter to US admiralty law of salvage in that the latter awards salvage rights over historic wrecks while the former is aimed at protecting wrecks *in situ*.

5 According to Murphy (2006, p. 82) *Jus cogens* "is sometimes referred to as 'super' customary international law". Although "International law even recognizes the possibility of norms from which states may not deviate under any circumstances, regardless of their treaty practice, a concept known as *jus cogens* (preemptory norms)", scholars think that these norms are very limited in number.

6 As discussed in more detail in later chapters, a prisoners' dilemma game is one where the dominant strategy of each player is not to cooperate with the other player(s). The outcome is worse than if they had cooperated.

7 Restatement (Third) of the *Foreign Relations Law* of the United States § 102(2) (1986).

8 "Conventional wisdom views CIL as a unitary phenomenon that pervades international law and international relations. Governments take care to comply with CIL, and often

incorporate its norms into domestic statutes. National courts apply CIL as a rule of decision, or a defense, or a canon of statutory construction. Nations argue about whether certain acts violate CIL. Violations of CIL are grounds for war or an international claim. Legal commentators view CIL to be at the core of the study of international law" (Goldsmith and Posner, 1999).

9 Even in the case of the territorial sea Goldsmith and Posner (1998) point out that there was never universal agreement over a common distance, the most typical claims being three or four miles, and that these claims changed over time to suit the interests of the countries concerned.

PART II

Historic wrecks, modern pirates

2

ECONOMIC ANALYSIS OF LEGAL REGIMES GOVERNING SALVAGE OF HISTORIC SHIPWRECKS[1]

1   Introduction

This chapter offers an economic analysis of international and US laws governing recovery of archaeological data from historic shipwrecks. The framework combines values of treasure salvage and archaeological knowledge. It is suggested that US salvage law – sometimes extended to international waters – gives insufficient protection to archaeological value, but that UNESCO's *Convention on the Protection of the Underwater Cultural Heritage* goes too far in the other direction. Two other legal regimes (government–salvager and inter-state agreements) are shown to have potential to further increase the social values recovered from historic shipwrecks. It is also suggested that a move toward maximizing social values would be promoted if the US admiralty courts tied the size of salvage awards more closely to the quality of the archaeological work performed.

Excavation of historic shipwrecks is a matter of dispute between archaeologists and others who support protection of the "underwater cultural heritage" and treasure salvagers who seek monetary values.[2] There is evidence that US courts are moving, albeit imperfectly, in the direction of promoting the recovery of both types of values. The ancient common laws of salvage and of finds were initially developed to govern salvage of ships and cargoes in immediate marine peril at a time when finding and recovering historic shipwrecks was technologically impossible. US admiralty courts are aware of the distinction between salvage and archaeological values and are trying to fashion salvage awards at least partly based on archaeological work done.[3] Wrecks lying in international waters may also benefit from this trend as US-flagged salvagers often seek property rights in them in US courts. However, many in the archaeological community question whether US courts under present laws can promote highest-quality archaeology by salvage companies. The issue is non-trivial, given that there are perhaps 50,000 wrecks off the US coast,[4] and one million worldwide.[5]

Problems with current US laws arise because an historic shipwreck combines private and public good characteristics. The private good is treasure that can be sold once a salvage company has been awarded property rights in an admiralty court. The public good is archaeological knowledge – the "underwater cultural heritage", collected by professional underwater archaeologists. Optimal production of a mixed good is unlikely, as the courts can award property rights in treasure but not in the underwater cultural heritage. In the case of an historic shipwreck, because salvagers work quickly, often with little regard for archaeological considerations – such as marking of finds in three-dimensional space and collection and preservation of historically important artifacts of low monetary value – salvage work creates an external diseconomy for archaeological value. If a mixed good is to be provided at the socially optimal level, a suitable legal governance regime is required. This chapter investigates the social efficiency of current US admiralty law as well as some other quite new governance regimes.

While US admiralty courts encourage salvagers to recover archaeological value, the underwater archaeology profession is highly critical of the results: the record, they say, is of poor archaeology largely because unqualified personnel are too-often used. The courts could set standards that they could monitor – such as requiring salvagers to employ *bone fide* underwater archaeologists that are given time for high-quality archaeological recovery of data and artifacts. But there is a monitoring issue: are the courts really going to get into the business of refereeing underwater archaeology reports that today is done by peer review within the archaeology profession? Besides, how competent would the courts be in striking a fair balance between the creation of archaeological value and the cost of creating it?

Public provision of public goods is widely practiced. In the case of historic shipwrecks such an agency could be a public university or museum, or other government-funded agency. Alternatively, a private supplier could be induced to supply the socially optimal quantity of a public good through a subsidy. Something close to the latter, discussed below, is that of the government–salvager partnership – whereby the salvager provides mainly non-archaeological inputs, and government some archaeological inputs.[6]

Salvage of historic shipwrecks in international waters is currently governed by the *United Nations Convention on the Law of the Sea* (UNCLOS III), which specifies that member countries recognize a "duty to protect objects of an archeological and historic nature found at sea" (Article 303(1)). The convention does not, however, abrogate admiralty law, thereby leaving in place the financial incentives (embodied in the laws of salvage and finds) to locate wrecks. Article 303(3) of the United Nations *Law of the Sea* states that "nothing in this article affects the rights of identifiable owners, the law of salvage or other rules of admiralty, or laws and practices with respect to cultural exchanges".[7]

An ongoing attempt to develop international law governing historic shipwrecks is that of UNESCO's *Convention on the Underwater Cultural Heritage*.[8] As discussed later, this is not a perfect governance device. In the meantime, US-flagged salvagers can turn to US courts and admiralty law for protection of property rights over sunken wrecks – even those lying in international waters. UNESCO's *Convention* in principle offers protection of archaeological value, to the virtual exclusion of for-profit treasure salvage. This governance regime that came into force in January 2009 reverses the positions of salvagers and underwater archaeologists. Property rights in salvage are not allowed, while, under certain circumstances, archaeological recovery is encouraged. An argument explored below is that even if the *Convention* does come into force it may not supercede US salvage law even in international waters.

Inter-governmental agreements – e.g. that for the *Titanic* – are another legal regime used to protect historic wrecks lying in international waters. These are used to protect sites from salvagers while promoting the interests of the governments concerned, leaving open the possibility of professional archaeology at a later date.

2 A model of comparative governance

Historic shipwrecks supply four kinds of social values: salvage value – as when cargoes of high monetary value are recovered, so returning them to the "stream of commerce"; archaeological value – as when careful investigation of an historic shipwreck uncovers interesting historical information; recreation value for hobbyist divers; and reef value – as when a wreck creates an artificial reef as a habitat for fish that may be of value to recreational anglers. In this chapter interest is focused on salvage and archaeological values for three reasons: these values can be large, sunken wrecks quite frequently combine them, and there is a social issue in that maximization of salvage value may destroy archaeological value.

Suppose that there are two types of organizations involved in extracting value from historic shipwrecks: salvage companies and archaeological teams financed by museums, universities and the like. Suppose too that the source of value of a wreck can be identified in advance; it would be natural for salvagers and archaeologists to partition the recovery of the value of wrecks according to their competencies. However, in practice, both types of value may be found on a wreck and, at the outset, the absolute and relative distribution of them is likely to be unknown. Also, in the "field", salvage companies are often the discoverers of sunken wrecks – mainly because they are the better financed, not least because they can profit from selling recovered treasure.

3 A salvage company's maximization problem

A salvage company is assumed to attempt to maximize profits from the salvage of a wreck. A reasonable supposition is that profit per *day* behaves something like as in Figure 2.1. There is negative profit during an initial "set-up period", when costs exceed the value of any recovered treasure. According to practitioners, peak daily treasure-salvage values are quite quickly reached – say, at about seven days, falling thereafter. By about fourteen days over a wreck the value of recovered treasure per day is about equal with daily operating costs – so profit per day falls to zero, and if the stay over a wreck is more prolonged it becomes negative.

According to Figure 2.1, *total* profit from salvaging treasure from a wreck is therefore maximized at fourteen diving-days over a wreck. These figures are only illustrative, and optimum dive-days over a wreck will vary from case to case; however, it is true that treasure hunters aim for rapid salvage and not prolonged stays over a wreck – as some of the quotes below indicate.

4 An archaeological team's maximization problem

Any archaeological values on an historic shipwreck should be added to treasure value to find the full value of a wreck.

While still a relatively new area in economics, several studies attempt to place values on cultural heritage goods – see, for example, the collected papers in Hutter and Rizzo (1997) and Navrud and Ready (2002). Contingent valuation is the most popular technique mainly because it has proven relatively easy to move over from the valuation of another class of public goods: environmental goods. Values of cultural heritage goods are often great – about $58 million per annum for visitors to Morocco to restore the Fez Medina (Carson et al., 2002), and

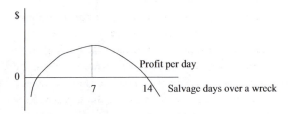

FIGURE 2.1 Daily profit from recovery of treasure

£7.3 million to remove air pollution stains from Lincoln cathedral (Pollicino and Maddison, 2002). A comprehensive review of cultural heritage valuation studies concludes that "people attribute a significantly positive value to the conservation or restoration of cultural assets" (Pearce et al., 2002, p. 265). A study that attempts to value archaeological knowledge and artifacts derived from historical shipwrecks is that of Throckmorton (1990). He points out that, "according to the Swedish tourist board, one million tourists spend an extra day in Sweden because of the *Vasa* [a seventeenth-century warship salvaged from Stockholm harbor in 1961 and placed in a museum]. At about $300 per day per tourist, this amounts to several hundred million dollars per year added to Sweden's economy" (p. 146). About 100,000 more people per year visited a museum in Kyrenia, Cyprus, after the artifacts and archaeological records of a fourth-century BC ship had been placed there for public inspection. And in 2002 about 30,000 people visited the *Mary Rose* exhibit (a recovered sixteenth-century English warship) in Portsmouth, England (*Mary Rose Annual Report*, 2002). These measures of the value of historic shipwrecks bear none of the sophistication of the other cultural value studies cited not least because the number of museum visits is unlikely to capture the full social value of the archaeological knowledge recovered. At the very least, non-use values should be added.[9]

Thorough collection of archaeological knowledge typically needs much more time than does salvage – for example, about 300 days were spent excavating the wreck of *La Belle* off the coast of Texas in 1997.[10] Thus, assume that net present archaeological value, NPV_A, increases with time spent over a wreck for a period much more prolonged than is the case for salvage.[11] Because of the external diseconomy created by salvagers, *daily* net present value of archaeological knowledge and artifacts collected by archaeologists depends both on the number of days spent by salvagers salvaging an historical wreck for commercial gain as well as the number of days spent practicing expert archaeological recovery. Rapid recovery of salvage value tends to destroy archaeological value due to damage done by salvagers to the archaeological site. There is plenty of evidence that rapid salvage of treasure destroys archaeological value. The International Congress of Maritime Museums describes a case:

> such an archaeologically very important find as the *Geldermalsen* should have been excavated in a scientific way. Correlation of the rather well documented information from the available archives and the excavation information is of utmost importance. This means registration of find places within the wreck, details on the ship structure, environmental information, etc. Without such scientific standards, no excavation should take place, in order not to lose the information, which is very important for a historical point of view. In fact, the cargo of the *Geldermalsen* has been looted [by salvagers] without concern for context and its commercial sale will entirely destroy the wreck.
>
> (quoted in Miller, 1987)

Hatcher, de Rham and Thorncroft (1987) say that "the academic moves slowly, carefully, methodically, with a program over many seasons. [The salvager] has to recover as much as possible as quickly as possible, preferably in one season, before rivals infringe on the site, and costs escalate out of the control of even very wealthy individuals" (p. 41). And in a similar vein, Dyson (1986) quotes the salvager of the *Geldermalsen*: "it was a race to get what they could before being interrupted by weather, rivals, pirates, or some government" (p. 114).

With respect to archaeological knowledge, the more time spent on excavation, the more knowledge that may be gained. Time spent during excavation is primarily devoted to intensive documentation and recovery. "Knowledge" that is ready for communication to peer groups and/or the general public derives from intensive analysis, synthesis and interpretation of the recovered data and artifacts. According to practitioners, time spent in the laboratory and the library can be twenty times longer than time spent diving over a wreck.[12]

However, it is reasonable to assume that the value of archaeological time spent over a historic shipwreck is subject to diminishing returns. As time goes by, the "big" finds are brought up with artifacts of lesser importance still remaining on the ocean floor.

Figure 2.2 shows the optimization problem. The two marginal curves are drawn only for their downward sloping portions which occur after the initial set-up time over a wreck has been completed. Marginal social benefit (treasure plus archaeological value) is assumed to be greater than marginal private benefit (treasure value only) on this particular wreck, as archaeological value is large. A treasure hunter's optimal number of diving days is T, while the optimum number of days to recover both treasure and archaeological values is much greater, at A days.

The objective of society is taken to be to maximize the social value derivable from an historic wreck.

The common law of salvage was initially designed only to return goods to the "stream of commerce" and was written when underwater archaeology was

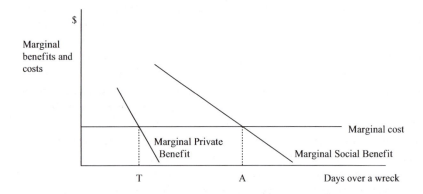

FIGURE 2.2 Optimizing days over a wreck

technologically near impossible. However, despite this historical origin, in the USA the law of salvage still governs recovery of shipwrecks – historic or not.

Assuming that a US court has awarded salvage rights to a salvage company, the latter has interest in working enough salvage and archaeological days to maximize the social value of a wreck only if it can monetize the social value of the archaeological knowledge and artifacts. In the likely case that a salvage company cannot monetize all or even most of the archaeological value, it will simply aim to work T days over a wreck (or close to T days), and social value will not be maximized. There is a need, therefore, to find ways to increase archaeological days spent over an historic shipwreck. In the following discussion four such models are discussed: salvage case law, government–salvager partnerships, inter-state management, and UNESCO's *Convention on the Underwater Cultural Heritage*.

5   US salvage law

Discussion of US salvage law is relevant not only because it applies to US waters but also because it is sometimes used by salvagers to claim rights over historic shipwrecks in international waters. Which law applies to the establishment of property rights in historic shipwrecks in US jurisdictions depends in large part on the location of the wreck. Relevant laws are salvage law, the *law of finds*, the *Marine Protection, Research and Sanctuaries Act* (1972), the *Abandoned Shipwreck Act* (1987), and related state legislation implementing the latter *Act* in state waters; in non-navigable state waters various laws may apply including common law, and state statutory or regulatory laws. However, none of these laws protects archaeological value to the extent implied by the *Archaeological Resources Protection Act* (1979, amended 1988). For example, there is no requirement that artifacts will remain the property of the US, or that archaeological records will be preserved by a suitable university or museum.[13]

Under the US law of salvage the original owner retains ownership of goods lost at sea but shares the value of recovered goods with the salvager. The salvage award is intended to compensate the salvager for "meritorious services" and to act as an inducement to others to perform such services.[14] The admiralty courts, in an effort to promote the recovery of archaeological data, also reward archaeological work done by salvagers. However, professional archaeologists are often highly critical of the scientific quality of such work.

The unsuitability of salvage law as it relates to the protection of abandoned historic shipwrecks is implicit in the *Abandoned Shipwreck Act* of 1987. The *Act* recognizes the multi-use values of historic shipwrecks. It says "that shipwrecks offer recreational and educational opportunities to sport divers and other interested groups, as well as irreplaceable State resources for tourism, biological sanctuaries, and historical research". The states are charged with the protection of natural resources and habitat areas, guaranteeing recreational exploration of shipwreck sites, and allowing for appropriate public- and private-sector recovery of shipwrecks consistent with the protection of historical values and environmental integrity of the shipwrecks and the sites.

However, following the *Brother Jonathan* case[15] in 1998 some expert legal opinion is that admiralty law of salvage supersedes the *ASA*.[16] The Supreme Court of the US said that states could not use the 11th Amendment for protection against law suits brought in relation to salvage law. Other opinion is more cautious, stating that some recent "cases have cast doubt on the propriety of applying the 11th Amendment to cases in admiralty" (McLaughlin, 1995, p. 178), and that the Supreme Court's unanimous judgment in the *Brother Jonathan* case "leaves unresolved numerous practical issues" (Sweeney, 1999, p. 185).

The *Marine Protection, Research and Sanctuaries Act* (1972) offers most protection to historic shipwrecks in US waters. It is unlawful to cause loss of or injury to any sanctuary resource, including historic shipwrecks. Fines can be substantial, amounting to $100,000 per day for willful misconduct. Such misconduct includes violation of archaeological sites. However, the area of jurisdiction of this *Act* is, as its name implies, restricted to marine sanctuaries, of which in 2013 there were just 16.

6 Admiralty courts and the protection of archaeological value

Admiralty law courts have fashioned rules rewarding salvagers' efforts to preserve archaeological data and artifacts. That is, they have adopted the doctrine of an "archaeological duty of care (ADC)" (Bryant, 2001). Thus, in some courts awards are larger for better archaeological work and in others an ADC is an element in establishing the property right in salvage. Bryant (2001) gives an example of the use of this latter requirement.[17] Examples of the former include the challenging in court of the exclusive salvage rights to the *Titanic* in 1996. The court, however, held that "the preservation of the archaeological integrity of the wreck as well as the preservation of the retrieved artifacts was evidence that the operation had been undertaken with due diligence" (Christie and Hildreth, 1999, p. 160). The salvagers of *The Nashville* were refused by a Federal District Court any salvage award because their handling of the property had increased the likelihood of the deterioration of the goods salvaged. In addition, in 1982 a Federal Court ruled that, in order to state a claim for a salvage award on ancient vessels of archaeological value, it is an essential element that the salvager documents to the admiralty court's satisfaction that it has preserved the archaeological value of the wreck. It is therefore apparent that US courts recognize the different values that may be contained in a shipwreck and that they have devised incentives for salvagers to gather archaeological data that they may well have otherwise destroyed.[18]

However, an important proviso concerns the type of archaeological data gathered by salvage companies. Is it of high archaeological value? There can be a vast difference between data gathered by non-specialist and specialist archaeologists. The latter most often will be concerned with gathering and interpreting data suitable for publication in peer-review archaeology journals. In other words, a specialist's archaeology can normally be expected to be of the highest quality. According to Robert Neyland, Chairman of the *Advisory Council for Underwater Archaeology*, no archaeological report written by a salvage company that he knows of has ever appeared in a peer-reviewed archaeology journal.[19] Thus, if it is an objective of the courts to induce salvage companies to be concerned with preserving the archaeological record, they are probably failing because salvage companies produce archaeological records of less than scientific standard.

One way to deal with this problem would be to require salvage companies to produce archaeological data suitable for processing into papers publishable in peer-review journals. This ought to induce them to employ professional archaeologists devoted to the collection of such data. Since such professionals would need to have some say as to the number of days needed for a dive, a move toward the social value-maximizing number of dive days would be expected. In other words, the courts could introduce standards that in effect use salvage companies as agents concerned with collecting high-quality archaeological data.

7 Government–salvager partnerships

The case of the seventeeth-century British warship HMS *Sussex* is an example of a different way forward. The British government entered into a partnering agreement with the American treasure salvager Odyssey Marine Exploration Inc. in 2002. The government gave assurances that "archaeological observers appointed by the government would be present throughout the whole recovery process. [And] an independent monitoring panel would be established in order that expert archaeological advice could be accessed at all stages of the project" (Dromgoole, 2004, p. 192). According to Odyssey, the HMS *Sussex* agreement "is the first time any government has entered into an agreement with the private sector for the archaeological excavation of a sovereign warship". A question is whether "during the process" monitoring of standards through government involvement is likely to be more effective in collecting and preserving the archaeological record than is the method of using the courts *post hoc* to reward whatever worthy archaeological work that was performed during a salvage operation. The very fact that the British government, under pressure from the archaeological community, chose the method it did suggests that it had become concerned with the likely quality of the archaeological record that an unmonitored salvage company would perform.

In 2011 the British government signed another contract with Odyssey Marine for the recovery of silver off of the SS *Gairsoppa*, a UK cargo ship sunk by a German U-boat in 1941. The wreck contains about 200 tonnes of silver worth about £150 million and lies in 4,700 meters of water in the North Atlantic, 300 miles off the Irish coast. It is therefore under the high seas – outside of Ireland's exclusive economic zone. The UK government (Department of Transport) agreement with Odyssey Marine is that Odyssey will keep 80 percent of the value of the silver recovered.[20]

The main advantage of government–salvager partnerships is that the government, because it employs archaeologists, is in a better position to monitor the quality of archaeological work performed than are the courts. This is especially so when monitoring is an on-going process from the beginning to the end of a "dig" that could take many thousands of work-hours. Moreover, the government can justifiably invest its own funds into a project – the return on the investment being to the public benefit.

8   Inter-state management

Another legal regime is that of inter-state agreements – either bilateral or multilateral – to manage designated wreck sites.[21] The case of the inter-state agreement between the USA, the UK, Canada and France concerning the wreck of the *Titanic* illustrates several important issues. First, each country has a direct interest in the wreck, as she was sailing from Southampton via Cherbourg to New York, and she sank on the Canadian continental shelf. Second, while emphasizing *in situ* preservation, the agreement allows for managed dives of either an archaeological nature or to protect artifacts from significant degeneration. However, the agreement was that "project funding shall not require the sale of recovered . . . artifacts or other things recovered", and the recovered artifacts "shall be kept together and intact in a manner that provides for public access . . . and its availability for educational, scientific . . . purposes" (UK Consultation Paper, quoted in Dromgoole, 2003, p. 6). In this respect, this inter-state agreement concurs with UNESCO's *Convention* (about to be discussed), in that sale of goods by salvagers is prohibited, yet it also allows for archaeological recovery – something that by Rules 1 and 2 of the *Convention* is not allowed. Third, enforcement of the agreement is by States Parties "regulating and authorizing" their own nationals and flag vessels. Fourth, the agreement is open for non-signatories to sign – an important provision given that other countries may eventually acquire the requisite recovery technologies.

9   UNESCO international law on historic shipwrecks

The UNESCO *Convention on the Underwater Cultural Heritage* favors archaeological values and appears to discount salvage value completely (for a similar view, see Bryant, 2001).[22] This is evident from the first two rules abstracted from the annex to the document:

> Rule 1. The protection of underwater cultural heritage through *in situ* preservation shall be considered as the first option. Accordingly, activities directed at underwater cultural heritage shall be authorized in a manner consistent with the protection of that heritage, and subject to that requirement may be authorized for the purpose of making a significant contribution to protection or knowledge or enhancement of underwater cultural heritage.

Rule 2. The commercial exploitation of underwater cultural heritage for trade or speculation or its irretrievable dispersal is fundamentally incompatible with the protection and proper management of underwater cultural heritage. Underwater cultural heritage shall not be traded, sold, bought or bartered as commercial goods.

It is clear that the *Convention* favors archaeological value to the virtual exclusion of salvage value. The value of salvage in returning goods to the circulation of commerce (such circulation presumably being the original intent when the goods were first shipped) is entirely discounted. This would appear to be the meaning of the last sentence of paragraph two: "*Underwater cultural heritage shall not be traded, sold, bought or bartered as commercial goods.*" Rather, as the opening sentence of the quotation says, "*The protection of underwater cultural heritage through* in situ *preservation shall be considered as the first option.*" This seems to imply that the *Convention* would rather leave goods untouched on a wreck site than have them recovered. Such a policy is extreme to say the least, given the very high salvage values that are possible. For example, the gold recovered from the steamship *Central America*, sunk in 1857 in 2,500 meters of water, is valued at up to $400 million.

According to Dromgoole (2004), the *Convention* "makes no provision in respect to ownership of underwater cultural heritage and was not intended to interfere with existing ownership rights" (p. 194).[23] This qualification may be taken to imply that the *Convention* applies only to abandoned wrecks. If so, it may run foul of the definition of "abandoned". As mentioned earlier, this is what happened to the USA's *Abandoned Shipwreck Act*. Absent an affirmative statement of abandonment by the previous owner, a wreck is not necessarily abandoned and would still come under the law of salvage. Could the *Convention* go the same way – US courts awarding rights and the treasure to salvagers of wrecks in international waters, saying that the law of salvage applies?

Dromgoole offers the further clarification that early drafts of the *Convention* tried to avoid the question of ownership by applying only to abandoned wrecks, but defining abandonment proved too difficult a task to undertake. So the final text applies to underwater cultural heritage, whether abandoned or not. The *Convention* makes no reference to, or provision for, ownership. Therefore, many questions are left open about the relationship between the provisions of the *Convention* and ownership rights, e.g. can an owner be prohibited from recovering its property in circumstances where *in situ* protection is considered a preferable option? Are owners free to dispose of their own property entirely, as they wish? There is no evidence that the draftsmen thought these questions through.[24]

10 Conclusions

In terms of the economic model developed here, the US courts salvager legal regime has the effect, in Figure 2.2, of moving salvagers to the right – increasing the number of dive days relative to the salvage optimum. However, given both the high costs of salvage operations and, according to at least some members of the underwater archaeology profession, poor quality of the archaeological work performed, it seems that neither the social maximum nor the archaeological maximum would necessarily be reached. But in an imperfect world careful use of the "archaeological duty of care" doctrine by the courts might still be the most effective means currently available to maximize the social values of historic shipwrecks. This is especially so given the reality that it is the salvagers that have the money to search for wrecks and that continued application of salvage law retains incentives for them so to invest it in search activities.

UNESCO's legal regime as defined by the *Convention* can be characterized as favoring archaeological value, given that it does not allow any salvage aimed at selling recovered cargoes or artifacts. In this case, if archaeological rescue were allowed, one would have to presume that the archaeological optimum would be reached. This is clouded however, given that the *Convention* states a preference for *in situ* preservation – that would make recovery of archaeological values difficult or impossible. Moreover, the US as a non-signatory of the *Convention* would not be bound by it. It would be free to apply its own laws to its flagged salvagers – even when the latter seek property rights in wrecks found in international waters. Given that US salvagers possess the most advanced salvage technology, and that this technology potentially can find up to 98 percent of historic shipwrecks (Dromgoole, 2003), an international agreement such as the *Convention* would seem to be ineffective as a device for protecting the underwater cultural heritage from treasure salvagers.

The perceived threat from treasure salvagers and lack of international agreement is driving two other responses for protection of the underwater cultural heritage. A regime constituted by the government–salvager agreement – that concerning the HMS *Sussex* being the first – in principle favors archaeological value more than does the US courts–US salvager regime. This largely depends upon a government's intent to collect archaeological value and so requiring salvagers to spend more time over an historic shipwreck. In the case of the HMS *Sussex* the British government does seem to have been pushed in this direction.

A fourth legal regime – that of inter-state management, such as those governing the wrecks of the *Titanic* and the *Estonia* – is also likely to give greater emphasis to the collection of archaeological value, again depending upon the intent of the governments concerned.

Notes

1 This chapter is based on a paper published with Thomas Miceli in *Ocean Development and International Law*, 36 (4), October–December, 2005, pp. 323–344.
2 As Roach (1998) notes, "Some salvors don't want to work under any type of archaeological guidelines no matter how reasonable. Some archaeologists want absolutely no private sector recovery of artifacts from shipwrecks."
3 Cases catalogued by Fletcher-Tomenius and Forrest (2000) and Roach (1998) when US courts have taken quality of archaeological work into consideration in determin-

ing size of salvage awards include RMS Titanic Inc. v. Wreck, 1996 AMC 2481, 2493 (E.D. Va. 1996); Klein v. Unidentified Vessel, 1985 AMC 2970, 2975 (11th Cir.); Deep Sea Research v. The Brother Jonathan 883 F. Supp 1343 at 1362; MDM Salvage Inc., 1987 AMC 537, 631 F.Supp 308 (S.D. Fla. 1986); Cobb Coin Inc. v. The Unidentified Wrecked and Abandoned Sailing Vessels, 549 F. Supp. 540 (S.D. Fla 1982); Columbus-America Discovery Group v. Atlantic Mutual Ins. Co., 1992 AMC 2705, 2728 (E.D. Va. 1994); 1995 AMC 1985, 2001, 56 F.3d 556, 569, 573 (4th Cir. 1995). See also Dromgoole (2003).

4 US Commission on Ocean Policy (2004) – the geographic area referred to is US territorial waters and exclusive economic zone. A Lake Champlain Maritime Museum document (1994) concurs with this estimate. The true number of historic shipwrecks in US waters is uncertain, as is exemplified by another estimate by the salvage company Sunken Treasure Inc. It estimated in a court case that about 50,000 shipwrecks were covered by the *Abandoned Shipwreck Act*, i.e. in US territorial waters alone (District Court of the Virgin Islands, Division of St Croix, Civil Action No. 1991/26, available online at www.vid.uscourts.gov/dcopinion/91cv0263_x01.pdf). The company also estimated that only five to ten percent of these wrecks were likely to be of archaeological value – an estimate repeated by Lake Champlain Maritime Museum (1994).

5 Rough estimate of the worldwide total by Robert Ballard, *Scientific American Frontiers*, PBS, June 2, 2004. He referred to historic shipwrecks as "time capsules".

6 Examples of salvager-supplied inputs include boats, and side-scanning sonar and remote operating vehicles. Salvagers many times perform much of the original research needed to locate a long-lost wreck. This is likely to involve archival work at historical registries and the tiresome work of systematically scanning the ocean floor. Archaeological teams supply archaeological expertise and specialized archaeological equipment. It is assumed that the researching/location-finding services provided by salvagers are so important that it would be a mistake to cut them out of archaeological recovery altogether.

7 O'Keefe and Nafziger (1994) say that with respect to the underwater cultural heritage the *Law of the Sea* as embodied in UNCLOS III is "murky". For example, it does not attempt to define preferential rights over a wreck between, say, the coastal state in whose non-territorial waters a wreck happens to lie, the flag state or the state of cultural origin.

8 UNESCO: United Nations Educational, Scientific and Cultural Organization based in Paris.

9 Peacock (1997) points to the need to do archaeology that gets people through the door may not be consistent with highest academic standards. However, it is reasonable to conclude that archaeological values of historic shipwrecks can be substantial.

10 Excavation of *La Belle* in Matagorda Bay, Texas, was dry behind a cofferdam. For details see "Sieur de La Salle's fateful landfall", *Smithsonian Magazine*, April, 1997.

11 According to private correspondence with Peter Waddell, from a diving and diving-logistics perspective the Red Bay, Labrador, project on several sunken Basque shipwrecks exceeded 14,200 hours, with 7,000 individual dives logged. This remains the largest underwater archaeology project ever undertaken in North America. The next most-worked sites are the Machault excavations (Zacharchuk and Waddell, 1986), on the Restigouche River in Quebec, with 5,000 diving hours, followed by approximately 1,100 hours by the United States Park Service on the USS *Arizona*. The Red Bay project used 6,300 hours (44 percent) excavating. The next most time-intensive activity (3,200 hours, 23 percent of the total) was recording (structural recording, mapping, tracing, elevations, note taking, timber tagging, and stratigraphies). Planimetric mapping of individual structural areas, the main input to the overall site plan, consumed 1,100 hours (8 percent) of dive time. Thus, excavation and recording accounted for two-thirds of the total dive time. Technical services were the next most time-consuming activity, accounting for 9 percent (1,300 hours). This included site set-up – for grids, datum lines, airlifts, air and hot water routing, temporary reburials and sandbagging. The remaining diving

hours, 24 percent of the total, are divided into nine different categories, each of which comprises one to six percent of total dive time.

12 Private correspondence with Toni Carrell.

13 Archaeological resources on US federal lands, including submerged lands, are by no means treated equally under US law. Land-based sites are granted much greater protection through quite recently passed laws than are historic shipwrecks – which still are largely governed by the ancient law of salvage.

   Thus, US law as expressed in the *Archaeological Resources Protection Act* (1979, amended 1988) gives extensive protection to archaeological sites found on land. The *Act* states that "archaeological resources on public lands and Indian lands are an accessible and irreplaceable part of the Nation's heritage", but that "these resources are increasingly endangered because of their commercial attractiveness". Moreover, "existing Federal laws do not provide adequate protection to prevent the loss and destruction of these archaeological resources and sites resulting from uncontrolled excavations and pillage". Thus, "the purpose of the Act is to secure, for the present and future benefit of the American people, the protection of archaeological resources and sites which are on public lands and Indian lands".

   Under the ARPA, permits are issued for the investigation of archaeological sites on the understanding that intended activity is "undertaken for the purpose of furthering archaeological knowledge in the public interest", and that "the archaeological resources that are excavated or removed from public lands will remain the property of the United States, and such resources and copies of associated archaeological records and data will be preserved by a suitable university, museum, or other scientific or educational institution". Penalties for violating the *Act* can be severe, the maximum sentence for a first offence being a $10,000 fine and imprisonment for up to one year, and twice these amounts for a second offence. The severity of the punishment is related to the archaeological and commercial value of the archaeological resources involved and the cost of restoration and repair of the site.

14 According to Collins (1999), the size of a salvage award depends upon two factors relating to the wreck – the degree of marine peril and the value of property recovered – as well as four factors relating to the salvagers: the risks incurred, their promptitude and skill, the value of the equipment used, and the amount of labor expended. These parameters are also critical in the UK's *Merchant Shipping Act* (see Darrington, 2002).

15 California v. Deep Sea Research Inc. (96–1400) 102 F. 3d 379.

16 This interpretation is found, for example, in Collins (1999) and Pelkofer (1999).

17 Cobb Coin Co. v. The Unidentified, Wrecked and Abandoned Sailing Vessel, 549 F. Supp. 540 (S.D. Fla. 1982).

18 Examination of the legal regime governing historic wrecks in England by Roberts and Trow (2002) also draws the conclusion that there is a mismatch between protection of archaeological and salvage values, and they call for new legislation giving greater protection to archaeological values. They also note that under the *Merchant Shipping Act* (1995) the Receiver of Wreck tries to promote the collection of archaeological data and artifacts as much as possible within the confines of the *Act*.

19 Private letter to author dated November 18th, 2002.

20 BBC, "Shipwreck of SS Gairsoppa reveals £150m silver haul", September 26th, 2011, available online at www.bbc.co.uk/news/uk-15061868.

21 UNESCO (1999) lists several examples, including those between France and the USA (1989) concerning the wreck of the CSS *Alabama*; between the UK and South Africa (1989) with respect to the HMS *Birkenhead*; between the UK and Canada (1997) over the wrecks of HMS *Erebus* and HMS *Terror*; and between Estonia, Finland and Sweden (1995) concerning the wreck of the *Estonia*, on which 757 people lost their lives.

22 Also relevant is the Council of Europe's *European Convention on the Protection of the Archaeological Heritage (Revised) 1992* that came into force in 2001. Unlike UNESCO's

Convention, it applies, as far as protection of underwater cultural heritage is concerned, only to territorial waters, but, similar to UNESCO's *Convention*, its principal aim is to preserve archaeological sites *in situ*. See Dromgoole (2004, p. 192).

23 A *Draft Convention* on the underwater cultural heritage written under the auspices of the International Law Association included a radical departure from the common law of salvage. In Article 1 it defined abandonment to have occurred when a wreck had been submerged for fifty years and when no recovery by the owners had been attempted within ten years after development of feasible recovery technology (O'Keefe and Nafziger, 1994). This definition of abandonment was not included in UNESCO's *Convention*.

24 Private correspondence with Sarah Dromgoole, June 14, 2004.

3

THE ECONOMICS OF MARITIME PIRACY[1]

1   Introduction

This chapter discusses the economics of international cooperation against maritime piracy. It begins with a short description of the cost of maritime piracy and describes international investment in enforcement against it. Next, pirate organization and a pirate business model are discussed, along with a brief discussion of what policies may be adopted to reduce piracy. Interactions between pirates and enforcement agents are then modeled in an equilibrium framework. It is then pointed out that as enforcement on the high seas is a mixed good – enforcement effort by country X also benefiting country Y – a free rider problem exists, and there will be under-investment in enforcement.

2   The nature, cost and scope of modern-day piracy

The International Maritime Bureau (IMB) records details of pirate attacks on shipping around the world. On a global basis, 2010 appears to be the peak year for piracy attacks ("actual and attempted incidents"), when 445 were reported. The next year saw a small reduction, with a bigger drop in 2012 to 297.[2] This downward trend seems to have continued in 2013.[3] "Personal violations" followed a similar trend, with 1,270 in 2010 and 662 in 2012. In the earlier year "hostage" was easily the largest category of violation, together with several cases of assault and injury, and eight sailors were killed – about the average for the period 2006 to 2010.[4] Hijackings and hostage-taking are practiced mainly by Somali pirates (Western Indian Ocean, Gulf of Aden and the Red Sea); while in South East Asia (especially Indonesia) piracy was primarily aimed at robbery. West Africa also contributes to maritime piracy.

Here are two chilling accounts of piracy incidents published by the International Maritime Bureau: 1) *"Asian Glory"*, a vehicle carrier, steaming, boarded January 1st, 2010, position 10:47N – 061:37E, about 620 nautical miles off Somali coast: "Pirates hijacked a ship underway and took her 25 crewmembers hostage. Pirates then sailed the ship to an undisclosed location in Somalia. It is believed a ransom was paid for the safe release of the crew and vessel." 2) *"Bet Fighter"*, a bulk carrier, steaming, boarded August 17th, 2010, position 03:17N – 105:29E, 12.6 nautical miles off Pulau Mangkai (Indonesia): "Six pirates armed with automatic guns and long knives boarded the tanker underway. They entered the bridge, and tied up the 2/O and the duty A/B. They entered the master's cabin and stole ship's cash. Pirates escaped with ship's properties, crew cash and personal belongings. Master reported the incident to an unknown warship in the vicinity."[5]

Cost of maritime piracy

The annual cost of piracy has been variously estimated to lie between $1 and $16 billion (Bellish, 2013; Bowden, 2010; O'Connell and Descovich, 2010; Wright, 2008). Of these, the most recent estimate is that of Bellish, who puts the total cost of Somali piracy in 2012 at $6 billion. These costs are made up of onboard security equipment and guards (29 percent), increased speeds (27 percent), military operations (19 percent), rerouting (5 percent), increased insurance premiums (10 percent), and increased labor (8 percent). These are mainly enforcement costs and the costs of avoiding being boarded. Hagemann (2010, p. 45) points out that these "costs lie where they fall", with each country paying the entirety of its own costs, even if its expenditures, especially on enforcement, also benefit other countries.[6] Some States Parties have taken on extra costs to aid in the establishment of "in-region" enforcement facilities – consisting of courts and prisons in Kenya and littoral states in the Gulf of Aden – under the Djibouti *Code of Conduct* of 2009.[7] Voluntary contributions have been made to a Trust Fund by South Korea and the United Arab Emirates.[8]

There are other costs in addition to these. In the absence of piracy, Fu et al. (2010) posit that all traffic between East Asia and Europe would use the shorter Suez Canal route and none the Cape of Good Hope route. They calculate an annual cost of container traffic reduction and diversion because of piracy of $30 billion, a number that is substantially greater than other estimates as it includes estimated values of lost consumers' surplus due to increased shipping costs being passed on to the end users.

3 Naval task forces

An interesting question concerns the forms anti-piracy investments have taken. Anderson (1995), looking at historical practices, points to economies of scale in this activity: when trade on a given shipping route was sparse individual merchant ships had to arm themselves, so duplicating investment. With greater amounts of trade several shipping companies reduced costs by banding together and hiring an armed ship for protection. With still greater traffic the least cost protection method turned out to be protection by a state's navy.

The international community has rallied to cooperate against piracy, with several naval task forces operating off the Horn of Africa. The European Union has Operation Atalanta with about 20 warships and 1,800 personnel. The USA has Combined Task Force 151 in the Horn of Africa area, while NATO has Operation Allied Protector – an escort system. Several individual countries also have warships in the area, including China, India, Saudi Arabia and South Korea. The EU also operates a voluntary information exchange where merchant and other ships transiting the area can coordinate with EU naval forces. Similarly, the US operates recommended transit corridors through the Gulf of Aden. The International Maritime Organization also collects and broadcasts information on piracy incidents.

However, curiously, in 2011 a Finnish warship, *Phojanmaa*, arrested 18 Somali pirates only to release them back onto Somali soil because "no country would take them and they had not offended against either Finnish shipping or Finnish nationals".[9] In the same year 16 suspected Somali pirates were arrested by a Danish warship, *The Esbern Snare*. The pirates were apprehended aboard a hijacked vessel and, according to NATO Allied Maritime Command, were holding two Yemeni hostages and were in possession of rocket launchers, assault rifles, ammunition, large quantities of fuel and two skiffs. However, the task force determined there were not sufficient grounds to prosecute, and the suspects were taken back to land.[10] If these facts are accurate, one has to wonder what evidence would be sufficient to bring suspected pirates to justice. Indeed, in the UK Julian Brazier, the Conservative Party's shipping spokesman (at the time not in power) commented that "It's shameful that so many pirates are being returned to do it again; the fault lies not with the hard-pressed naval commanders but the ridiculous rules of engagement and operating instructions they are being given by their political masters" (Ungoed-Thomas and Woolf, 2009).

In fact, although shipping traffic off the Horn of Africa is vast, protection against piracy by the world's navies is not the whole story. Initially the shipping companies did not favor the use of onboard armed guards, but from 2009 onward there was an increasing trend toward merchant ships arming themselves – just as if traffic was sparse. Thus, in 2011 they spent about $530 million on on-board security, and this approximately tripled to $1.53 billion in 2012.[11]

4 Pirate organization

The more efficient is a pirate organization the greater is the probability of the perpetrators *not* being caught on any given attack against shipping and, it can be supposed, the greater is the value of the booty captured. Indeed, Leeson (2007), using historical examples argues that pirate organizations developed so as to render piracy an efficient enterprise.[12] As a criminal organization, participants were outside of the rule of law, yet they had to have incentives in place to encourage cooperation. To achieve incentive alignment between the pirates – aimed at maximizing the take of booty from piracy voyages – the rank and file had to be satisfied that they would enjoy fair shares and would not be expropriated by the captain and the group around him. To achieve this, the pirate organization, in the heyday of piracy, 1690–1730, used elected captains who had charge only when the ship was in a conflict. Otherwise, the quartermaster, also elected, had charge of the ship. Pirate ships had agreed-upon constitutions governing things like compensation for wounded men, the sharing of booty, restrictions on the captain's privileges, and allowable punishments for sailors who broke the rules.

Somali pirates likewise have developed a social organization. Thus, certain "ports in Somalia . . . have been identified as havens for pirate gangs . . . Within these ports the pirates rely on facilities for shelter, food, and buildings to keep hostages. A key characteristic shared by these port cities that make them advantageous for pirate gangs to be based at is they are strongly armed, have sympathetic populations, and are in areas beyond the control of the local Somali Transitional Federal Government (TFG)" (O'Connell and Descovich, 2010, p. 33).

Based on interviews conducted by Bahadur (2009, 2011) with pirate leaders in northern, central and southern Somali ports, we can see that a number of factors have helped to create a group identity among Somali pirates:

1   Many pirates are ex-fishermen and hold the complaint that foreign fishing vessels intrude into Somalia's Exclusive Economic Zone, severely reducing fish stocks and harming the fishermen's well-being. Somali pirate attacks on foreign shipping are therefore legitimate, aimed only at levying a "tax". This justification for legitimacy is heightened by the fact that, as a failed state, Somalia has no national government to look after the fishermen's interests, so they must look after their own.
2   Boyah, a pirate clan leader of 500 men in the North, claims that everyone who seeks the position of pirate must see him and swear allegiance until death, natural or otherwise. This leads to low turnover within the group.
3   Many Somali pirates, at least those based in the North, are ex-Coast Guard recruits and therefore share something of a common background and training. The same is true for the ex-militiamen who have become pirates.

4   Somali piracy is a repeated profitable "game" that would be expensive in terms of forgone income if any pirate or pirate leader chose to renege on his commitments to the group. One interviewee claimed to have earned $350,000 in the first three years he was a pirate.

5 Piracy business model

The Somali piracy business model was developed some time early this century and is based on the profit-motive with profit sharing (Minney, 2010; O'Connell and Descovich, 2010).[13] There is even a "stock exchange" in Harardhere, where pirates can raise money to purchase the tools of the trade, and which also allows non-pirates to share in the profits of piracy. According to Minney (2010), "One wealthy former pirate named Mohammed took *Reuters* around the small [stock exchange] facility and said it had proved to be an important way for the pirates to win support from the local community for their operations, despite the dangers involved" . . . "Four months ago, during the monsoon rains, we decided to set up this stock exchange. We started with 15 'maritime companies' and now we are hosting 72. Ten of them have so far been successful at hijacking" . . . "The shares are open to all and everybody can take part, whether personally at sea or on land by providing cash, weapons or useful materials . . . we've made piracy a community activity" . . . "Shareholder Ms. Sahra Ibrahim, 22 years, whose initial stake was a rocket-propelled grenade received as part of the settlement when her husband divorced her, says: 'I have made $75,000 in only 38 days since I joined the 'company'" Minney (2010).

It makes sense that the more efficient is the pirate organization(s), the greater will be the economic rents that can be extracted from international shipping.

6 An economic model of piracy

Let *pr* be the probability of *not* being caught *and* prosecuted on any given piracy attack, which we assume is the same for all attacks (i.e. attacks are independent events). We can ask: what is the probability of *not* being caught on "*n*" attacks? Call this cumulative probability *CPR*, where

$$CPR = (pr)^n \tag{1}$$

For example, suppose *pr* = 0.8 (an 80 percent chance of getting away after a piracy attack). Then the probability of committing five attacks without being caught is $0.8^5 = 32.8\%$, while the probability of committing 11 attacks without being caught is $0.8^{11} = 8.6\%$.[14]

The expected net return from becoming a pirate as a function of the planned number of attacks, *n*, is

$$E(NB(n)) = CPR(n)[n(\$booty - \$wage)] - (1 - CPR(n))(\$jail) \tag{2}$$

where *CPR(n)* is again the cumulative probability of *not* being caught during those *n* attacks (so *(1 − CPR(n))* is the probability of being caught); *$booty* is the value of the "prize" gained per act of piracy; *$wage* is the opportunity cost of piracy per attack (i.e. the wage given up that could have been earned by a pirate in a legal job); and *$jail* is the implicit expected monetary cost of spending time in jail should a pirate be captured and jailed for an act of piracy.

A risk–neutral pirate will choose *n* to maximize (2). The resulting first-order condition (assuming an interior solution) is given by:

$$[1 + n\ln(pr)](\$booty - \$wage) = -\ln(pr)(\$jail) \qquad (3)$$

where the left-hand side is the marginal benefit of one more attack, and the right-hand side is the marginal cost.[15] The determination of the optimal number of attacks, *n**, is shown graphically in Figure 3.1.[16] As an example, let ($booty − $wage)/ ($jail) = 10, meaning that the net booty is ten times the expected cost of spending time in jail. For *pr* = 0.8, we obtain *n** = 4.38. It follows that *CPR(n*)* ≈ 38%, or the pirate perceives a 38 percent chance of not being caught during his career.

If we assume that as the number of pirate attacks grows the value of booty collected per attack increases – perhaps because more experienced pirates become better at locating high-value targets (a learning-by-doing effect) – then the marginal benefit of piracy may rise with the number of attacks by a given pirate. If this effect is strong enough, then there would be no limit to the number of attacks. That is, the MB function in Figure 3.1 could be positively sloped. In this case a person would plan on becoming a pirate for life and not limit himself to a given number of attacks.

Two other factors that would increase the optimum number of attacks for a pirate are a low opportunity cost of piracy, *$wage*, and a low value placed on jail time. In the Somali context of poverty with few alternatives to piracy, both of these terms can be assumed to be low. Notice too that it can be supposed that the greater

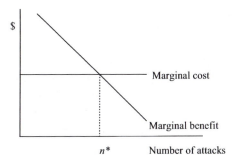

FIGURE 3.1 A pirate's optimal number of pirate attacks

is the efficiency of a pirate organization, the higher is *pr* (the probability of not being caught on an attack), and/or the greater is *$booty*, the further to the right in Figure 3.1 is the marginal benefit curve. In other words, an efficient organization also induces individual pirates to remain longer in the business.

7 Policies to reduce the number of pirate attacks

Policies that could be adopted to reduce the number of pirate attacks can be seen by observing the components in equation (3). Specifically, we can ask what policies will have the effect of lowering the marginal benefit of piracy (i.e. shifting the MB curve leftward) and/or raising the marginal cost of piracy (i.e. shifting the MC curve upward). Thus:

1   Cut the value of booty, *$booty*. As booty usually takes the form of ransom payments, at least in the case of Somali piracy, this might be difficult if not dangerous to achieve. Attempting to bargain ransom payments downward from the levels now prevalent could well risk hostages' lives.
2   Raise the opportunity cost of piracy by increasing *$wage*. However, to raise wages outside of piracy in Somalia would require substantially moving Somalia toward being a working state with a proper government, rather than a failed state. This would require a major effort on the part of the international community.
3   Similarly, aiding the Somali Transitional Government to take charge of the whole of Somalia, or at least its coastal regions, would be a step toward disrupting the efficacy of the pirate organization. A more "normal" land-based enforcement authority (i.e. a government with "normal" controls over its territory) would raise the marginal cost and lower the marginal benefit of piracy by increasing the probability of detention after any given number of acts of piracy. Moreover, the formation of such a government could lead to an increase in the opportunity cost of piracy (*$wage*), as well as substantially reduce the reward for piracy, *$booty*, as Somali pirates lose their safe havens both to hold hijacked ships in Somalia's territorial waters and to hold hostages in safe havens on land. This point is consistent with the empirical findings of de Groot, Rablen and Shortland (2011), who find that increasing the efficacy of government beyond the level found in coastal Puntland (Northern Somalia) leads to a decrease in the "production of pirate activity".
4   Cut the chances of getting away after an attack – that is, cut *pr*, thereby also cutting *CPR* and reducing the number of planned attacks by pirates.[17]
5   Increase expected jail time and, therefore, *$jail*.[18] The USA certainly took a stride down this route when in February 2011 it imposed a detention sentence of thirty-three years on a detained Somali pirate.[19] However, so far other countries have not handed out such severe sentences.

8 Interaction between shipper and pirate activity

The amount of shipping activity, y, and pirate activity, x, in a given area of ocean space are interdependent. The amount of pirate activity depends directly on the amount of shipping activity because piracy is likely to be more profitable when more targets are available – a predator–prey relationship. Conversely, the greater is the amount of pirate activity the lower will be the amount of shipping activity because some shippers will divert to other routes.

Figure 3.2 shows the pirates' best response function, $\hat{x}(y; \bar{p}, \bar{s})$, as positively sloped and that of the shippers, $\hat{y}(x; p^+, s^+)$, as negatively sloped. Equilibrium best responses on these reaction functions are initially at point A, where it is clearly shown that the amount of shipping activity is lower than it would be in the absence of piracy – the maximum occurring at the vertical intercept of the $\hat{y}$ function.[20]

It is further assumed that the amount of pirate activity is negatively related to both the probability of being caught and punished, p, as well as the size of the sanction imposed, s (years in prison).[21] Hence, an increase in p or s shifts the $\hat{x}$ function to the left, as marked in Figure 3.2. Conversely, enhanced enforcement that raises p, or stronger punishments increasing s, make shippers feel safer and the $\hat{y}$ function shifts to the right. A new equilibrium occurs at point B. Notice that in Figure 3.2 an increase in p or s reduces pirate activity and increases shipper activity.[22]

9 A free rider problem

As we saw in Section 2, enforcement against maritime piracy is costly. Moreover, enforcement on the high seas is a mixed good in that the enforcement efforts of a given country's navy benefits not only its own merchant shipping (a private benefit) but also the merchant shipping of other countries, which is an external benefit. The provision of mixed goods is likely to be sub-optimal because those countries enjoying the external benefit of safer seas cannot be charged for the service.

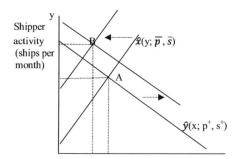

FIGURE 3.2 Interaction between shipper and pirate activity

Here is an argument showing that, with a mixed good, provision in the absence of coordination between countries will be sub-optimal. Section 4 in the next chapter also tackles this matter from a more descriptive angle.

Begin by assuming a single enforcement agency as opposed to the actual case of multiple enforcement agents policing against piracy on the high seas. A single enforcement agent will observe the social marginal benefits (i.e. benefits to the international community as a whole SMB $= \sum_{i=1}^{n} MB_i, i = 1, 2, 3, \ldots n$ countries) and marginal costs of enforcement, MC, and optimize by setting SMB $=$ MC. For example, state policing in, say, Connecticut is paid for by a single payer. A rational enforcement agent will set the social benefit of an extra unit of enforcement equal to the marginal cost of an extra unit of enforcement. This is shown in Figure 3.3, where E_1 is the optimal level of enforcement.

With multiple enforcement by countries, $i = 1, 2, 3 \ldots n$, optimum enforcement is now SMB $= \sum_{i=1}^{n} MC_i$. However, assume that the MBs are ranked $MB_1 > MB_2 > MB_3 > \ldots MB_n$. This could be because country 1 has most shipping passing through an area where piracy is prevalent, country 2 the second most, and so on downward.

In principle, each country sets its MC equal to its own perceived MB. So country 1, with the highest MB, sets $MB_1 = MC_1$ and makes an investment in enforcement accordingly. Suppose that this investment is $300 million per year. The other countries would all do the same thing – setting their own MBs equal to their own MCs. The MB of country 2 might be $200 million, that of country 3 $150 million, and so on downward.

So country 1 will invest $300 million in enforcement. However, all the countries with lower MBs than MB_1 see that enforcement expenditure is already greater, at $300 million, than their respective MBs, so they don't see a need to invest at all. Accordingly, the countries $i = 2, 3 \ldots n$ enjoy a free ride on the enforcement expenditure of country 1.

In Figure 3.3 this means that the level of enforcement is only E_2, which is below the socially optimal level. Enforcement units between E_2 and E_1 should be supplied, because SMB $>$ MC, but the free rider problem means that they are not.

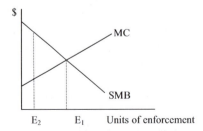

FIGURE 3.3 Optimal and sub-optimal enforcement against piracy

The upshot of this analysis is that although apparently large amounts of money are being spent on enforcement against maritime piracy, enforcement is sub-optimal because of an enduring free rider problem, itself made possible by the nature of the international public law underpinning the *Law of the Sea Convention*. This argument is consistent with the fact, stated at the beginning of this chapter, that pirates are often released after being captured. This is because prosecution and imprisonment would be an extra expense and one incurred on behalf of some other country – the flag state, the country where the owners are citizens, or the countries from where the crews are drawn, which are often not the same as that of the navy doing the capturing.

10 Problems arising from trying pirates in States Parties' courts

Trying pirates far from where their crimes were committed is expensive. Per-pirate prosecution cost is estimated at between five and seven times more expensive outside the Horn of Africa region than in the region (such as in Kenya, Seychelles, Somaliland); for example, the cost is $52,000 in-region, versus $246,000 in Europe and $336,000 in the USA (Bowden, 2010). Moreover, legal questions can arise concerning the relevance of national laws to the crime of piracy, if such laws even exist; as Dutton (2011a) points out, many countries such as Denmark do not even have national laws governing the crime of maritime piracy. And problems can arise for civilian courts given that the arresting agent is a military rather than a police authority.

These issues are illustrated in the following case. A German ship flying a German flag, the MV *Taipan*, on route from Djibouti to Mombasa, was boarded by 10 Somali pirates on April 5th, 2010, 500 nautical miles east of Somalia. The Dutch naval vessel HNMLS *Tromp* happened to be nearby and a contingent of its marines landed from helicopters on the MV *Taipan*; after a skirmish, all suspects were arrested.[23] After being held in chains for several days on the *Tromp* the suspects were passed on for trial in Germany.[24] The trial took place in the Youth Chamber of the Hamburg Criminal Court, Room 337, Strafjustizgebäude (Criminal Court Building), Sievekingplatz 3, 20355 Hamburg, beginning November 22nd, 2010.

The court proceedings indicate several difficulties in putting pirates on trial far from their homes.[25] Without legal documents, suspects' ages were hard to determine, and were never known for sure; but age is relevant as persons have to be over fourteen years to stand trial in a German court. Second, problems arose with the simultaneous translations into Somali language of legal proceedings being held in German, especially technical terms, thus questioning the fairness of the trial from the defendants' point of view. Third, naval officer-witnesses had to travel long distances from their ships (and/or home country) to the trial in a foreign country. Fourth, as military personnel, some witnesses were restricted from giving evidence on certain military matters that the defense thought relevant. Evidence had to be collected, in this case by Dubai detectives, and then transported to the German court – with a German detective having to travel to Dubai to collect it. Fifth, fingerprinting of evidence (for example, of guns found on the MV *Taipan*) was not performed, as it is not the practice of the arresting naval force. Sixth, an important question was raised over whether evidence gathered through interviews on the *Tromp* was found through "interrogation" of suspects or through "voluntary statements". If the former, and without proper legal procedures being followed (such as the court-issue of an arrest warrant), some evidence might not be allowed in court. Finally, the fact that the accused were not told their rights was a violation of German, Dutch and international law. The German court had to rule on this and decided that as the statements were made on a Dutch ship they could be introduced into proceedings. However, there was an extra complication that a Dutch court would later have to rule on regarding admissibility.

11 Conclusions

In some areas of the world maritime piracy is far from being inconsequential, and merchant shippers and countries are investing resources against it. This chapter examines economic aspects of this relationship between pirates and enforcement agencies. Unfortunately, because enforcement by a country's navy and courts benefits not only that country but other countries too – because enforcement has external benefits, it's a mixed good – there is under-investment in enforcement. International public law aspects of enforcement against maritime piracy are the subject of the next chapter.

Notes

1 This chapter and the next are based on three papers written with Thomas Miceli and published in *Ocean Development and International Law* (2011), *Maritime Policy and Management* (2013) and the *Scottish Journal of Political Economy* (2013).
2 ICC-IMB Piracy and Armed Robbery against Ships Report – *Annual Report, 2012*.
3 ICC Commercial Crime Services, April 2013, available online at www.icc-ccs.org/.
4 ICC-IMB Piracy and Armed Robbery against Ships Report – *Annual Report, 2010*, Tables 7 and 8.
5 *Ibid.*, pp. 48, 41.
6 He was referring to the UK's Operation Headquarters in Northwood, which had been established in 2008 as the operational headquarters for EUNAVFOR, the umbrella for the European Union's naval forces off the Horn of Africa (and the first joint maritime operation by the EU).
7 This *Code of Conduct* is discussed in more detail later in this chapter.
8 Alshihad News and Analysis, "S. Korea pledges US$500,000 to anti-piracy trust fund", April 24th, 2011, available online at http://english.alshahid.net/archives/20085. Emirates 24/7 News, "UAE donates $1.4m to fight piracy: Money will go to Counter-Piracy Trust Fund", April 19th, 2011, available online at www.emirates247.com/news/uae-donates-1–4m-to-fight-piracy-2011-04-18-1.382219.
9 *Icenews*, April 27th, 2011, available online at www.icenews.is/index.php/2011/04/27/18-captured-pirates-released-without-charge/.

10 "Danish warship captures Gulf of Aden pirates", *Terradaily*, available online at www. terradaily.com/reports/Danish_warship_captures_Gulf_of_Aden_pirates_999.html.

11 Source: Oceans Beyond Piracy, The Economic Cost of Somali Piracy 2012 and 2011, *On Earth Future*.

12 See also Guha and Guha (2011) on this matter.

13 For an amusing view of this model see M. Lynn, "Out cutlasses and board: a plan for our age", *Financial Times*, February 11th, 2011.

14 We could also ask: what is the probability of being caught on, say, the second attack, given the probability of not having been caught on the first attack of 0.8? This probability is $0.8 \times 0.2 = 0.16$, where 0.8 is the probability of not having been caught on the first attack, so being able to go on the second attack, and 0.2 is the probability of being caught on the second attack. Notice that given two attacks the probability of being caught can be calculated as $1 - (0.8 \times 0.8) = 0.36$, or as $0.2 + 0.16 = 0.36$.

15 Note that $\ln(pr) < 0$ given $0 < pr < 1$.

16 Note that the marginal benefit is decreasing in n given $\ln(pr) < 0$, and the marginal cost is constant.

17 If pr is cut from 0.8 to 0.6 (i.e. the capture rate is doubled from 0.2 to 0.4), the optimal number of planned attacks per pirate falls from 4.38 to 1.86, all else equal.

18 If jail time is increased, say, twofold, then the ratio ($booty − $wage)/($jail) (the "mark-up") would be cut in half. If the mark-up fell from 10 to 5 as a result of this change, the optimal number of attacks per pirate would fall from 4.38 to 4.28, holding pr fixed at 0.8.

19 Abduwali Abdukhadir Muse was charged with in 2009 kidnapping, hijacking and hostage-taking for his role in the seizure of the *Maersk Alabama* container ship and two other vessels in the Indian Ocean. See MSNBC news, available online at www.msnbc. msn.com/id/41615693/ns/us_news-crime_and_courts/.

20 In fact, point A is the Nash equilibrium.

21 Notice that pr is the probability of not being caught and prosecuted, while p is the probability of this happening.

22 Notice that increased enforcement that increases p or s, or both, could lead to *more* piracy depending on the extent of the shifts in the functions in Figure 3.2. It could be that stronger enforcement will induce so much more shipping into an area that pirates will take more risks to get at it. In Figure 3.2 it is assumed that this is not the case.

23 "Pirated German ship rescued – EU NAVFOR HNMLS Tromp retakes pirated MV Taipan" Monday, April 05, 2010, available online at www.odin.tc/eng/articles/231-Pirated-German-ship-rescued—EU-NAVFOR-HNMLS-Tromp-retakes-pirated-MV-Taipan. asp.

24 The Dutch were not willing to put the suspects on trial themselves; however, under Universal Jurisdiction – any country can prosecute (on universal jurisdiction see Randall, 1988).

25 This information is summarized from a blog of the trial: "Reclaiming the Seas", available online at http://reclaim-the-seas.blogspot.com/p/reports-from-court-case.html.

4

MARITIME PIRACY AND INTERNATIONAL LAW

1 *Law of the Sea Convention*

For centuries enforcement against piracy on the high seas has been customary international law. In modern times the *Convention on the High Seas*, 1958, codified this customary international law.[1] More recently the *United Nations Convention on the Law of the Sea* (1982, ratified 1994) took over the articles of the 1958 *Convention* virtually verbatim.[2] It also extended international law governing piracy to include the EEZs.[3] The navy of any country can arrest a pirate ship of any other country. Arrests may not be made in the territorial zone, except with the permission of the coastal state.[4]

According to Article 100 of the 1982 *Convention*, "all States shall cooperate to the fullest possible extent in the repression of piracy". But as neither "cooperate" nor "fullest possible extent" are defined anywhere in the *Convention*, there is room for each country to "cooperate" as it sees fit. Thus, a country may choose to send naval forces or not – and if does, whether to make arrests and incur prosecution costs or not, or, simply, to let the suspects go.

Article 101 defines the acts that constitute piracy, emphasizing "any acts of violence, detention of crew or passengers or any act of depredation, committed for private ends by the crew or the passengers of a private ship . . . or against another ship; also the taking over of a ship used/to be used in acts of piracy". The term "private ends" is important as it includes robbery, and hijacking for ransom and personal profit. It does not include acts of terrorism that are aimed at political ends. Article 103 defines a pirate ship as "intended by the persons in dominant control to be used for the purpose of committing one of the acts referred to in Article 101". Article 105 states that "On the high seas, or in any other place outside the jurisdiction of any State, every State may seize a pirate ship or aircraft, or a ship taken by piracy and under the control of pirates, and arrest the persons and seize the property on board. The courts of the State which carried out the seizure may decide upon the penalties to be imposed, and may also determine the action to be taken with regard to the ships, aircraft or property, subject to the rights of third parties acting in good faith." This is the important point in customary international law referred to above. Also important is Article 106 that governs seizures at sea "without adequate grounds", that would create a liability for the arresting state to the flag state. What constitutes "adequate grounds" is defined in Article 103 as "intent" or "in control". In either instance an arresting navy has to make a judgment, and may release suspects when reported facts suggest that neither "intent" nor "in control" were present.

Despite the existence of this international law, very often arrested suspects are simply let go, apparently in many cases to commit the crime of piracy again and again. Thus, over the period from August 2008 to September 2009, navies in the Horn of Africa region disarmed and released 343 pirates, while only 212 others were handed over for prosecution (US Central Command, 2009).[5] Also, the UN Security Council reports that 90 percent of apprehended pirates are released, and that some of them are captured more than once (United Nations Security Council, 2011). At issue in this chapter is this: why are suspected pirates being let go rather than being prosecuted?

2 *Ad hoc* explanations or cooperation failures

Two explanations have been put forward for the failure of international cooperation to bring maritime pirates to justice. First, the *Convention*'s relevant Articles have not been written into some countries' national laws, thus creating jurisdictional issues. As Dutton (2010, p. 3) has observed: "The apparent reasons for this refusal to accept these judicial burdens are many: for example, inadequate or non-existent national laws criminalizing the acts committed, concerns about the safety and impartiality of local judges, the difficulties of obtaining and preserving evidence, and fears that if convicted, the pirates will be able to remain in the country where they are prosecuted."

Second, evidentiary problems might arise if suspected pirates were not actually caught in the act of piracy. *The Esbern Snare* case referred to in the last chapter is an example of this, and on the face of it appears to be an application of Article 106 of the *Convention* – liability for seizure without adequate grounds. However, we are not at all persuaded by this argument, as suspects had been spotted far out at sea using the fast skiffs favored by Somali pirates and in possession of hijacked vessels, hostages, and piracy equipment such as grappling hooks, firearms and even rocket propelled grenades.

The position here is that both of the foregoing arguments for releasing maritime pirates are *ad hoc* and result from a more fundamental problem. This is that under the *Convention*, unavoidably, maritime piracy outside of the territorial seas is enforced by multiple enforcement agencies, which as explained in the last chapter entails radically different incentives compared with the case of a single enforcement agent operating entirely within a State Party's jurisdictional boundaries.

3   Provision of global public goods

As discussed in the last chapter, policing, whether domestic or in international waters, has public good characteristics because, if it is effective, it reduces crime for everybody. Provision of global public goods is quite rare in history, and seems best to coincide with the existence of a global hegemon (Kindleberger, 1986), or "preponderant actor". Two examples in the maritime context are the UK in the nineteenth century, which provided a good deal of maritime security, and the establishment by the USA – with cost-sharing with the UK – of the International Ice Patrol following the sinking of the *Titanic* in 1912.[6] Two cases of a preponderant actor in high seas fisheries are discussed in Chapter 12.

4   The economics of enforcing laws against maritime piracy

In principle, an economic approach to the control of maritime piracy is a direct application of the general theory of law enforcement, as first examined by Gary Becker (1968) and refined by Polinsky and Shavell (2000).[7] The theory relies on two fundamental claims: first, that potential offenders (criminals or pirates) respond to the threat of legal sanctions in deciding whether or not to commit illicit acts – that is, they are rational maximizers; and second, that an enforcement authority stands ready to enforce those sanctions by expending resources to apprehend and prosecute any offenders who violate the law. If either of these assumptions fails to hold, then threatened legal sanctions will not be effective in reducing piracy.

In the context of ordinary crime, there is ample evidence that most offenders do in fact behave rationally in the above sense, especially when committing property crimes. This is reflected by empirical studies showing that increases in the likelihood or severity of punishment do reduce the crime rate. (See, for example, Shepherd, 2002.) And since the primary motivation for maritime pirates is material gain, whether derived from the confiscation of cargo or the seeking of ransom for hostages, it seems reasonable to suppose that they too are acting in a rational way.

The next question concerns the enforcement of laws against piracy, and it is here that problems emerge. Optimal enforcement of laws against ordinary crime requires the existence of a single enforcer, usually a city or state government, that has both the will and the resources to carry out the threatened sanctions (assuming, of course, that laws against crime have been enacted – an assumption that, as we have seen, is not always met in the case of piracy). Enforcement of international laws against piracy, in contrast, necessitates the cooperation of multiple nations in order to achieve optimal deterrence.[8] In practice, however, there are several reasons for the general lack of such cooperation.

First, the gains from deterring piracy consist of the savings in lost profits and other costs incurred by all countries engaged in shipping along routes threatened by pirate attacks. Thus, each country has an interest in reducing piracy in proportion to its share of those costs – as was argued in the last chapter, enforcement has a private good characteristic. As noted above, however, the deterrence of piracy, like law enforcement in general, has public good qualities in the sense that actions by any one country to apprehend offenders will benefit all countries. Thus, each country has an incentive to free ride on the efforts of others. It follows that, in the absence of some mechanism that obligates countries to contribute to a unified enforcement effort, the level of enforcement will likely be sub-optimal in the same way that public goods will be underprovided if solely financed by voluntary contributions.

A second reason countries will tend to under-invest in enforcement against piracy concerns the cost of prosecuting and punishing detainees. If those costs are borne entirely by the apprehending country, then countries will have an incentive to avoid them, especially if the offender's acts were not against the apprehending country's vessels (as in the Finnish example described in Section 3 of the last chapter). This creates a kind of "reverse rent-seeking" problem, in which countries seek to avoid being the first to apprehend a pirate in the hope that someone else will incur the resulting costs. Note that both of the above problems are due to the collective nature of enforcement of international laws, and will arise in any law enforcement context where crime overlaps jurisdictional boundaries and there does not exist an over-arching government or enforceable mutual aid treaty to induce cooperation. For example, similar problems plague the enforcement of laws against drug trafficking (Naranjo, 2010; Poret, 2003), as well as prosecution of the "global war on terror".

A third enforcement problem, unrelated to the collective action issue, concerns the credibility of threats to actually impose sanctions once a pirate is apprehended. Specifically, once an offender is caught, the apprehending country may simply choose not to spend the resources necessary to detain, prosecute and punish him. This issue is largely ignored in the economics of crime literature,[9] where it is generally assumed that threats to prosecute criminals are credible, but it is amplified in the context of piracy because of the absence of a unified enforcement authority that can develop a reputation over time for carrying out threatened sanctions. As the above anecdotes show, this outcome is not an uncommon one.

A final issue concerns the choice of the sanction to be imposed on a convicted pirate. If individual countries choose their own sanctions, there will likely be considerable variability in the nature and severity of the sanction, and some countries may have no sanctions at all against piracy. There will also be differences in criminal procedure and evidentiary standards. In theory, international agreements can specify uniform sanctions and procedures, but philosophical differences regarding appropriate punishments (e.g. disagreements over the death penalty or sympathy with the pirates) will make this difficult. And besides, for the reasons already noted, pre-specified sanctions may not be viewed as binding by the country that actually apprehends a pirate and has to bear the cost of imposing them.

5   Attempts aimed at promoting greater international cooperation

In the preceding section it was argued that States Parties will tend to under-invest in provision of maritime enforcement because of its public good nature. Thus, if maritime policing is to be provided at anything like the socially optimal level, some degree of increased international cooperation needs to be organized beyond commitments made in the *United Nations Convention on the Law of the Sea* Articles 100 to 107. In fact, several such efforts have been attempted. The UN Security Council in 2008 issued Resolutions 1816, 1838, 1846 and 1851, which exhorted States Parties with warships in the Horn of Africa area to cooperate and to undertake greater efforts to capture and bring pirates to justice. Resolution 1816 allowed states cooperating with the Somali Transitional Government (STG) to pursue pirates in Somalia's territorial waters; Resolution 1838 urged States Parties to protect shipping engaged in World Food Program activities; Resolution 1846 extended the period in which States Parties' warships could enter Somalia's territorial sea; and Resolution 1851 enabled States Parties to pursue Somali pirates ashore. But none of these resolutions *required* States Parties to step up their anti-piracy efforts.

Another attempt at international cooperation occurred in January 2009 under the auspices of the International Maritime Organization (IMO). Seventeen regional governments met in Djibouti to discuss issues related to piracy, with nine of them signing the *Code of Conduct concerning the Repression of Piracy and Armed Robbery against Ships in the Western Indian Ocean and the Gulf of Aden*. The signatories declared their intention to cooperate "to the fullest possible extent" to repress piracy (IMO, 2009). The specific aims are to improve communication between states, increase the capacity of regional states to arrest and prosecute pirates, and to improve the capabilities of their coast guards.

Yet another attempt at promoting international cooperation against piracy was held in Dubai in April 2011 at the instigation of the Dubai government and international shipping interests, with about fifty countries in attendance.[10] Apart from a few commitments to contribute financially to the setting up of enforcement facilities in Horn of Africa regional countries, nothing much concrete seems to have come out of this conference.

By contrast, an attempt at cost-sharing, functioning since 2006 and now with seventeen contracting parties, is the *Regional Cooperation Agreement on Combating Piracy and Armed Robbery against Ships in Asia*, which practices information sharing and performs anti-piracy patrols.[11] According to Noakes (2009) these efforts have met with a good deal of success.

6   Three proposed solutions to overcome free riding

This section discusses three responses aimed at removing the free rider problem associated with control of maritime piracy. The first proposes the use of the International Criminal Court to try pirates, the second advocates extension of the *SUA Convention* to piracy as well as to terrorism, and the third suggests an extension of certain parts of civil aviation law to govern enforcement against maritime piracy. The following paragraphs briefly describe these proposals and what may be important drawbacks associated with them.

Use the International Criminal Court

Dutton (2011b) suggests trying pirates in the International Criminal Court (ICC). She points to a number of advantages: a) no new international institution is needed as the ICC already exists; b) piracy under customary international law is a crime against the international community; c) under the *Rome Statute* the ICC can be used even when national courts are unwilling or unable genuinely to carry out the investigation or prosecution; d) the cost of using ICC relative to the current cost of prosecuting cases in Kenya would not be prohibitive.

In light of the analysis offered in this paper, this suggestion also has the particular advantage of possibly reducing the free rider problem that leads to the underfunding of the prosecution of pirates. Under the Rome Statute that established the ICC and its governing Assembly there would be, if the same financing system was carried over, international sharing of the cost of prosecuting pirates. As described by Romano and Ingadottir (2000, pp. 4–5), the Rome Statute lays out how the ICC is funded: the Court and its governing Assembly are financed from assessed contributions from States Parties who are members of the ICC (in 2011 there were 114); these contributions are based on a scale adopted by the UN for its regular budget (itself based on "capacity to pay"), and also come from funds provided by the UN and approved by the General Assembly. Voluntary contributions are also welcomed.

In addition, the ICC could operate more efficiently as a piracy tribunal than if each state had to proceed on its own. This is true for several reasons. First, use of the ICC would avert the need for costly duplication of judicial resources. Second, it would allow judges and prosecutors to specialize in the prosecution of piracy cases. Third, the court could adopt standardized practices and procedures for gathering, evaluating and presenting evidence. For example, the costs of trials could be reduced by having witnesses, located perhaps thousands of miles away from the ICC, give evidence by live-video – which is specifically allowed for by Rule 67 of the ICC's "Rules of Procedure and Evidence Adopted by the Assembly of States Parties".[12] Finally, use of the ICC would alleviate the need for States Parties to justify to domestic audiences the costly prosecution of pirates whose acts did not specifically target that nation's vessels.

However, as Dutton (2011b) acknowledges, if the ICC were to take over the prosecution of pirates, its Statute would have to be modified to allow it to do so. It is beyond the scope of this book to venture an opinion on the likelihood of such a modification occurring, but it is worth noting that any countries that have thus far chosen not to contribute to enforcement of the *Law of the Sea* against piracy, or to contribute to the financing of the same, could take the stance of attempting to block any such changes to the Rome Statute or otherwise refuse to finance prosecution of pirates by the ICC. Nevertheless, it is most interesting that Dutton (2011b) recognizes these relevant financial problems and has suggested a way to resolve them.

Apply SUA1988

The *Convention for the Suppression of Unlawful Acts against the Safety of Maritime Navigation (SUA1988)* is aimed at illegal acts on the high seas, though in this case it targets acts of terrorism rather than piracy. There are 149 signatories, and Article 6 requires that *SUA*'s legal provisions be written into national laws, with signatories agreeing to prosecute any suspects delivered to them. However, only those states with some connection to the offense in question are allowed to prosecute, which does little to address the multi-jurisdiction problem. Still, the *SUA Convention* is clearer than the *Law of the Sea* in terms of spelling out the obligations of States Parties, which would help alleviate an important source of free riding.

Noakes (2009), the chief maritime security officer for the Baltic and International Maritime Council (BIMCO, a ship-owners association), argued before a US House of Representatives Committee that *SUA1988* can and should also be used to combat piracy, and moreover that it is incorrect to think that this *Convention* applies only to terrorism and not to piracy on the high seas. Indeed, the Introduction to *SUA1988* recognizes that the States Parties to the *Convention* are "deeply concerned about the world-wide escalation of acts of terrorism *in all its forms*". The next paragraph makes clear that the unlawful acts it had in mind are "against the safety of maritime navigation, . . . jeopardize the safety of persons and property, seriously affect the operation of maritime services, and undermine the confidence of the peoples of the world in the safety of maritime navigation" (Noakes, 2009).

However, *SUA1988* grew out of UN General Assembly Resolution 40/61 in 1985, itself a response to terrorism on the *Achille Lauro* in 1985, and Resolution 40/61 is clearly aimed at terrorist acts at sea and not piracy. Moreover, the following paragraph in the preamble to *SUA* addresses motivations for criminal acts at sea and they are clearly related to terrorism. Thus, "Recalling resolution 40/61 of the General Assembly of the United Nations of 9 December 1985 which, *inter alia*, 'urges all

States unilaterally and in co-operation with other States, as well as relevant United Nations organs, to contribute to the progressive elimination of causes underlying international terrorism and to pay special attention to all situations, including colonialism, racism and situations involving mass and flagrant violations of human rights and fundamental freedoms and those involving alien occupation, that may give rise to international terrorism and may endanger international peace and security'".

Kontorovich (2009) points out that "the reluctance to use *SUA* as a basis for jurisdiction may be due to a lack of guidance about the precise applicability of the treaty" (p. 4). In fact, we know of one such case of "guidance" – the stated opinion of the US legislative attorney R. C. Masson (2010), working for the Congressional Research Service. Masson implies that *SUA* is directed at piracy as well as terrorism at sea. However, this is only "guidance" and at this time the US position on *SUA* and piracy remains unresolved. Anyway, as far as we are aware, the argument for applying *SUA 1988* against piracy has not been taken any further.

Apply civil aviation laws

There are several Conventions under the United Nations International Civil Aviation Organization (ICAO), and Kilpatrick (2011) argues that one or more of these may be applied against maritime piracy. Most relevant is the *Hague Convention*, 1970. It compels states to either extradite or to prosecute airplane hijackers. It also requires signatory states to punish terrorist acts through "severe penalties" through domestic laws. Kilpatrick (2011) argues that the widespread acceptance of the *Hague Convention* by major economic powers arguably establishes customary international law that binds both signatories and non-signatories alike. This however begs the question of whether customary international law is in fact binding. Even so, Kilpatrick points out that "despite significant challenges, these international agreements, domestic laws, United Nation resolutions, and leveraging mechanisms have worked to establish a regulatory regime designed to prevent and deter aircraft hijackings. By strengthening airport and aircraft security, prosecuting hijackers and terrorists, and imposing de facto sanctions on states that provide safe havens for such offenders, aviation security has evolved into a viable legal framework that may contribute to solutions in other sectors facing similar issues" (p. 10).

However, the reason why the civil aviation conventions suppressing aircraft hijackings have been widely adopted among states is probably not because of the creation of customary international law. Rather, as the world's largest airline market, United States legislation has a significant impact on global regulation because foreign airlines and flights from foreign airports that do not meet United States security standards are effectively prohibited from accessing its lucrative market. Moreover, countries are more strongly motivated to move against aircraft hijackings because each single incident is most likely to affect more people, say, 250 on an airplane versus 20 on a ship; aircraft hijackings seem also to be much more prominent in the media than are maritime hijackings, and they are more deadly – one bomb can instantly kill hundreds of people. In other words, US leadership in devising effective international laws against maritime piracy is much less effective than it was in civil aviation, or, in the terminology of Chapter 12, while it could be a preponderant actor in civil aviation it cannot be in maritime piracy.

7 Conclusions

The background to this chapter is that in recent years more captured maritime pirates have been released by the warships that captured them than were passed on for prosecution. An argument put forward here is that *ad hoc* explanations for this failure are not the whole story – namely, that many countries have not written relevant international law (Articles 100 to 107 of the *United Nations Convention on the Law of the Sea*, 1982) into national law, and that evidence is usually insufficient to prosecute suspects. Rather, it is argued that there is a more encompassing argument: that maritime enforcement as governed by current international law has the nature of a public good, or, at least, a mixed good, and as such suffers from free rider problems. That is, as the shipping of no one country can be excluded from the benefits of reduced crime created by enforcement expenditures by other countries, incentives for all actors to invest in enforcement at an optimal level are lacking. In particular, it has been argued that aversion to incurring costs that benefit others helps to explain why countries are in no rush to write international law into national law, and also why there is a preference for letting arrested suspects go rather than going to the expense of putting them on trial and imprisoning them.

Ultimately, the blame for failure to bring so many captured maritime pirates to justice lies with the nature of international public law, which, while requiring "cooperation" (Article 100 of the *Convention*) nowhere defines what is meant by it. This allows signatories to choose their preferred degrees of "cooperation". In this regard, as Article 100 is not a binding contract, requiring a pre-specified "cooperation", one should not be surprised that what cooperation is offered is too often insufficient.

Notes

1 1958 *Convention*, Articles 14 to 21.
2 1982 *Convention*, Articles 100 to 107.
3 1982 *Convention*, Article 58(2).
4 Except in the case of Somalia, which is allowed under a UN Security Council resolution.
5 US Central Command (2009), "Pirate Attacks on the Rise off Somali Coast", B. K. Dandridge, Sept 29th, available online at www.centcom.mil/press-releases/pirate-attacks-on-rise-off-somalia-coast. See also Ungoed-Thomas and Woolf (2009), who describe captured Somali pirates "routinely" being released.
6 In the case of the International Ice Patrol, all costs were initially shared with just one other country – the UK – even though shipping from other countries also benefit from the broadcasting of iceberg positions (Wiswall, 1983). The underlying reason was that US and UK shipping "internalized" enough of the benefits of knowing where icebergs

were to justify paying the full costs of running the Patrol. It was not until 1956 that an international agreement was signed with other countries to share costs (*The Agreement Regarding Financial Support for the North Atlantic Ice Patrol*, January 4th 1956, 7.U.S.T. 1969, T.I.A.S. Number 3957, 256, U.N.T.S. 171). Even so, signatory nations account for only about one-half of shipping benefiting from the services of the International Ice Patrol (Amacost, 1995). Non-payers are free riders.

7   See Hallwood and Miceli (2011) for a formal application of this theory to the control of piracy, on which this section is based.

8   Since enforcement is costly, optimal deterrence will not generally result in *complete* deterrence of piracy. Rather, resources should be devoted to enforcement up to the point where the marginal savings from deterring an additional act of piracy equals the marginal cost of those resources. See Hallwood and Miceli (2011) for details.

9   But see Boadway, Maceau and Marchand (1996) and Baker and Miceli (2005).

10 See *Al Jazeera*, "Dubai hosts anti-piracy conference", April 18th, 2011, available online at http://english.aljazeera.net/news/middleeast/2011/04/20114186721819166.html.

11 See the ReCAAP website at www.recaap.org/.

12 First session New York, 3–10 September 2002, Official Records ICC-ASP/1/3. It is an open question how the ICC would handle video evidence should the USA ever accede to the Rome Statute. Under Federal Rules of Evidence, Rules of Criminal Procedure, Rule 26 requires that testimony be given in open court, a provision that is consistent with the 6th amendment to the US Constitution that guarantees a defendant the right to confront their accuser(s) in person.

PART III

Enclosure

5

ENCLOSURE OF THE OCEANS

1 Progression of ocean governance regimes

From the seventeenth century onward it was usual for coastal states to claim a 3-nautical mile territorial sea – about how far an onshore canon could fire. The rest of the ocean was high seas and not subject to national laws – though customary international law applied, see Chapter 1. Ocean resources were effectively open access. However, in 1945 through the *Truman Proclamation* the USA claimed the resources on and under its continental shelf, setting off a progression of ocean enclosures as other countries followed suit – a kind of "land grab". Accordingly, in 1947 Chile and Peru, both with narrow continental shelves, claimed 200-nautical mile exclusive economic zones, and many other countries then chose to do so. In fact, from 1982, under the *Law of the Sea*, Part V, Article 55, a country is allowed to claim its continental shelf out to 350 nautical miles if the continental shelf extends that far. These enclosures account for 38 million square nautical miles of ocean space – about 36 percent of ocean surface area, 90 percent of its commercial fisheries and 87 percent of its oil reserves.[1]

Codification of enclosure claims was attempted at the 1958 *United Nations Convention on Law of the Sea* (UNCLOS). Coastal state sovereign rights over the adjacent continental shelf were recognized out to the 200-meter isobath or beyond if exploitation was possible. Beyond these markers and in the water columns above, the high seas regime ruled. The following UNCLOS, in 1960, attempted further codification but achieved little. More than a decade later, in 1973, UNCLOS convened for nine years, eventually agreeing to the 1982 *Law of the Sea*. This was ratified in 1993, entering into force in 1994. The *LOS* recognizes 200-mile exclusive economic zones, with coastal states having sovereign rights over the continental shelf and water column above it. Also recognized are sovereign rights over the continental shelf out to 350 miles. Rights of transit passage in the 12-mile territorial seas were affirmed.

Negotiation over rights to deep sea mining continued until 1994, when, in July, the *Implementing Agreement* was signed, entering into force two years later. This is the closest nations have come to managing the oceans under the *common heritage of mankind* doctrine. It allows commercial companies to mine the deep seabed, but under regulation by the International Seabed Authority – so access to high seas mineral resources is not free; see Chapter 23. At this point in time, deep sea mining for polymetallic nodules is not commercially viable but could become so in the near future. There are also international agreements covering high seas living resources that are discussed in subsequent chapters.

Box 5.1 lists the various marine boundaries now in force.

BOX 5.1   MARINE BOUNDARIES

a) Distances from land are measured from *base lines* that are defined in the *UN Convention on the Territorial Sea and Contiguous Zone* (1958) and in UNCLOS (1982) as the low water mark. Quite complex definitions are used to draw base lines across bays, river mouths and indented coastlines.

b) *US states waters* reach three miles into the ocean, as defined in the 1953 *Submerged Lands Act*. States are required to abide by the "public trust doctrine" to protect the interests of the general public in, for example, the management of fishing, research, recreation and cultural heritage. The Federal government retains powers over navigation, national defense and power generation.

c) *The territorial sea* reaches 12 miles out from the base line.

d) *The contiguous zone* is recognized under international law as ocean space 12 to 24 miles out from a base line. A US state has limited authority here over matters such as customs and immigration control.

e) *The Exclusive Economic Zone (EEZ)* covers the ocean 12 to 200 miles from a base line. A nation has sovereign rights over exploitation and management of marine resources, living or otherwise, in the water column, and on and below the sea floor.

f) *If the continental shelf* extends beyond 200 miles, a country's EEZ is effectively extended to cover it.

g) *The high seas* lie beyond the continental shelf.

2 Why enclosure?

With respect to the question "why enclosure?", Harold Demsetz (1967) argued that a change in property rights would occur when the added value of the newly defined property rights exceeded the cost of bringing those rights into existence. An historical example is the change in access rights to beaver hunting areas among Native Americans after the French had opened trading posts in the seventeenth century in the maritime provinces of northeast North America. Prior to the surge in demand for pelts, hunting was open-access at least to 1648; but by 1723 a good deal of enclosure was observed. During the intervening period over-hunting had led to the introduction of pre-defined hunting grounds, with boundaries marked by the scorching of trees; essentially, a set of enclosures was created to exclude those without access rights.

A similar thing has happened with the oceans. Growth in world population has raised demand for the resources of the oceans and, together with new harvesting technologies – introduced especially after WWII – the resources of the oceans have effectively changed from being virtually non-depletable by people who fished for them only in small wooden boats, to being all too depletable in the new age of the industrialization of the oceans. Thus, over-hunting provided an urgent need for a new system to manage the oceans.

At the same time, new technologies, such as faster coast guard boats and radar, reduced the cost of policing, so making possible more effective policing of defined maritime boundaries.

Figure 5.1 shows that as demand for a depletable resource increases, the demand curve shifting from D_1D_1 to D_2D_2, the social loss caused by open access also increases. Thus, production of the good, say, beaver or cod, involves an external cost as one hunter raises the cost of hunting for others as wild stocks are thinned out. When

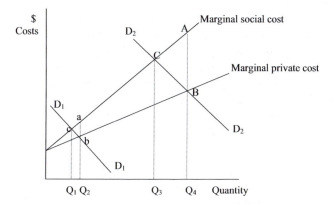

FIGURE 5.1 Worsening social loss as demand increase in the presence of external diseconomies

demand is low, the social loss, or deadweight loss, is only the area abc, which may be small enough to not justify a change away from open access. However, after demand has increased, the social cost caused by open access is much greater, at area ABC. To avoid this greater loss it may be worthwhile to incur the cost of changing property rights. Dividing an area of land (or ocean) into small lots, with only a few designated hunters allowed on each of those lots, is a possible solution. With fewer hunters per lot, the hope is that they are better able to confer with one another to find arrangements that will reduce their over-hunting. For example, they might agree to a closed season. Similarly, by excluding foreign fishing boats, enclosure of the oceans held out the promise of more rational ocean use under national regulations.

Without sovereign rights (or management through an international organization under a *common heritage of mankind* doctrine), costly conflict between states can and does occur over the use of ocean space. For example, economic growth and population growth in East Asia is putting greater pressure on marine resources there – especially fish and offshore oil. However, largely owing to historical rivalries and complex coastlines that make the drawing of boundaries difficult, enclosure under internationally recognized boundaries is quite rare in the area. Indeed, only eight of a total of 70 maritime boundaries in the region have been drawn (Blake et al., 1998).

The result is that the incidence of international disputes over ocean resources is high. Naval engagements sometimes happen – e.g. in the South China Sea between China and the Philippines over the Spratly Islands in 1998 and 2013. Indeed, boundaries in the South China Sea are disputed by all the coastal states: China, Vietnam, the Philippines, Malaysia and Brunei. Sometimes fishing boats are accompanied by warships, and international investors in offshore oil exploration don't want to come to the area. Disputes over the Spratly Islands can be more subtle: in 2006 the Vietnamese government failed to halt strikes aimed at Taiwanese companies operating in Vietnam, and it was suggested that this was to protest against Taiwan building a landing strip on one of the islands also claimed by Vietnam.[2] To back up its allies against the Chinese claim to virtually the whole of the South China Sea, in July 2010 the US Secretary of State, Hillary Clinton, declared that the USA had a national interest in freedom of navigation there. Then, in 2012–2013, an especially ugly dispute arose between Japan and China over the seas surrounding the Senkaku (Japanese name) – Diaoyu (Chinese name) Islands in the East China Sea. Japan enforced its claim by, among other things, ramming Chinese vessels fishing in the area. China responded by boycotting the purchase of Toyota and Honda vehicles produced in China – sales falling by almost 50 percent in September 2012. Chapter 7 offers a more complete discussion of economic aspects of disputes of maritime boundaries.

3   Optimal number of subdivisions of a common access resource

We can think of the enclosure of the oceans under sovereign rule as responding to the benefits and costs of doing so. The following discussion will help in understanding why enclosure outside the range of old cannon shot only began as late as 1945.

The total benefit of subdivision of an ocean space is due to a reduction in the cost of over-harvesting. This cost is the deadweight loss, ABC, in Figure 5.1. Following Field (1989), it is assumed that the smaller the geographic area of a subdivision, the fewer the number of bargainers will be on it – thereby reducing bargaining costs and, through greater social pressure on known members of a social group, reducing free riding by non-participants in conservation measures. For example, if a large area hunted by 100 strangers is divided into twenty enclosures, each enclosure will on average have five hunters per zone, who, we can presume, become known to one another. In a national context, hunters from a given country may have greater solidarity than a larger group made up of hunters from many different countries.

Figure 5.2 shows the total benefit of enclosure as a positive function of the number of subdivisions. The TB function shows diminishing returns to enclosure, as even a small number of subdivisions can be assumed to substantially reduce over-harvesting, leaving less and less marginal benefit from an ever larger number of subdivisions. Thus, the marginal benefit of increasing subdivision is a decreasing function. Decreasing marginal benefit is shown by the decreasing slope of the TB function.

However, policing costs are incurred in enforcing the boundaries of the subdivisions, and the more subdivisions there are, the greater the total length of all the boundaries taken together. Total cost, therefore, is an increasing function of the number of subdivisions. We assume that the marginal cost of subdivision increases – hence the increasing slope of the TC function in Figure 5.2.

Given the TB and TC functions in Figure 5.2, the optimal number of subdivisions occurs where net benefit is greatest – or, where MB = MC. This is with S* subdivisions.

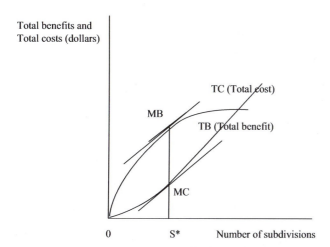

FIGURE 5.2 The optimal number of subdivisions

Figure 5.2 can be used to explain some historical events in ocean enclosure. In early times, the resources of the sea were so plentiful that over-harvesting was not a problem – hence the total benefit of enclosure was close to zero – and the TB curve lay near or along the x-axis. Also, the total cost of policing the oceans was high, so that the TC curve rose steeply in Figure 5.2. Thus, the optimal number of enclosures was small or zero.

However, as harvesting technology advanced, over-harvesting became an increasing problem, and so the benefits of reducing it through enclosure increased. Now, the TB function began to arc upward above the *x-axis*. Also, given advances in policing technology, the TC function began to pivot downward.

It is indeed significant that the *Truman Proclamation* in 1945 claiming the resources on and under the US continental shelf coincided with the development of technologies capable of exploiting them – offshore oil exploration in particular.

4 A microeconomic example of the optimal enclosure

The preceding model suggests that subdivisions are of "medium" size in the sense that S* is somewhere in the middle of the range where the total benefit exceeds the total cost of enclosure. This also appears to be true at the microeconomic level, as exemplified by the Maine lobster fishery. According to Acheson (1979, 1988), at one time lobster fishermen divided into small groups, largely based on their home port, and defended the boundaries around their enclosures. Exclusion was performed by various means, such as leaving threatening notes in traps, verbal abuse and cutting free intruders' lobsterpots. It seems that only just enough "policing" effort was expended so as not to provoke retaliation, and only one or two traps would be cut loose.

The prediction of our model is that population growth and greater demand for lobsters will lead to even more enclosure, as the benefits of exclusion increase due to increasing external diseconomies of over-harvesting. Indeed, this is what we have found with respect to the enclosure of the oceans as a whole. However, in the Maine lobster fishery, even as population grew the opposite trend occurred; enclosures grew in size (there are fewer of them) rather than shrank.

The explanation for this is that as population and demand for lobsters grew the incentive for "outside" lobstermen to encroach also increased. An increasing frequency of encroachment had the effect of raising the cost of defending the boundaries of each enclosure. As Acheson (1988) observed, "The present disposition of lobster fishing territories is a function of the costs and benefits of territorial defense. On the mainland, men in harbors on the ends of peninsulas have not found it worthwhile to defend their territorial boundaries against more desperate men from upriver. As a result boundaries have broken down and the area where mixed fishing is allowed has increased" (p. 83).[3] In Figure 5.2 this shows up as an *upward* pivot of the TC function and a reduction in the optimal S* – i.e. larger enclosures.

5 Enclosure by coastal states versus governance through an international organization

Here, we ask: what economic reasons explain why enclosure of the high seas, or, at least the most productive part of them in 200-mile exclusive economic zones, won out over governing them through an international organization?

As with other national boundaries, at least part of the answer has to do with military power. It is perhaps no coincidence that the world's preeminent military power was the first to claim its continental shelf.

Leaving the military power argument aside, efforts made from the 1950s to the 1970s in the United Nations aimed at managing the oceans through an international organization based on the idea of the oceans as a *common heritage of mankind*, in which all people, not just those of the coastal states, would benefit. However, the idea failed to catch on in a significant way. This is not to say that governance of the remaining high seas is also beyond international organization. Far from it: the International Maritime Organization – with over 40 Protocols under its belt – plays a central role in managing many aspects of international shipping, there are many (unfortunately weak) international agreements in force governing high seas fisheries and marine mammals, and the International Seabed Authority is in place to manage deep sea mining.

What then are the main economic reasons for enclosure of the oceans winning out over international governance? If enclosure is economically rational then it must be that the benefits of enclosure – net of costs of enclosure – were greater than the net benefits of international governance.

Three disadvantages of international governance are:

1   A recurrent theme in this book is that any agreement on international governance is difficult to reach because countries have divergent interests and there can be incentives to free ride on the efforts of other countries. Since enclosure to some extent reduces the need for international negotiations (it doesn't in the case of straddling fish stocks), rational management rules can in theory be more quickly agreed.[4] If this argument is accepted, benefits of ocean resource management will be higher under enclosure than with international governance.

2   Policing is easier and less costly if interested parties, especially in the fishing industry, accept them as being desirable. It is possible to argue that nationals of a given country will find rules set by their own legislatures in some sense more legitimate than rules set in a far-off international organization. If this argument is accepted, then policing costs under enclosure will be lower than under international governance.

3   If governance of the oceans were through international organizations, coastal states would worry about how the economic rents generated by international governance would be divided between the members of the organization. In

other words, international governance is more risky than national governance, and the latter is a risk-reduction tool. With enclosure, a coastal state has a degree of certainty over what increased economic rents are available to it, should it choose efficiently to manage its ocean resources. In an international organization this degree of certainty is not so high, as the members may choose to allocate benefits in all sorts of different ways.

The next chapter extends our discussion of ocean enclosure – the drawing of lines in the sea – by recognizing that marine boundaries are often disputed. The discussion will emphasize how the balance between "dispute costs" incurred by a pair of countries in dispute, and the expected economic rents of marine resources in the area under dispute can affect if and where a boundary is drawn, and if not, whether countries will agree to a joint development zone.

Notes

1 See Asgeirsdottir (2008) and Encyclopedia of Earth (2013).
2 *The Economist*, January 28th, 2006.
3 Similarly, Acheson (1988) writes that "For people in harbors on the open sea, it has not been worthwhile to repel the invaders. While incursions from upriver communities mean more competition and a subsequent reduction in both catches and revenues, attempts to stop the invasions would cause a great deal of trouble, perhaps even a fully fledged lobster war, with huge financial losses, problems with the law, and worse" (p. 82).
4 Australia, New Zealand and Norway are cases where rational management in their exclusive economic zones is occurring. The US and the EU are examples where it is not.

6

AN ECONOMIC ANALYSIS OF DRAWING LINES IN THE SEA

1   Introduction

Under customary international law open access is allowed in disputed ocean space, and economic theory suggests that under open access resources will be over-exploited with resource rent dissipation. In the case of fisheries there is ample evidence for this, Myers and Worm (2003), for example, reporting that industrial fishing has reduced fish stocks by as much as 90 percent of their levels of fifty years earlier. There is therefore an urgent need for improved fisheries management, and given that the international community has largely rejected oceans management under the *common heritage of mankind* doctrine, a necessary step is to agree ocean enclosures.

However, agreement on maritime boundaries is proving to be drawn-out and fractious. Of 430 potential maritime boundaries only 210 have been agreed – 49 percent of the total, a percentage that overstates progress as potential boundaries between islets in the South China Sea are not included in this figure, and disputed islands are treated as belonging to the state that currently occupies them. Moreover, boundary agreements often do not cover all jurisdictional issues – for example, fisheries management *and* delimitation of the continental shelf. Agreements may also not cover the full length of a potential boundary.[1]

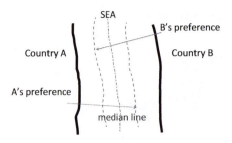

FIGURE 6.1 Disputed lines between facing shore states less than 400 miles apart

In this chapter we offer an analysis of the broad economic factors that lead countries with disputed maritime boundaries either to agree or not to agree them (Section 2). These disputes could be between facing shore countries – as in Figure 6.1 – or between adjacent countries that dispute a lateral boundary. Section 3 illustrates the economic modeling with reference to negotiations over Arctic marine boundaries. Section 4 and, in more detail, in Chapter 7, we look at an actual disputes resolution compromise, the joint development zone (JDZ), that is short of agreeing boundaries yet allows for more efficient economic use of ocean space.

2 Economic analysis

The economic analysis begins by asking what the inducement to agree a maritime boundary is. The answer depends upon the expected *net* returns, or, net resource rents, derived from drawing such a boundary between a pair of counties.

Suppose the situation shown in Figure 6.1, where two countries, A and B, dispute over which of three possible maritime boundary lines is to be drawn – the one favored by A, the one favored by B, or a compromise median line. If A's boundary prevailed, B would obtain a smaller area of ocean space over which it had sovereign rights, and vice versa if B's boundary prevailed. However, under international law a common boundary must be agreed and cannot be imposed by one country upon another. One of four choices is possible for a given country, say, country A:

1 Agree to the other country's preferred boundary: A agrees to B's preferred boundary;
2 agree a compromise boundary (neither A's preference nor B's, but the median line); alternatively, agree to a JDZ, so setting aside issues of sovereign rights behind an agreed boundary, but still allowing for improved resource management;
3 country A accepts B's offer to agree on A's preferred boundary; or,
4 agree to no boundary, so the dispute continues.

Assume also that the ranking of resource rents available to a given country is:

highest with its preferred boundary: e.g. country A gets its preferred boundary;
lower with a compromise boundary – the median line, or with a joint development zone;
lower still with a boundary set by the other country – A agrees to B's boundary; and
least of all if no boundary is set.

This ranking makes sense as resource rents, in principle, could be maximized when
a sovereign has independent management rights over a tract of ocean space that has
been delineated on its own terms; lower when two sovereigns have agreed a compromise boundary or a JDZ; and lowest with open access, as no sovereign is able to
impose a rational system of resource management.

Assuming no boundary has yet been drawn, a country will rationally not agree
to a compromise boundary (with its lower economic rent) if the expected *increase* in
resource rent from gaining sovereign rights behind its preferred boundary exceeds
the cost of continuing a boundary dispute. The expected increase in resource rent
from the ocean space defined by this preferred boundary depends on four variables,
as set out in equation (1). Thus,

$$E(\text{increase in resource rent}) = \sum_{t=1}^{T} \left(\frac{pr_t(\$rent)_t}{(1+r)^t} - \frac{(1-pr)_t\$x_t}{(1+r)^t} \right) \tag{1}$$

where *E(increase in resource rent)* is the expected present value of the increase in
resource rent; pr_t is a decision maker's subjective probability of gaining sovereign
rights over its preferred boundary in any given year $t = 1 \ldots T$; r is the decision
maker's rate of time preference; $\$rent$ is the annual rent that would be earned if
sovereign rights were won over the preferred boundary; $\$x_t$ is resource rent earned
even with no boundary being drawn (i.e. there is open access to the disputed ocean
space by the States Parties concerned). Note that pr_t may change from year to year
as can both the rate of time preference, r, and expected value of annual rent. The
probability of winning sovereign rights, pr_t, may change with other circumstances –
for example, if the opposing state's bargaining strength is thought to have increased,
pr_t for the other state may well decrease. The rate of time preference, r, a measure
of the degree of impatience, may change if, for some reason, reaching an agreement
is thought to have become more urgent. Melting sea ice and, consequently, less-
costly access to offshore hydrocarbons or fisheries resources would almost certainly
increase impatience (measured by a rise in r) as valuable offshore resource become
newly accessible. Furthermore, aggregate *resource rents* can change for various reasons; for example, if newly gathered geological data indicates greater hydrocarbon
deposits than previously envisaged, or, again, in the case of the Arctic Ocean, melting ice allows access to previously inaccessible resources.

If a boundary is not agreed, a boundary dispute continues. However, there is a cost of maintaining a dispute. The expected discounted present value of dispute cost is:

$$E(dispute\ cost) = \sum_{t=1}^{T} (\frac{(1 - pr)_t\ (\$dispute\ cost)_t}{(1 + r)^t}) \tag{2}$$

where $(1 - pr)_t$ is the subjective probability of not having sovereign rights in year t, in which case an annual dispute cost is incurred. These costs may be low – just the cost of a negotiating team – but they could be substantial; for example, as when warships have to accompany fishing boats or when actual military conflict breaks out. Or, dispute costs could be incurred outside of maritime issues, as is implied by Van Dyke (2007) when he observes that Korea and Japan have an incentive to agree maritime boundaries so that they "can strengthen their relations in other areas and promote the mutual prosperity of their citizens" (p. 205). And, as another example, when in September 2010 China threatened to suspend sales of rare earths (crucial inputs for some manufactured products) to Japan after the latter had arrested the captain of a Chinese fishing vessel accused of fishing in Japanese waters that are disputed by China.[2]

The net advantage of continuing a boundary dispute is calculated as:

$$E(\underline{net}\ resource\ rent) = E(increase\ in\ resource\ rent) - E(dispute\ cost) \tag{3}$$

or,

$$E(NRR) = (equation\ 1) - (equation\ 2) \tag{4}$$

The payoffs in Figure 6.2 represent the present value of expected *net* resource rent, E(NRR), defined in equations (3) or (4) as the *probability weighted expected increase in resource rent* from a given tract of disputed ocean *less* the cost of continuing a boundary dispute with the other country. In other words, a country looks at what the value of its ocean resources could be with enclosure and subtracts from this their value without an agreed boundary as well as the cost of continuing to dispute a boundary with the other country. E(NRR) is used in our analysis of whether a pair of countries will agree on one of three potential boundaries, or will continue disputing sovereign rights over a particular ocean tract.

Figure 6.2 is understood as follows. If E(NRR) is positive for both countries each country wants nothing less than its preferred maritime boundary because dispute cost is low relative to the expected increase in resource rents gathered behind those preferred boundaries. Thus, in the northwest box the boundary dispute continues – recall that it is being assumed that expected resource rents are highest given a country's preferred boundary compared with a compromise boundary.

COUNTRY B

	Positive net resource rent	Negative net resource rent
Positive net resource rent	**Dispute continues**	**Line favors country A**
Negative net resource rent	**Line favors country B**	**Compromise boundary or JDZ agreed**

(Left label: **COUNTRY A**)

FIGURE 6.2 Ocean boundaries: Dispute and settlement

Now suppose that E(NRR) is positive for one side but negative for the other party. This situation favors agreement on the boundary favored by the "positive" side. Thus, in the northeast box, E(NRR) is positive for country A, so it will continue to insist on its preferred boundary, but negative for country B. In terms of our economic model, country B has no incentive to prolong the boundary dispute as dispute cost is greater than the expected gross benefit of prolonging the dispute, so it will agree to the boundary preferred by country A. Country B thereby avoids future dispute costs but still gains some increase in resource rent, though not as much of an increase had the boundary been drawn on its terms.

If the signs of E(NRR) are reversed, negative for country A and positive for country B, we move to the southwest box in Figure 6.2. In this situation the boundary favored by country B will be agreed. Country A sees both a negative net return from continuing to pursue its favored boundary but some increase in its resource rents behind the boundary favored by country B.

Finally, in the southeast box E(NRR) is negative for both countries. In this case both would want to abandon insistence on their particular favored marine boundary because of the relatively high dispute costs. This situation is ripe for agreement on a compromise boundary – the median line in Figure 6.1, for example. Another possibility is that instead of a mutually agreed boundary, a joint development zone (JDZ) could be established – as in the Timor Gap between Australia and East Timor (Timor Leste). An advantage of a JDZ is that neither party has to give up its claim to its preferred boundary. A disadvantage is that ocean management with joint sovereigns may be less efficient than with a single sovereign; for example, biologically sensible fishing quotas may be harder to set if the fishing industries of two countries have to be satisfied.

We now turn to a discussion of the dispute over Arctic marine boundaries, and we will see how our economic model helps to understand it. We will also, in

Section 4, briefly describe some JDZs, before, in Chapter 7, looking in more detail at bargaining over the Timor Gap JDZ.

3 Arctic marine boundaries

At issue is whether and how quickly marine boundaries in the Arctic Ocean are likely to be drawn – so enhancing prospects for efficient hydrocarbon extraction. With earlier and more extensive melting of the Arctic's summer ice cover, accessibility to these resources is improving,[3] and estimates of Arctic Ocean hydrocarbon deposits show them to be large.[4]

Even though in August 2007 a Russian flag was planted on the seabed at the North Pole, apparently claiming a large portion of the Arctic Ocean for Russia, this has no force in international law. According to Article 77 §3 of the United Nations Conference on *Law of the Sea* (UNCLOS), gaining sovereign rights over ocean space must pass through an international legal process. However, the flag planting alerted the four other Arctic coastal states – Norway, Denmark (through possession of Greenland), Canada and the USA – to consider their own positions on boundary delimitation.

According to UNCLOS, Article 57, coastal states may have a 200-mile exclusive economic zone. On this basis, the Arctic Ocean has a "doughnut hole" where no country has sovereign rights and is accordingly "high seas". However, as we know, there is an exception to the 200-mile limit in the case where a country's continental shelf extends beyond it to as much as 350 miles from its coastal baselines. The extent of a country's continental shelf is to be determined by the coastal state concerned – Article 76 §4(a) – but it cannot unilaterally claim that shelf when it is also claimed by another country. Delimitation has to be by mutual agreement, and claims are to be submitted to the UN Commission on the Limits of the Continental Shelf (Article 76 §8). Recognized sovereign rights, according to Article 44 §4, give rights to the exploitation of "mineral and other non-living resources of the seabed and subsoil together with living organisms belonging to sedentary species". And Article 81 says that "the coastal State shall have the exclusive right to authorize and regulate drilling on the continental shelf for all purposes".

Russia claims that the Lomonosov Ridge is an extension of its continental shelf, running through the North Pole and onward toward Greenland. If the Russian claim was recognized in international law, Russia would be able to add about 460,000 square miles of what otherwise would be Arctic Ocean high seas – about one-third of the latter's area. Any minerals recovered from this area would belong to Russia, or entities licensed by Russia, and would not be available to the international community under the *common heritage of mankind* doctrine.[5]

Other Arctic Ocean coastal states dispute the Russian claim to the Lomonosov Ridge. Both Denmark and Canada claim that it is an extension of their own continental shelves. Even though settlement, if and when it comes, would be through the Commission on the Limits of the Continental Shelf, because this institution has no enforcement powers the states themselves would have to recognize each other's claims.[6] Thus, according to Article 83 §1 of UNCLOS, disputes between coastal states with opposite or adjacent coasts shall be through international law: "The delimitation of the continental shelf between States with opposite or adjacent coasts shall be effected by agreement on the basis of international law, as referred to in Article 38 of the Statute of the International Court of Justice, in order to achieve an equitable solution."

Our economic model of drawing lines in the sea indicates that both the expected value of ocean resources – say, Arctic offshore oil – and the probability of a given country obtaining international agreement on a preferred boundary are relevant to the eventual outcome. Thus, while the summer melting of the ice cap likely raises country A's expected value of Arctic Ocean space, $rent$ in equation (1), this is not to say that this will make the countries in dispute over boundaries less likely to agree a compromise or even go to war over them.[7] Country A also has to think about the chances of getting an agreement on its preferred maritime boundary, pr_i in equation (1), but this probability could well fall as the countries concerned anticipate larger revenues from offshore oil production. This probability would fall if country A reasons that country B will become more resolute, hardening its position, because it does not want to give away valuable resources to country A. Therefore, and para-doxically, increased access to Arctic Ocean resources could well promote a desire for compromise on boundaries.

Another factor that could contribute to agreement on Arctic marine boundaries is if the pair (or more) of countries concerned are fairly confident that offshore oil in a given area exists, but are not quite sure as to exactly where. Indeed, this is likely to be the case because not that much offshore oil exploration has been done in the Arctic. Thus, the countries concerned will want the legal certainty that comes with resolution of a boundary dispute, but they will not necessarily be as stubborn as to where that boundary should be drawn. This type of uncertainty could be modeled in equation (1) as increasing the discount rate, r (indicating great risk in expected returns), so reducing expected returns. If this happened, a pair of bargainers could be moved from the northwest quadrant in Figure 6.2, where a dispute continues, to the southeast quadrant, where each party seeks compromise.

Uncertainty over the exact location of offshore hydrocarbons may well have aided Norway and Russia in reaching agreement on a marine boundary between them in the Barents Sea.[8] Article 5 of this treaty makes it perfectly clear that the two countries have little or no idea as to where offshore oil deposits might exist. For example, paragraph one begins "*If* a hydrocarbon deposit extends across the delimi-tation line . . ." and several other paragraphs deal with the ramifications of this "*if*".[9]

4 Joint development zones

A half-way-house arrangement between *not* agreeing boundaries and sovereign rights behind a "line in the sea" is that of a joint development zone (JDZ) whereby countries agree to share use of a resource – say, offshore oil, or marine fisher-ies. "JDZ" here is used as a generic term covering sharing agreements described variously as "provisional agreements", "provisional measures zones", "international fisheries committees" and "reciprocal fishing access" (Xue, 2005). Alternatively, Blake and Swarbrick (1998) also define four categories of JDZ:

> *geological cooperation*, whereby geologists determine the location of mineral deposits and national production quotas are allocated according to some boundary formula;
>
> *joint operations*, whereby there is equal sharing of production regardless of which side of a theoretical boundary it occurs (for example, Germany–Netherlands share production in the Groningen gas field);
>
> *united exploitation*, where a single operator produces offshore oil and gas, and production is allocated according to some sharing formula (90–10 in some oil fields in the Timor Gap for example (King, 2002)); and
>
> *shared sovereignty*, as between Saudi Arabia and Sudan in the Red Sea.

Under UNCLOS (1982) Article 74, JDZs are legal entities governing ocean management in cases where boundaries of exclusive economic zones (EEZs) cannot be agreed between party states.[10] In such cases, Article 123 of the *Convention* requires state parties to cooperate in marine conservation.[11]

By the mid-1990s only 15 offshore JDZs existed (Blake and Swarbrick, 1998).[12] This small number may be surprising given that in agreeing to a JDZ a state does not necessarily relinquish its claim to sovereign rights. A claim is simply put on hold for possible resolution at a future date. Moreover, assuming that resource management under a JDZ arrangement improves on that of open access – for example, improving fisheries management, economic rent can be expected to increase – even if it has to be shared with another country.

Over the last ten years the pace of formation of JDZ agreements seems to have been stepped up, especially in East Asia. Thus, China and Japan signed a joint fisheries agreement in 1997. China ratified JDZs with Vietnam in 2004 – a fifteen-year fisheries agreement in the Gulf of Tonkin – and with South Korea in 2000 for fisheries management (see Keyuan, 2005; Xue, 2005). In 2005, China, Vietnam and the Philippines signed the *Tripartite Agreement for Joint Marine Seismic Undertaking in the Agreement Area in the South China Sea* (Ministry of Foreign Affairs, Vietnam[13]).

If neither enclosure nor a JDZ is agreed, the two countries concerned remain in dispute and efficient management of the relevant ocean tract remains impaired. How, in this situation, might agreement be reached?

5 Reaching agreement on marine boundaries

The foregoing economic analysis can be used to highlight some strategies that one or more coastal states may adopt in an effort actively to reach agreement on the boundaries it prefers. This means moving from the northwest box in Figure

6.2 – with no agreed boundaries, in the case of country A – to the northeast box (or, in the case of country B, the southwest box). The less likely a protagonist thinks that it can win on its own terms, the more likely it will settle on the terms of another coastal state.

What actions might a country take? Answers may be found by inspecting the formula for expected net resource rent, E(NRR), equation (3).

"Play for time"

This is making sure that the other side knows that a boundary is unlikely to be agreed for many years into the future. If successful, this:

a   reduces pr_t in equation (1) – so reducing *E(increase in resource rent)*; and
b   by increasing *(1 – pr_t)* raises the size of equation (2), the expected cost of maintaining a boundary dispute.

However, as delay reduces the expected increase in resource rents of both countries, this strategy is feasible only for the country with the lower rate of time preference, *r* – in which case its expected net resource rent falls least. High rates of time preference indicate impatience, but in the case of the Arctic at this point in time it is impossible to know which of the coastal states are most impatient.

"Agitate"

This could involve, for example, taking the other country to the International Court of Justice, as is allowed for under Article 38 §1 of UNCLOS, or arguing for an international adjudicator, or pursing the other country in the civil courts for compensation if a country thinks that its rights have been impaired – all tactics used by East Timor in its dispute with Australia.[14] Such tactics would raise the expected dispute cost of continuing a boundary dispute, so increasing the value of equation (2).

"Appeal to the international community"

This points out the "unfairness" of the other side's boundary claims. An example of this is, again, (poor) East Timor's complaint against (rich) Australia that the latter will not agree to "fair" maritime boundaries (specifically the end points of the Indonesia–Australia line of demarcation agreed in their 1972 *Treaty* that, according to East Timor, impinge on its waters). Such an appeal might be effective if the rich country did not want to lose face in the international community (perhaps impairing its credentials as a good foreign aid giver). A successful appeal would, in effect, raise the rate of time preference – the discount rate, applied to expected resource rents by, in this example, the rich country. However, it does not seem that matters have gone this far in the Arctic Ocean boundary dispute; but it is a tactic that Greenland could use, should it obtain independence from Denmark.

Raise the other side's dispute costs by *other means*, as, for example, in 2006 in the Spratly Islands marine boundary dispute between Vietnam and Taiwan. The China–Japan boundary dispute also referred to earlier is another case in point.

6 Conclusions

This chapter offers a microeconomic framework through which to understand bargaining over marine boundaries. The economic model takes into account resource rents expected from a contested tract of ocean space as well as expected dispute costs incurred in claiming those resource rents under sovereign rights. When expected resource rents are high relative to dispute cost a country will continue to insist on its preferred marine boundary. When this is true for both countries the prospect for agreement on a maritime boundary is dim.

However, it is demonstrated that improving summer access to Arctic Ocean resources – hydrocarbons as well as fisheries – is likely to encourage coastal states to agree marine boundaries, as, indeed, Norway and Russia have recently done. Alternatively, the countries concerned could set aside their boundary dispute and agree to some sort of provisional arrangement – as is allowed under the United Nations *Law of the Sea*. Several such joint development zones already exist and could serve as models for jointly developing Arctic Ocean continental shelf resources.

Notes

1 Information kindly supplied through private communication by the International Boundaries Research Unit, Durham University, May, 2007.
2 *Financial Times*, September 23rd, 2010.
3 See, for example, on rising temperatures Bekryaev, Polyakov and Alexeev (2010), and on diminishing ice sheet cover Comiso (2003).
4 According to the United States Geological Survey (2008), "the occurrence of undiscovered oil and gas in 33 geologic provinces thought to be prospective for petroleum. The sum of the mean estimates for each province indicates that 90 billion barrels of oil, 1,669 trillion cubic feet of natural gas, and 44 billion barrels of natural gas liquids may remain to be found in the Arctic, of which approximately 84 percent is expected to occur in offshore areas." These estimates represent, respectively, 13 percent of world undiscovered oil, 30 percent of undiscovered gas, and 20 percent of undiscovered liquid hydrocarbons.
5 The *common heritage of mankind* doctrine has been invoked in relation to various branches of international law – e.g. the *Law of the Sea*, the *Antarctic Treaty*, outer space law, environmental law, human rights and humanitarian law. See Turack (2002).
6 For the US to access these institutions it would need to ratify the UNCLOS.
7 The possibility of war over Arctic Ocean boundaries is raised by Irvin Studin in "The melting of the polar ice signals the end of Pax Arctica", *Financial Times*, August 30th, 2012.
8 *Treaty between the Kingdom of Norway and the Russian Federation Concerning Maritime Delimitation and Cooperation in the Barents Sea and the Arctic Ocean*, available online at www.regjeringen.no/upload/SMK/Vedlegg/2010/avtale_engelsk.pdf.
9 As the *Financial Times* reported (April 28th, 2010): "Under the deal, each country will get roughly half of the disputed area covering 175,000 sq km of the Barents Sea and the

Arctic Ocean. It is not known how much oil and gas is at stake but large gas fields exist on either side of the zone, leading geologists to predict more reserves in between."

10 Article 74: Delimitation of the exclusive economic zone between States with opposite or adjacent coasts.

11 Article 123: Cooperation of States bordering enclosed or semi-enclosed seas.

12 Examples of JDZs include the *Australian–Indonesian 1989 Timor Gap Treaty*; *Australia–Papua New Guinea Treaty* (1978); and Malaysia–Thailand treaties (1979 and 1990 – Gulf of Thailand). Japan and South Korea formed a JDZ. Malaysia also has a JDZ with Vietnam (1993). In the Middle East there are JDZs between Saudi Arabia and Sudan and Saudi Arabia–Bahrain (1958). There is one between Qatar and UAE (1963). In Europe, France and Spain jointly exploit the Bay of Biscay (1973 agreement). Norway has a JDZ agreement with Iceland (1980) and another with the UK (1976). The UK has a JDZ with Argentina (1995).

13 For information on this agreement see www.mofa.gov.vn/en/tt_baochi/pbnfn/ns050314164241.

14 King (2002).

7

DIVISION OF ECONOMIC RENTS IN THE TIMOR GAP

1   Introduction

This chapter presents a case study of the drawing of lines in the sea. While the negotiations have been complicated it should be noted that, even though national interests run deep, agreements on seabed boundaries, fisheries boundaries and a joint development zone have been achieved under international law, and that at no point have warships been deployed – as they have, for example, in the South China Sea and East China Sea disputes referred to in Chapter 6.[1]

The Timor Sea lies to the northwest of Darwin, Australia, and south of the island of Timor, which is itself divided into West Timor (a part of Indonesia) and what is now East Timor – see Figure 7.1. Almost from the beginning of the period of enclosure of the oceans, division of the Timor Sea has been disputed by three entities: Australia, Indonesia, and then a succession of parties that have governed what is now the independent country of East Timor. These parties were Portugal as the colonial power to 1975, Indonesia as the occupying power, 1975–1999, the United Nations as the interim administrator, 1999–2002, and now the independent country of East Timor.

International law would seem to favor Australia's claim to the Sahul Shelf, which extends up to 313 miles from Australia's coast. On its northern edge the continental slope plunges for over 1.7 miles into the Timor Trough, the latter situated only about 50 miles off the southern coast of East Timor. As Heyward et al. (1997) explain, the Sahul Shelf "is considered to be a recently drowned part of the Australian continent

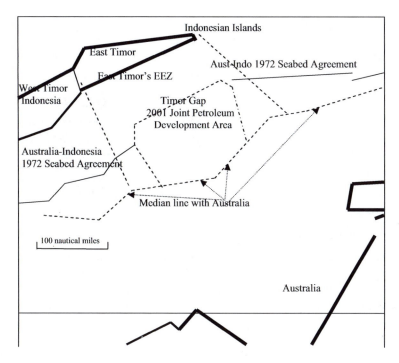

FIGURE 7.1 The Timor Gap between East Timor and Australia

. . . as recently as 18,000 years ago, most of the Sahul Shelf was exposed . . . Extensive palaeo-river channels, some up to 150 km long and 5 km wide, connect the Bonaparte Depression to the old shoreline" (p. 8). The significance of this is that under UNCLOS Articles 76 (para. 6) and 77 (para. 1) a country can claim the seabed resources of its continental shelf out to 350 miles from its coast.[2]

However, another consideration is that Article 83 (para. 4) states that "Where there is an agreement in force between the States concerned, questions relating to the delimitation of the continental shelf shall be determined in accordance with the provisions of that agreement." As we shall see, Australia has had seabed agreements in the Timor Sea predating UNCLOS coming into force. Even so, it remains something of an open question as to why Australia has not pressed its claims, especially given that it is the predominant military power in the region. Cotton's (2003) meticulous analysis of the issue indicates why no conclusive reason can be given as to why Australia has not pressed its seabed claims more firmly. He says that Australia's position "may derive from generosity mindful of East Timor's plight, or amount to an implicit recognition of the compelling nature of East Timor's claims, or be intended as leverage in order to increase the chances of major infrastructure being sited in Australia, or even represent a pragmatic judgment that generous revenues for East Timor will lessen the new nation's calls on Australian aid" (p. 31).

Indeed, between 1999 and 2003 Australia gave East Timor Australian$3.9 billion in foreign aid (Cotton, 2003, p. 27) Or, then again, "given that the exploitation of the oil and gas resources of the gap will exhaust within 30 years, it is difficult to interpret Australia's strategy as anything other than playing for time (and revenue)" (Cotton, 2003, p. 32).[3]

Thus, even after more than thirty-five years of negotiations, seabed boundaries south of East Timor in the Timor Sea have not been agreed. However, as we saw in Chapter 6, a pair of countries can "agree to disagree" and create a joint development zone. This is what Australia and East Timor have done, and this provides the legal framework in which oil companies now operate.

2 Timeline

The timeline of claims of sovereign rights over the part of the Timor Sea known as the Timor Gap begins in 1953, when Australia claimed its continental shelf that it said extended close to the island of Timor. However, three years later Portugal claimed sovereign rights up to the median line between East Timor and Australia. Thus, overlapping claims had been posted. The United Nations Conference on *Law of the Sea* sets the median line between opposite shore nations closer than 400 miles apart as the line of demarcation, but with the complication that a country is also allowed to claim its continental shelf.

In 1962 Australia granted prospecting rights to the oil company consortium of Arco, Aquitaine and Esso, and one year later to a second consortium composed of Woodside Petroleum, Burmah Oil and Shell. By 1970 the Timor Sea was known to have hydrocarbons in commercial quantities.

Then in 1972 a *Seabed Agreement* was signed after a two-year negotiation between Australia and Indonesia demarcating the seabed boundary between the two countries. Two important features of this agreement are that the boundary is closer to Indonesia than is the median line. As Indonesia has possessions both west and east of East Timor, but not East Timor itself, there was (and remains) a gap in this line of demarcation – the so-called "Timor Gap". Negotiations during the period 1971–1974 between Australia and Portugal to close the Timor Gap came to nothing, as Australia insisted on a demarcation according to its definition of its continental shelf, while Portugal insisted on the median line.

During these negotiations a combination of favorable geological reports and the quadrupling of oil prices led Australia to think that the Timor Sea was an extremely valuable oil province. And in January 1974 Portugal granted exploration rights to Petrotimor – a consortium led by the US company Oceanic Exploration along with several Portuguese interests. The concession area was out as far as the median line with Australia and overlapped exploration permits granted by the Australian Federal and Western Australian governments.

In 1975 Indonesia invaded East Timor, following Portugal's stated intention to decolonize, but before legal decolonization had occurred. With the loss of its head office in Dili (East Timor), Petrotimor abandoned its concession area. However, Portugal, the displaced legal authority, said that it would continue to support Petrotimor's legal claims.

By 1978 Australia had granted petroleum leases in six areas of the disputed Timor Sea. Elf Aquitaine's Australian manager said:

> No one would want to find oil there without knowing who owns it. But we are not expecting any major problems because of the border lines already agreed to by Indonesia on either side of the disputed area. If these two lines are just joined together, there will be no trouble at all.
>
> (Quoted in King 2002, p. 18)

This is why a valid legal regime is necessary, and why, despite the continuing lack of agreement over seabed boundaries, a joint development zone was created.

Significantly, in 1981 a *Provisional Fisheries Surveillance and Enforcement Agreement* was signed between Australia and Indonesia, dividing responsibilities along the median line between the two countries. This included East Timor, as at the time it was incorporated into Indonesia. Even so, in 1984, with Australian–Indonesian negotiations over a seabed boundary still going nowhere, Australia suggested a joint development zone with 50–50 sharing of resource rent taxes. However, as this indicated that Australia recognized Indonesia as the sovereign power in East Timor, Portugal protested.

In 1989, with Indonesia still in control of East Timor, the *Timor Gap (Zone of Cooperation – a joint development zone) Treaty* was signed by Indonesia and Australia. The Timor Gap is called "Zone A" in the treaty, but the treaty did not agree seabed boundaries. Instead there was an agreement to share on a 50–50 basis resource rent in the Timor Gap. Portugal called this agreement a "blatant and serious breach of international law." The East Timor resistance leader José Ramos-Horta wrote, "Australian oil companies would be well advised not to jump into the Timor Gap area. A future government of an independent East Timor would certainly review all oil exploration agreements". Despite these uncertainties, heightened activity in the zone of cooperation followed, with 42 wells being drilled, finding 400 million barrels of oil and three trillion cubic feet of gas in several small to medium fields.[4]

Two years later, in 1991, Petrotimor (holder of a 1974 Portuguese-granted exploration permit) was invited by Australia to bid for a new permit. The company refused, pointing out that it already held a permit for what turned out to be an oil- and gas-rich bloc that included the $1.6-billion Bayu-Undan gas project developed by Phillips Petroleum. The same year, Portugal took Australia to the International Court of Justice, and in 1995 the Court found that it was difficult to see how Portugal could help the East Timorese people, but it did state the right of a people to self-determination.

Two years further on again, a *Delimitation Treaty* was signed by Australia and Indonesia, which was intended to finalize boundaries between the two countries. Oil and gas production in the Timor Gap continued to grow, with the Elang-Kakatua field producing a $240 million annual revenue 1998–2002, with production levels of 24 million barrels per day. The three oil reservoirs in, or straddling, the Timor Gap (Sunrise-Troubadour, Bayu-Undan and Elang-Kakatua) were estimated in 2000 to contain 500 million barrels of oil, worth $17 billion at then ruling prices.[5]

East Timor had never accepted the Indonesian takeover and struggled against the military occupation. Ultimately, the Indonesians left following an affirmative vote for independence in East Timor. In the 2001 *Interim Agreement* the UN, as the interim administrator of East Timor, agreed a resource rent sharing formula in the Timor Gap with Australia. East Timor was to get 90 percent and Australia 10 percent. In the longitudinal boundary straddling the Great Sunrise oil–gas field the split is 20–80 in Australia's favor. The same year Petrotimor claimed its concession with the UN Transitional Administration, and it launched a legal action for recognition of its concession rights in the Australian Federal Court, seeking $2.85 billion in damages. Phillips and the Australian Commonwealth counter claimed.

In 2002 there followed the *Timor Sea Treaty* between Australia and newly independent East Timor. It covers "Zone A" of the 1989 *Treaty*, and created the Joint Petroleum Development Area. Incorporated from the 2001 Interim Agreement is the 90–10 split, while the 20–80 split became an 18–82 split.

> The agreement gave an estimated $7bn to East Timor over 20 years and nearly $1 billion to the Australian government, down $3 billion on the previous agreement with Indonesia. Gas and oil in the Australia/East Timor Joint Petroleum Development Area was valued at $22 billion. East Timor would also get royalties from 30 per cent of the adjoining $27 billion Greater Sunrise Field.
>
> (King, 2002, p. 39)

However, East Timor still calls for a redrawing of the longitudinal lines defining the western and eastern boundaries of the Gap. It claims that Australia and Indonesia had drawn these to East Timor's disadvantage. Redrawing would put all or most of the large Greater Sunrise field into East Timor's waters. Indeed, as Cotton (2003, p. 29) notes, some international legal opinion is that there is a case for enlarging the area of East Timor's seabed rights – especially spacing the longitudinal (north–south) lines further apart into what are now Indonesian waters. However, Australia has resisted this as it would most probably involve reopening the seabed boundary issue with Indonesia that had been settled in the 1972 *Seabed Agreement*. There is some justification therefore in claiming that Australia has benefited from bilateral negotiations over its seabed boundaries and that the outcome might turn out to be different in trilateral negotiations. For example, if trilateral negotiations were opened with a view to "enlarging East Timor's seabed rights", and if Indonesia agreed to moving the longitudinal boundaries into what are now its waters, it might want to be compensated by moving the seabed boundary with Australia further from its own coast. This, of course, is speculation, but it does indicate the delicate balance that has so far been achieved in agreeing seabed boundaries and the joint development zone in the Timor Sea.

3 Conclusions

What we have then is a long series of failed negotiations over East Timor's seabed boundaries. Instead there is agreement to share resource rents in a joint development zone. East Timor, though, still wants to redraw these boundaries – out to the median line with Australia and longitudinally with Indonesia both to its west and east.

There are a number of reasons as to why East Timor's ocean boundaries are still disputed despite decades of negotiations and a series of Treaties.

First, Australia claims most of the Timor Sea on the basis of international law – that a country has a right to claim its continental shelf. Australia claims that the Timor Trough between itself and East Timor marks the edge of its continental shelf, and it rejects the median line boundary in favor of the continental shelf boundary – both of which being justified under international law.

Second, although three countries have coastlines along the Timor Sea (Australia, Indonesia, and East Timor and its precursor entities) Australia has always insisted on bilateral negotiations. The earliest of these bilateral negotiations was with Indonesia and led to the *Seabed Agreement* of 1972. This set a seabed boundary favorable to Australia. King (2002) explains that this outcome occurred because Indonesia was at the time in receipt of Australian economic and military aid and felt it should reciprocate the relationship by giving something in return. Also, following massacres of ethnic Chinese in Indonesia during the 1960s, an agreement with Australia lent renewed international legitimacy to Indonesia.

No agreement on a seabed boundary had been agreed between Australia and Portugal, the latter sticking to the median boundary principle. Portugal was removed from the picture in 1975 following the Indonesian invasion of East Timor. This again left Australia negotiating with Indonesia over a seabed boundary in the Timor Gap. No boundary was agreed. However, under the 1989 *Timor Gap (Zone of Cooperation) Treaty*, 50–50 resource rent sharing was agreed. That gathering offshore hydrocarbon resource rents was an uppermost consideration for Australia is suggested by the fact that in 1981, under the *Provisional Fisheries Surveillance and Enforcement Agreement*, Australia had agreed to a fisheries-policing boundary based on the median line principle.

The next Australian bilateral agreement was in 2001, with the UN acting as administrator for the newly liberated East Timor. Under the *Interim Agreement* resource rents from offshore hydrocarbon production were to be shared 90–10 favorable to East Timor. Again no seabed boundaries were agreed.

Then there was the bilateral negotiation with East Timor that led to the *Timor Sea Treaty*. This is largely based on the 1989 *Timor Gap (Zone of Cooperation) Treaty* that defined the geographical space of the Timor Gap (i.e. was decided earlier between Australia and Indonesia), and the 2001 *Interim Agreement* that decided the 90–10 split, but 20–80 split for the Greater Sunrise straddling oil–gas reservoir.

In an annex to this treaty a minority report points to the unequal bargaining positions of East Timor and Australia (see Joint Standing Committee on Treaties, 2002). It calls for more generous treatment of East Timor – to avoid a "failed" state close to Australia – and calls for use of the International Court of Justice to settle the disputed boundaries. However, none of this has occurred.

When East Timor called for the redrawing of its longitudinal (north–south) boundaries with Australia, Australia refused, saying that this would upset its bilateral treaty with Indonesia. At this point in time Australia has "locked in" favorable seabed boundaries and uses an agreement with a third country to not negotiate with East Timor. Moreover, Australia has refused international arbitration, having in March 2002 withdrawn from international arbitration on seabed boundaries in the International Court of Justice and the International Tribunal for the *Law of the Sea*. These criticisms aside, it is still true that Australia has agreed to share resource rents on what it claims is its continental shelf in the Timor Sea, and most significantly of all, not a warship has been deployed to the area to enforce perceived rights.

Notes

1 This chapter owes a lot to the work of King (2002).
2 Article 76 (6) says that "the outer limit of the continental shelf shall not exceed 350 nautical miles from the baselines from which the breadth of the territorial sea is measured", and according to Article 77 (1), "The coastal State exercises over the continental shelf sovereign rights for the purpose of exploring it and exploiting its natural resources."
3 According to Article 76, para. 8 of UNCLOS, "Information on the limits of the continental shelf beyond 200 nautical miles from the baselines from which the breadth of the territorial sea is measured shall be submitted by the coastal State to the Commission on the Limits of the Continental Shelf." Furthermore, "The Commission shall make recommendations to coastal States on matters related to the establishment of the outer limits of their continental shelf. The limits of the shelf established by a coastal State on the basis of these recommendations *shall be final and binding*" (italics added). However, Australia withdrew the issue of its maritime boundary dispute with East Timor from both the International Court of Justice and the International Tribunal of the *Law of the Sea* in March 2002.
4 Confirmed reserves in the Jabiru field in the Timor Gap put at 214 million barrels with annual production of about 42,000 barrels per day.
5 *The Economist*, December 2nd, 2000.

PART IV

Fisheries economics

8

ECONOMICS OF THE FISHERY

1   Some data on US and world fishing

An open access fishery illustrates "the tragedy of the commons", with in many cases fish stocks being depleted 90 percent or more. Table 8.1 shows this for US New England commercial fish landings, comparing the years 1960 (a year quite early in the industrialization of the oceans), the peak year, and the most recent year, 2011. In most cases landings increased dramatically to the peak year, which were typically thirty or more than forty years ago. Following the peak year, landings then crashed by an astonishing 90 percent or more.[1]

It is also a tragedy that effective management of these fisheries would have allowed more fish to be sustainably caught than at today's depleted levels, at lower costs and with larger economic rents.

Indeed, over-fishing is a worldwide tragedy. Lost economic benefits are estimated to be about $50 billion annually, and over an extended period, 1974–2004, the cumulative worldwide loss is about $2 trillion; moreover, these losses do not count those in the fish processing industry, or the costs that can be imputed to lost biodiversity (World Bank, 2009).[2] It has also been estimated that the annual worldwide catch of

TABLE 8.1 USA New England: Annual commercial landings, metric tons

	1960	Peak year	Peak year landings, metric tons	2011 landings, metric tons	Percentage increase 1960 to peak	Percentage decline from peak in 2011
Cod	15,991	1980	53,192	7,948	233	85
Halibut	112	1965	148	25	32	83
Haddock	53,803	1962	60,858	5,709	13	91
Flounder, plaice	1,376	1982	15,128	1,386	999	90
Flounder, yellowtail	13,624	1983	31,410	1,810	131	94
Flounder, summer	752	1976	4,939	1,976	557	60
Flounder, winter	8,262	1981	17,082	2,075	201	98
Flounder, windowpane	–	1985	4,113	5.4		99
Bass, striped	95.8	1973	918	631	858	7
American shad	196	1967	341	12	74	96
Redfish	64,153	1960	64153	2,010	0	97

NOAA, Office of Science and Technology, *Annual Commercial Landing Statistics*, available online at www.st.nmfs.noaa.gov/commercial-fisheries/index

wild fish, which was about 82 million tons in the early 1990s, could have sustainably been about 125 million tons with effective fisheries management (FAO, 1997a).

Over-fishing is a feature of most segments of the world's fisheries, with all 200 fisheries monitored in the FAO study being described as "fully exploited". The later World Bank study confirmed this, saying that 60 percent of the world's marine fish stocks were "underperforming assets" in 1974; this rose to over 75 percent in 2004, with the remaining 25 percent being of low-grade fish. It is apparent that the world ocean fish catch is only being maintained by moving on to less desirable species as higher-value species are fished out. Thus, when turbot and halibut were fished out, fishers moved on to species that used to be thrown back – whiting and spiny dogfish, for example. The world fish catch has also been boosted by fishing in more distant waters – the Falkland's EEZ in the south Atlantic being a case in point. Even so, Myers and Worm (2003) report collapse of fish biomass throughout the world's oceans. Thus, comparing catch per hundred hooks of predatory fish such as tuna from the beginning of "industrialized" fishing in the early 1950s to the time of their study, the decrease was between 70 percent and 90 percent in all of the following areas: tropical Atlantic, subtropical Atlantic, temperate Atlantic, tropical Indian, subtropical Indian, temperate Indian, tropical Pacific, subtropical Pacific, temperate Pacific, Gulf of Thailand, South Georgia, Southern Grand Banks and Saint Pierre Banks.

By some estimates the US fish catch is only half as valuable as it would be if its stocks were allowed to recover. In its EEZ as a whole the *volume* of finfish catches peaked in 1995, thereafter falling. The *volume* of shellfish catch has been flat for about thirty years. The *value* of finfish catch has been falling since 1994 due to both the lower catch and the fact that lower-value fish are substituting for higher-value fish (e.g. whiting for halibut). The *value* of the shellfish catch is increasing and is now greater than that of finfish.[3]

Over-fishing is not the only cause of the falling US fish catch. A full three-quarters of this catch depends on US estuaries mainly as habitats for juveniles. However, the ecological function of many estuaries is itself deteriorating due to worsening pollution, eutrophication and loss of wetland – see the discussion of coastal wetland management in Chapter 18.

The collapse of the oceans fisheries has occurred alongside an increase in the worldwide fishing fleet of about 75 percent from the mid-1970s to about four million decked and un-decked boats in 2004 (World Bank, 2009). Moreover, new technologies have been introduced. Today, trawlers can trawl four nets from a single boat instead of just one; gill nets 40 miles long are used; in less developed countries motorization of fishing vessels is extensive; fishing fleets are accompanied by freezer mother-ships; planes are used for spotting; and fishing boats are fitted with directional sonar to find schools of fish.

Fitzpatrick (1996) estimated that the technological coefficient, a parameter of vessel fishing capacity, grew at a rate of 4.3 percent per annum since the early 1970s. But the trend of his catch/capacity index shows that worldwide fishing productivity fell by a factor of six between 1970 and 2005 (p. 16 and Figure 19). At the same time, average catch per fisher has declined worldwide by 42 percent from more than five tons annually in 1970 to only 3.1 tons in 2000 (World Bank, 2009, p. 13 and Figure 15). The same study found that the global marine fish catch could be achieved with approximately only one-half of current global fishing effort – a finding supported by the FAO (1997a) study that reported that in the case of Norway, which has successfully introduced fish management arrangements and whose fleet has been cut by two-thirds, a smaller fleet catches just as much fish.

2 Sustainable yield

There is some scientific support for the belief that if left alone the size of many biological populations, including marine fish, will follow a logistic curve – like that in Figure 8.1, or something similar (see Hjort, Jahn and Ottestad, 1933). Thus, if some event, such as over-fishing, decimated a population, its recovery would initially be slow, progressively speed up to some maximum rate, and then slow again (see, for example, Post et al., 2002, and Russ and Alcala, 1996, 2004).[4] The governing factors are the environment, such as water temperature and the availability of food. Assuming that these factors are stable over time, when the fish population is small the fish have plenty to eat, births easily outrun deaths and the population grows quickly. However, as the population becomes larger, the growth rate eventually slows as the excess of births over deaths declines. Eventually maximum carrying capacity is reached.

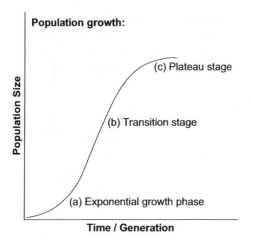

The slope of the logistic curve = Δ population/Δ time. Assume Δ time = 1 year, then Δ population is the annual growth in fish population. The latter is shown on the vertical axis of Figure 8.2.

FIGURE 8.1 Fish population over time

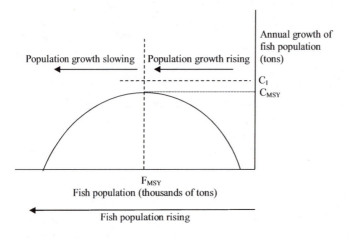

FIGURE 8.2 Maximum sustainable yield

Growth of the fish population is given by the slope of the logistic curve. In Figure 8.2 growth of the fish stock, measured in tons, is shown on the vertical axis as a function of population size – shown on the horizontal axis. Notice that the figure is drawn with the origin on the right – population rising moving leftward. It has been drawn this way to help the argument in Figure 8.3. You can see that when the fish population is small the absolute increase in the population is also quite small. However, with a larger stock, the tonnage of fish added per year increases.

At the point marked C_{MSY} in Figure 8.2, the amount of fish added to the population each year is at its maximum, and thereafter growth in the stock declines. The term "sustainable" means that if only the annual growth is taken, the fish population will remain constant. Thus, if the fish population is equal to F_{MSY} in Figure 8.2, the maximum sustainable yield can be taken each year. Either side of F_{MSY} the sustainable yield is lower.

At any population size a catch greater than the sustainable yield will reduce the population. For example, if C_1 is taken the population will fall, and if it was to be taken year after year, the population would approach zero.

3   How much fish to take to maximize the social surplus?

What quantity of fish is it socially optimal to take, given an objective of maintaining the fish population at a given level? One view is that it is optimal to take the maximum sustainable yield. After all, the MSY yields the most fish per year while also stabilizing the fish population at P_{MSY} in Figure 8.3.

However, given that fishing incurs costs, the MSY is not the socially optimal, rent-maximizing catch. Taking account of revenues and costs, the optimal catch is *less* than the MSY and the optimal fish population is greater than P_{MSY}.

The economist's view is that the objective should be to maximize the "profit" from fishing activity, where profit is the difference between total revenue and total cost. In fact, just to repeat, when dealing with a natural resource, instead of using the term "profit" the related concepts *of economic rent*, or *social surplus*, are used. We now turn to explore these propositions with the aid of Figure 8.3.

Total revenue earned catching fish = price of fish multiplied by size of the catch. For convenience we assume a constant unit price of fish, so total revenue varies only with the size of the catch. We know the size of the catch from Figure 8.2 – which is reproduced in the lower half of Figure 8.3. The upper part of Figure 8.3 plots the total revenue curve. Notice that it mirrors the yield curve in the lower part of the figure.

To further simplify, assume that fishing effort is accurately measured by the number of hunting (fishing) days at sea. Supposing that fishermen are self-employed, the cost of a day's labor fishing is what a fisherman could have earned in the next best job. In other words, cost is a fisherman's *transfer earnings*. Assuming that transfer earning is constant, the total cost of fishing effort is a linear function, and is drawn as such in the upper half of Figure 8.3.

From the TR and TC functions we easily deduce the *marginal revenue* and *marginal cost* of fishing effort. These are given by, respectively, the slopes of the total revenue and total cost functions. Furthermore, we know that profit maximization occurs when marginal revenue = marginal cost. In terms of Figure 8.3 this equality occurs where the respective slopes are equal, and this occurs at a fishing effort of E_{MEY}.

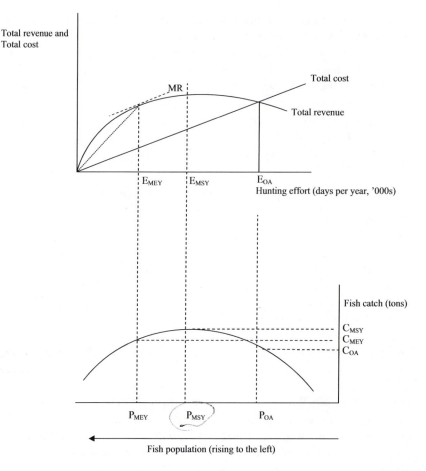

FIGURE 8.3 Optimal fishing effort, catch, population and economic rent

Look too at the size of the catch in the lower part of Figure 8.3. It is C_{MEY} – which is less than the C_{MSY}. Also, observe the optimal size of the fish population. This is P_{MEY} – which is a larger population than that associated with the maximum sustainable yield, P_{MEY}.

4 Optimal yield

The total cost function in Figure 8.3 includes only the private cost of fishing, specifically fishers' transfer earnings. However, fishing can involve external costs. For example, MEY in herring fisheries may reduce the food source for other sea creatures, and non-selective fishing gear can destroy habitats and cause large and wasteful by-catches. Watling and Norse (1998) compare disturbance of the seabed by mobile fishing gear to forest clear-cutting – that is, as a threat to biodiversity and economic sustainability, because of the crushing, burying or exposing of marine animals and the disturbance of the young stages of commercially important fishes. They estimate that about one-half of the world's continental shelves are trawled or dredged annually and, worse, fishers return to the same places at intervals far shorter than the time required for benthic ecosystem recovery. Similarly, Morgan, Tsao and Guinotte (2007) point out that deep sea coral protection is wrongly treated as a secondary issue; rather, improved habitat would increase fish stocks and reduce the probability of population crashes. The US Commission on Ocean Policy (2004) said that "unintentional catch of non-targeted species by recreational and commercial fishermen, commonly known as by-catch, is a major economic and ecological problem" (p. 244). And the Pew Oceans Commission (2003) asserted that "the principal objective of fishery management should be to protect the long-term health and viability of fisheries by protecting, maintaining and restoring the health, integrity, productive capacity and resilience of the marine ecosystems upon which they depend".

To take account of external costs, the total cost function in Figure 8.3 should pivot upward so as to incorporate both private and external costs of fishing effort. In that case optimal fishing effort would move to the left of E_{MEY}, and social economic rents would be reduced. However, the fish stock would increase as the optimal fish catch was reduced.

The effect of habitat destruction in one fishery on another fishery is shown in Figure 8.4, which allows for negative biological spillovers between fisheries. For example, trawling for one type of fish may damage the habitat and, therefore, the ability of another type of fish to reproduce. This shifts the second fishery's TR curve downward from TR_1 to TR_2. In the absence of this negative spillover, the socially optimal effort in this negatively impacted fishery is E_{MEY1} with associated economic rent of AB; but with the negative biological spillover, optimal effort is only E_{MEY2} with the smaller

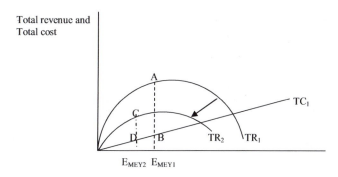

FIGURE 8.4 Optimal yield allowing for a negative biological spillover from another fishery

economic rent of CD. It is apparent therefore that fisheries policy based on optimal yield in a given fishery should take account of biological spillovers between fisheries. The case discussed in Figure 8.4 suggests that fishing effort in the fishery causing the spillover should be reduced further than in the absence of a spillover, and/or fishing gear in that fishery should be changed so as to remove the spillover.

Precautionary approach

The problem of negative spillover effects from one fishery to another and back again from the second fishery to the first fishery – dynamic effects – has led some marine scientists and economists to emphasize the idea of a precautionary approach to fisheries policy. A precautionary approach is needed because the extent of spillovers between fisheries is not well understood, certainly not well enough to be able to develop a known-to-be-correct equation along with its correct parameters that in turn can be maximized in order to find the MSY or MEY.[5] All the better therefore to take a precautionary approach, to be on the safe side, to reduce catches below what might seem to be safe levels based on not well-understood metrics – not, therefore, to fish to the edge of what might be disaster. Indeed, the precautionary approach is written into the UN *Straddling Fish Stocks and Highly Migratory Fish Stocks Agreement*, discussed in Chapter 13.

5 Tragedy of the commons

We know from Figure 8.3 that the *socially optimal* hunting effort is E_{MEY}, that the optimal catch is C_{MEY} and that the optimal fish stock is P_{MEY}. If a social planner was given authority over a previously unexploited fish stock and had all the relevant information, in the interests of maximizing the social surplus she would impose a fishing quota, a total allowable catch, of C_{MEY}. The outcome, however, is very different when fishing is left to the "free market" – to the individual decisions of many individual fishermen and women.

Free market organization of fishing leads to over-fishing, what has been called the tragedy of the commons. The tragedy is that in Figure 8.3, instead of the socially efficient, economic rent-maximizing set (E_{MEY}, C_{MEY}, P_{MEY}), free market open access ends up with the socially inefficient open access set of (E_{OA}, C_{OA}, P_{OA}). In other words, the operation of the unfettered market leads to too much fishing effort, a smaller than optimal fish stock and a smaller than possible fish catch. Moreover, all economic rent is competed away.

6 The market and the tragedy

It is quite easy to understand why the unfettered market leads to a tragedy of the commons in the fishing industry. From Figure 8.3 we know that the socially optimal hunting effort is E_{MEY} days, where the marginal cost of an extra day's fishing equals the marginal revenue of that extra day of effort. However, at E_{MEY} the average cost of another day's fishing is less than the average revenue that can be earned from that day's fishing. What can be earned per day is more than cost per day, so it pays to go on adding days fishing beyond E_{MSY}. To see this in Figure 8.3, recall that average revenue equals total revenue divided by days of effort – this is the slope of the ray from the origin in the top part of Figure 8.3. Likewise, average cost is the slope of the TC function. Clearly, as at E_{MEY}, AR > AC "free market" fishers have an incentive to go out fishing for at least one more day. Indeed, as it is true that AR > AC all the way to E_{OA}, fishing will continue up to the latter (excessive) amount of effort. In the process, economic rent will be exhausted; effort and fishing costs will rise – though the fish catch will fall, and so too will the fish population.

7 Driving a fish stock to extinction

It is worthwhile storing a commodity if the expected rate of price increase is great enough to justify the cost of storage (Hallwood and Edwards, 1980). This is said to be the case with blue fin tuna.[6] When frozen to –60°C, it can be preserved for many years before eventual sale on the market. But with this fish becoming scarcer in the wild, and the possibility that it could become extinct as a commercial species, the expected rate of price increase may be high enough to justify fishing even at a financial loss today. Thus, in Figure 8.5, fishing effort may be pushed beyond E_{OA} to E_{OAWS} ("open access with storage"), where fishing cost incurred today is greater than total revenue. If all the catch was sold on the market today, fishers would incur a loss of $xy in Figure 8.5.

However, suppose that fishers, or the wholesalers that they sell to, can borrow money to finance the loss $xy plus any storage costs at the rate of interest r_1 while the rate of increase of market prices is expected to be p_1. If p_1 exceeds r_1 storage is expected to be a profitable activity – in which case hunting effort will be pushed

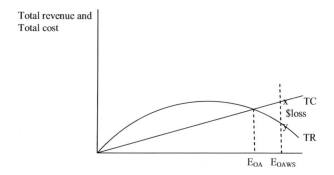

Hunting effort (days per year, '000s)

FIGURE 8.5 Increased hunting effort with storage

beyond E_{OA} in Figure 8.5 – but the reduced annual catch and smaller fish stock will not be of concern for private market actors, fishers and storage specialists, because they are engaged in a profitable activity.

There is a more general lesson here. Even if there was a monopoly fishing organization such as state control of a fishery, it is still possible that E_{MEY} in Figure 8.3 will not constitute optimal fishing effort even with its associated large annual catch, fish stock and economic rent. Our discussion of optimal fishing effort in Figure 8.3 implicitly assumed that fishers used a zero-percent discount rate – that is, they were indifferent as to what date a given level of profit was earned, say, $100,000 this year or next year. However, if fishers have a time preference – if they prefer larger profits today even at the expense of lower profits next year – they will increase hunting effort beyond E_{MEY} in Figure 8.3, with corresponding adverse impacts on fish stocks and the size of the catch in later years.

Even a government that has effective control over a fishery under the law may find it rational to allow excessive fishing effort for political or economic reasons. If a commercial fishing lobby is strong, as in the US and the EU, governments may "buy" votes by allowing excessive fishing effort compared with the social optimal. Similarly, a government chooses to allow an excessively large fishing industry to remain in existence because it is less expensive than various fishing industry policies it could adopt, such as paying fishers to leave the industry.

8   A comparison of open access with private ownership fisheries

The foregoing analysis of open access fisheries makes a number of predictions that can be tested. In comparison with a properly managed fishery, open access has a number of undesirable properties. In particular, it results in lower profits, a smaller fish population, smaller catches, larger fishing effort, and lower productivity per worker or per boat.

This tragedy of the commons is well illustrated by the sea scallop fishery either side of the boundary dividing Canadian and US waters on Georges Bank. Although on the US side the fishery was managed through "command and control" – see Chapter 9 – due to management failures, it was effectively open access. By contrast, on the Canadian side rights-based fishing was instituted in 1986 – a system that creates incentives for fishers to achieve maximum economic yield (also see Chapter 6). Repetto (2001) found that on the Canadian side the biomass of four- to seven-year-olds – i.e. larger specimens of greater commercial and biological value (because they are more fecund) – was large, while on the US side it was small. The US biomass was also more variable than the Canadian. The Canadian take of the less-desirable three-year-olds was zero percent of the total harvest, and that of four- to seven-year-olds was 20 percent, the remainder being of seven-year-olds (or older). By contrast, the US take of the less-desirable three-year-olds was 20–50 percent and that of four- to seven-year-olds 50–80 percent of the harvest. Moreover, the Canadians substantially reduced the number of boats in the industry from 67 to

28 over the period 1990 to 1999, while there was no reduction in the size of the US scallop fleet. Also, the catch per day on Canadian boats was about one ton, while on US boats it was estimated to be only 0.4 tons; and while the Canadian fishery was profitable, Repetto estimated that the US boats were loss-making.

Some new management measures were adopted on the US side in 1994, including the creation of three closed areas, a pause on new permits, and reductions in days at sea, as well as gear and crew restrictions. However, these measures did not have any noticeable effect on the fishery until 1999 (Hart and Rago, 2006). Thus, during 1994–2005, the biomass of sea scallops in the US sector of Georges Bank increased by a factor of about 18, and this appears to be due to the area closures, the biomass of those areas coming to account for 80 percent of the scallop biomass on the US side of Georges Bank. Recruitment beyond the closed areas did not increase, but it did so with the closed areas in the Middle Atlantic Bight (Hart and Rago, 2006). The latter is an obvious beneficial feature that is relevant to the discussion of the economics of marine protected areas in Chapter 17.

Notes

1 In the broader area of the Northwest Atlantic, spanning from Long Island Sound northward to the Arctic Sea and including the high seas, the total catch peaked in the mid-1960s at about 4.5 million tons, falling to less than two million tons in the mid-1990s. Catches of Atlantic cod peaked at about 1.8 million tons in the late 1960s, falling to an insignificant amount thirty year later. The catches of hake, haddock and other cod are also much reduced from their earlier peaks. Catches of demersal fish are also heavily down, including those of American plaice, yellowtail flounder and witch flounder.

2 These losses are worse than in an earlier estimate that put the worldwide loss at $15–30 billion per annum (FAO, 1997a).

3 National Marine Fisheries Service, various documents.

4 Some evidence of logistical growth was found by Russ and Alcala (1996); they observed predator fish recovery on a Philippines coral reef after fishing there stopped when it became a marine protected area. They report that a slow increase was seen in the first three to five years (reflecting delayed recruitment and a natural delay to the period of maximum individual mass growth), followed by an increasing rate over the next four years.

   Russ and Alcala (2004) monitored predatory fish populations over a seventeen-year period on two coral reefs in the Philippines and estimate that recovery times were fifteen years on one reef and forty years on the other. Because the logistic curve is symmetric around the inflection point, the MSY occurs at exactly 50 percent of the maximum environmental carrying capacity of a fish species. Thorson et al. (2012) investigate whether this is true, finding that MSY occurs at an average of only 40 percent in their database of 147 fish stocks. Fish like anchovies and herring have lower values, while others such as cod and hake have higher ratios than this average. They point out that by adding a "shape parameter" the original model is easily replicated.

5 As Richards and Maguire (1998) write, "more research is required to quantify uncertainties associated with reference point definitions and their practical application in a management context. In addition, future research will emphasize environmental issues with extensive data requirements, such as ecosystem impacts of fishing. Data collection will remain a core business activity; agencies must address the costs of maintaining shared and documented data archives over the long term" (p. 1545).

6 Documentary film, *The End of the Line*, Roberto Mielgo, 2009.

9

MANAGEMENT OF FISH STOCKS
(Biomass)

1 Introduction

We saw in Chapter 8 that over-fishing characterizes many fisheries around the world, and that in some cases fish stocks are as low as only 10 percent of their preindustrial fishing levels recorded in the 1950s. We also saw that with reduced fishing effort in a fishery *more* fish can be caught because fish stocks could recover. Properly designed fisheries management is a win–win–win–win game producing larger fish stocks, larger catches, less fishing effort and greater profits. The *proviso*, though, is "properly designed" because most of the many fisheries management systems that have been tried show little or no evidence of win–win–win–win.

In this chapter we will discuss the economic characteristics of some of the main fisheries management methods, explaining why those that are ineffective are so, and we will also discuss the economic characteristics of some management methods that have turned out to be effective.[1] Moreover, it is not as if the fishers and fisheries managers do not know how to manage fisheries in a way to approximate maximum economic rent; rather, the failure is one of political will.

2 Management methods

Until countries claimed 200-mile Exclusive Economic Zones (EEZ), a single country had jurisdiction only over its territorial waters. As a result, into the 1970s and in earlier times management of fish stocks beyond the territorial sea was a matter of international negotiation, but absent the *Fur Sea Treaty* of 1911 (see Chapter 11) there was no success.

However, as most fish stocks live on continental shelves, the creation of 200-mile EEZs put a different complexion on fisheries management. Now the search for solutions became one of a search for national solutions. The exceptions to this general rule were (and remain) fish stocks that straddle between national jurisdictions and high seas fisheries, such as tuna – examined in Chapters 13 and 14. In this chapter we concentrate on national management solutions where "game playing" between fishers and governments is at the national level. *A priori*, the chances of success are greater when a game is played in a single jurisdiction because ultimate power – the policing authority – to impose solutions lies with the sovereign, should it want to exercise it. As we will see, sovereign powers have often failed to find sensible solutions to the problem of over-fishing even in their own jurisdictions.

EEZs have been successful in excluding foreign fishing vessels. Thus, according to the FAO (1997b), prior to their introduction catches by distant water fishing fleets in the Northwest Atlantic amounted to over one-half of the total catch in several fisheries; for example, Canadian catches of cod in the early 1970s were only about one-quarter of the total catch in the area. By the early 1980s, however, distant water fleets accounted for only about 12 percent of the total catch, the rest being taken by the USA, Canada and Greenland. Unfortunately, stock recovery was short-lived because national fishing fleets moved in to replace the fishing effort of the distant water fleets.

3 Methods of coping with open access

Several methods are used to manage fish stocks toward the social optimum, where the sustainable catch is at a level that maximizes economic rent. Results are mixed, with several management methods being ineffective. The main management methods are listed in Box 9.1. These are divided into *command and control* methods – the government sets rules – and the *creation of property rights*. We will discuss an example from each main section – specifically, the methods of total allowable catch (TAC), vessel catch limits, limited licensing, and time and area closures. We will also discuss what is widely, though not universally, regarded as the best practical alternative to

---

BOX 9.1   FISHERIES MANAGEMENT METHODS

Regulations – "command and control"
   Limitation of output
      Total allowable catch (TAC)
      Vessel catch limits
   Limitation of input
      Limited licensing
      Individual effort quotas
      Other gear restrictions (e.g. mesh size)
   Technical measures
      Size and sex selectivity
      Time and area closures
Creation of property rights
   Individual quotas (IQ) and individual transferable quotas (ITQ)
Landing fees

---

command and control – the creation of property rights – both individual quotas (IQs) and individual transferable quotas (ITQs). Finally, an alternative to these that has not been tried anywhere – a landing fee on fish – is briefly discussed.

Before getting down to the specifics of each management system we will discuss a common problem with all command and control techniques.

4   National fisheries management through "command and control"

To understand the general economic background of the problems of command and control fisheries management, let's review the idea of the supply and demand for labor. In this case the demand for labor is from a large fishing boat looking for crew. Such a demand curve in Figure 9.1 is downward sloping – more crew being demanded at a lower wage. The supply of labor is determined by workers' willingness to work and is assumed to be at the fixed wage W_1. Thus, the wage is W_1, and L^* units of labor are hired by the fishing boat captain.

You will recall that the demand for labor depends upon how much physical output the last worker adds to output (measured, say, in pounds of fish), together with the price of that output (fish in this case). Assuming a fixed price of fish, multiplying these two things together gives the *marginal revenue product of labor* and the MRPL curve is the demand for labor curve.

Now suppose that a law is passed aimed at reducing fishing effort that stipulates that the amount of labor that the fishing boat can hire per year has to be reduced from L^* to L_1. What are the implications of this law?

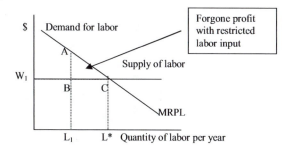

FIGURE 9.1 Fishing effort reductions

As less labor is employed, fewer fish will be caught and, assuming a fixed price of fish, the boat's total revenue will fall. Second, observe that at L_1 units of labor input the MRPL at A is greater than the wage, W_1. In other words, what the L_1th unit of labor adds to the boat's revenue is greater than what it adds to its costs (which is equal to the wage). The boat therefore forgoes profit on this unit of labor and it does so on each of the units between L_1 and L^* units. The area ABC measures lost profit.

The boat's owners will recognize that they can increase profits if they can catch more fish. As the law prevents them from employing more labor, they will turn to other means of increasing the catch. For example, they may mechanize previously unmechanized activities or make more trips to the fishing grounds.

The conclusion must be that when a combination of inputs is needed to catch fish, passing a law to limit the use of any one of them does not necessarily mean that fewer fish will be caught. Rather, the law is an inconvenience to be got around by substituting other inputs for the legally limited input. In fact, as we shall see, "*command and control*" laws are more than just an inconvenience; they waste resources raising the cost of fishing, but have minimal impact on the amount of fish caught and the size of fish stocks.

5 Total allowable catch – Derby fishing and capital stuffing

Total allowable catch limits are widely used around the world, with the European Union using TAC limits for 36 fish species,[2] and the US using TAC limits as a method of managing fish stocks in all of its eight Regional Fish Management Council areas. In principle, the system is straightforward: the government determines and announces TAC landings and closes a fishery when the TAC is reached. In the short-run the objective usually is to increase the fish stock by setting the catch at less than its biological rate of increase. In Figure 9.2, given an overriding concern to maximize economic rent, in the long-run the fishery will move from point A to point B.

If successful, the fish population will rise from its "over-fished" level, corresponding to E_1 effort, to that with the lower effort level, E_2. With a TAC-only policy, effort

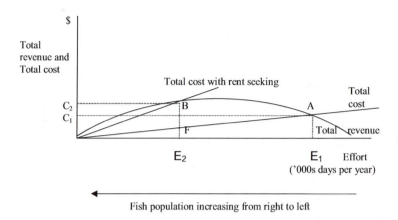

FIGURE 9.2 Total allowable catch

in a fishery will fall from its open access level because fishers know that the fishery will be closed as soon as the TAC is reached. Thus, supposing that closure happened half-way through the season, and that prior to the policy's introduction fishing effort was evenly spread through the season, this would mean that effort exerted later in the season wouldn't be used and total fishing effort would fall correspondingly. Even so, with the larger fish population the sustainable catch rises from C_1 to C_2.

Unfortunately, this is not the end of the matter because the TAC policy raises profits only *for those who catch fish.* This leads to a number of problems.

First, fishers have to catch fish before the fishery is closed and this causes a *race to fish* – so-called *Derby fishing.* Fishers therefore aim to get out as early in the season as possible. It also leads to *capital stuffing,* with fishers buying faster boats (to get back and forth from the fishing grounds more quickly), and bigger boats (so that they can stay out fishing for longer). The result is that the total cost curve in Figure 9.2 pivots upward, in the limit until it cuts through point B with all economic rent being dissipated. This is a situation of rent seeking, with expected economic rent being dissipated on expenditures designed to capture it.

Second, with less effort being put in, but by fewer boats, there is likely to be a trend toward concentration in the fishery – smaller, less efficient boats getting pushed out. Also, with declining manpower needs, the same happens to some workers. This can be a problem when small fishing communities depend on fishing but find their source of livelihood moving away. Moreover, with shorter fishing seasons, employment in fishing will be less steady than it used to be.

Third, the race to fish leads to fish being taken early in the season, causing a glut and necessitating freezing in order to spread consumption out over time; quality is degraded.

According to the OECD (1997), these adverse effects of TAC management – race to fish, shorter fishing seasons, capital stuffing and fewer vessels – are well supported by the evidence, but with one additional problem. Catches were most often above the TAC, so that fish populations did not recover. In other words, while the TAC system raised fishing costs it did little or nothing to achieve the objective of raising fish stocks and catches.

6 Vessel catch limits

Vessel catch limits limit the amount of fish a vessel can land per trip or per period of time, such as one month. The US has used this method of fisheries management at one time or another for several fish species; numerous other countries also use the technique.

As fishing has to stop when a catch limit is reached, in the short-run effort is reduced from E_1 to E_2 in Figure 9.3. But at E_2 there is an economic rent equal to BC that induces activity on the part of fishers to garner it. Incumbent vessels are likely to make more trips per week, to use larger engines so that they can travel faster, and other vessels might well enter the fishery. Effort therefore increases from E_2 to, say, E_3. Unit costs of fishing also increase – as catch per trip falls – so the total cost curve swings upward to TC_2. All economic rent is again wasted on rent seeking, though fishing effort is likely not to return to its initial level at E_1.

Thus, although profitability is not likely to increase, reduced effort at E_3 compared with E_1 holds out the prospect of larger fish stocks and larger catches. However, these beneficial effects are likely not to materialize because fishers have an incentive to land only high-valued fish, throwing back lesser specimens, often dead. This is the problem of *high grading*.[3]

The evidence on vessel catch limits provided by the OECD (1997) indicates that over-fishing was not reduced and resource conservation didn't occur, but enforcement (policing) costs increased to monitor vessel catches. Moreover, vessel catch limits in combination with a total allowable catch were also ineffective. Only vessel catch limits in combination with limited licenses showed positive results.

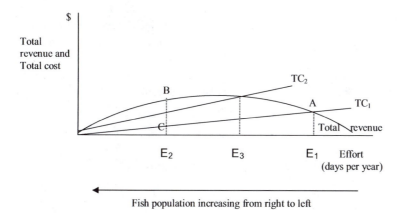

FIGURE 9.3 Vessel catch limits

7 Licenses

Licenses are used in many fisheries around the world. They can be attached to a boat, gear, or to a person, and they may be sold or given away. The distribution of licenses is problematical because this determines who is and who is not able to enjoy the expected increased profitability of a fishery should the policy be effective. One method that has been tried in an effort to reduce tensions over rent-seeking is to issue licenses to all interested parties and then to buy some of them back, or to allow attrition to reduce the number of fishers over time.

If the license system reduces effort, in the short-run license-holders earn an economic rent – as was the case in Figures 9.2 and 9.3. However, each license-holder has an incentive to practice capital stuffing, substituting inputs for the input constrained by the license, and better gear may be used – e.g. two trawls instead of one. Neither is there an expectation that the race to fish will end. Ultimately, costs rise and pressure on the fishery increases – though not to the unconstrained level. There could be a positive effect on both the level of the catch and the fish population, although OECD (1997) found only limited evidence of this.

8 Time and area closures

Time and area closures are also widely used around the world. They amount to the sovereign laying claim to its submerged lands and regulating accesses, too often as desperation measures introduced when it's all too obvious that a fishery is over-fished. Time closures may be introduced to allow juvenile fish to grow to a good size, and area closures – such as in estuaries, coastal wetlands, around reefs, or out to sea over low topography but promising seabed features (scallop beds, for example) – are used to protect the habitat of young fish.

As will be discussed in Chapters 16 and 17 – in reference to, respectively, coral reefs and the economics of zoning – time and area closures help to reduce externalities (e.g. protecting young fish in one area raises the abundance of adult fish in a related area) and so raise the levels of fish stock inside the protected area and, potentially, outside of it as well. For example, Hart and Rago (2006) find that the establishment of a closed area in the US Middle Atlantic Bight scallop fishery led to increased recruitment downstream from it. These are the main beneficial effects of time and area closures. However, used in isolation, time and area closures do nothing to move fishing effort away from that of open access to the social optimum that maximizes economic rent.

9 Creation of property rights: Individual quotas

An individual quota (IQ) gives a fisher the right to catch a specified amount of fish or proportion of a determined total allowable catch. An individual quota is a property right that can be used year after year. If the quota is transferable it becomes an *individual transferable quota* (ITQ) that can be bought and sold. The greatest difficulty

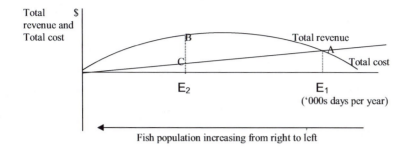

FIGURE 9.4 Individual quotas and individual transferable quotas

with both IQ and ITQ, as with limited licenses, is in their initial allocation because some fishers become excluded from a fishery while those that receive a quota allocation are able to participate in a more productive fishery that yields larger profits.

IQ and ITQ are little-used in the USA, but they are a popular management technique in many other countries – New Zealand having the most species fished with individual quotas. The view among many experts is that ITQs are the best possible fisheries management system, provided that the available biological information allows for the setting of a sensible TAC.

The effects of IQs are shown in Figure 9.4. Initially there is open access, effort is at E_1 and there is no economic rent. Assuming a period where quotas are set at a level that allows the fish stock to recover, an effective quota system will reduce effort to the rent maximizing social optimum at E_2. Economic rent increases from zero to $BC and both the fish catch and fish population are larger. All of these effects rely on the TAC being properly set by biological standards.

If the system adopted is individual quotas – not transferable, and most usually allocated according to historical catch shares – there is some danger that some high-cost fishers will remain in the fishery. An important advantage of a system of ITQ is that high-cost fishers can sell their quotas to more efficient fishers.

Other advantages of IQ and ITQ are that they eliminate the race to fish, encourage a catch to be spread out over a whole season and, as effort is reduced, by-catch is also likely to be reduced.

The worst disadvantages of IQ and ITQ mainly occur at the quota allocation stage, where rent-seeking disputes can be intense. Another disadvantage is that quota ownership may become concentrated, so closing-out small-scale fishers and, possibly, small isolated ports.

10   Landing fees

Use of landing fees, essentially a harbor side tax on fish, has been suggested by Gylfason and Weitzman (2002), but, despite its desirable properties, at the present time it is not used in any of the world's fisheries. A landing fee would be payable

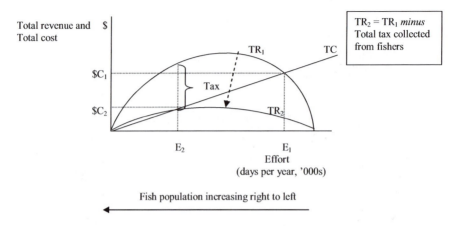

FIGURE 9.5 Using a landing tax to reduce fishing effort

on landed fish. It would act to contain over-fishing by reducing revenue-after-tax, therefore reducing the incentive to harvest fish. This is explained as follows: suppose a landing fee is levied on fish, of which t percent is incident on the suppliers – the fishers. This reduces the net price of fish they receive. As a result, for any given level of effort, *net* total revenue falls. This reduction in total revenue at each level of effort is shown in Figure 9.5 where the total revenue function shifts downward from TR_1 to TR_2.

Still assuming open access, effort will drive on to where TR = TC. The difference now is that $TR_2 < TR_1$ because of the landing fee. The result is that effort is reduced from E_1 to E_2 and the fish stock increases in size. An ideal landing fee would optimize the catch – effort should be at the level that maximizes economic rent. At E_2 effort *gross* total revenue, along TR_1, is greater than TC. This difference represents the social surplus. A properly set landing fee on fish therefore is able to improve on the unregulated open access outcome.

In practice it would be possible to vary the landing fee as the fish population changes – lowering it as the population rises. Another advantage is that there is no need to regulate and monitor fishing effort or fishing techniques as fishers simply supply effort according to the new net-of-tax total revenue schedule. There is no need for command and control in a landing fee system.

Notice too that the economic rent is collected by the government through landing fees. This is no loss to fishers as, with open access effort, E_1, they are not earning economic rent in any case. Government revenues raised through the landing fee could be used to subsidize adjustment in the fishing industry – paying for displaced fishers to be retrained, for example.

The main difficulties with a landing fee system are discovering the correct tax rate, which requires knowledge of the elasticity of demand and the effect of the tax on the fish stock and optimal catch; the political problem of taxing food – something which governments have found politically difficult to do; and the fact that fishers have an incentive to evade the tax.

A tax on the insurance-cost of vessels: Jensen (2002) suggests that taxing the insurance cost of fishing vessels would lead to a reduction in over-capacity in the fishing industry, as well as enable the government to enjoy a share of the rent. He estimates that a 2.6 percent annual tax would reduce the Danish fishing fleet by about 20 percent over ten years. He does not discuss, however, the effect of this tax on either substitution between inputs – e.g. fishing gear added to the remaining vessels – or whether fishers would compensate by reducing the proportion of the value of vessels covered by insurance.

11   Iceland and a possible resource depletion charge

Gylfason and Weitzman (2002) have suggested a fisheries tax for Iceland – a major fishing nation. The main management institution would be an open market fisheries committee (OMFC) that would be charged with maximizing the return on fisheries to the Icelandic state as the sovereign owner of the fisheries resources. A species-specific harvest payment, or resource depletion charge (RDC), would be calculated on the day of landing and paid by fishers. The charge would be paid as-if-in-kind as a percentage of the wet fish landing. In practice the RDC would be paid in Icelandic krona.

The species-by-species RDC could be varied monthly according to scientific and harvest data collected by the OMFC. If the stock of a species is thought to be falling below optimal levels, so that future catch size would decline, the RDC would be increased. If collected data suggest abundant stocks, the RDC could be lowered.

12   The Coase theorem and private solutions to over-fishing

Ronald Coase (1960) stated two propositions relating to the management of open access resources, such as fisheries:

1   Under certain circumstances individuals will come to an agreement to increase the social surplus above the level of the "bad outcome" – the Nash equilibrium.
2   The efficient use of a resource does *not* depend on the assignment of property rights.

Figure 9.6 sets the scene. There are two fishers, A and B, and they can either agree to constrain fishing rights – to manage the fishery collectively – or to remain with open access, "unimpaired" rights. The payoff matrix indicates that the social surplus can be increased from $4,000 ($2,000 each) to $20,000 – a gain of $16,000. But this game is a prisoners' dilemma because each player has a dominant strategy to "play" unimpaired rights – that is to say, even if they agree to constrain rights, in a one-off game each has an incentive to cheat. The Nash equilibrium of the game

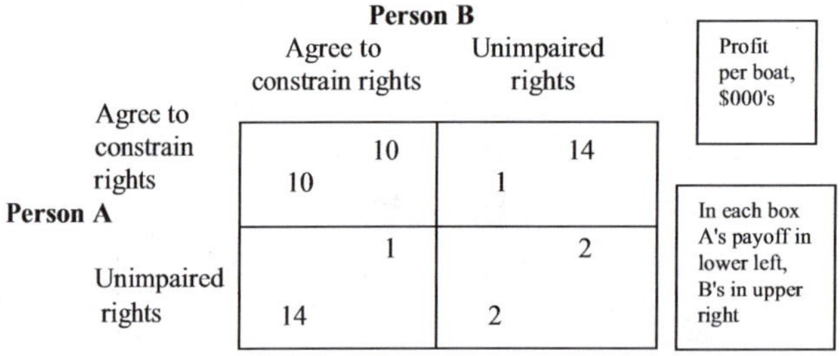

	Person B	
	Agree to constrain rights	Unimpaired rights
Person A Agree to constrain rights	10 / 10	14 / 1
Unimpaired rights	1 / 14	2 / 2

Profit per boat, $000's

In each box A's payoff in lower left, B's in upper right

FIGURE 9.6 Prisoners' dilemma and constraining fishing rights

is in the southeast box, where neither player has any further incentive to change their strategies (behavior).

Proposition I

The Coase theorem says that if transaction costs (including negotiation, monitoring and enforcement costs) are lower than the gain from moving from the "bad outcome" – the Nash equilibrium – to the "good outcome" (that is Pareto efficient) the parties will, in principle, be able to reach the cooperative solution to maximize the social surplus – in the northwest box of Figure 9.6.

State sponsored solutions to the prisoners' dilemma: All of the fisheries policies discussed so far in this chapter are state-sponsored solutions. The sovereign observes over-fishing, concludes that private solutions have not been found, and steps in to impose its own solutions – such as the command and control policies, or the introduction of property rights.

State-sponsored solutions work best when new fisheries laws – introduced to cope with the prisoners' dilemma problem that the private sector is failing to resolve – fit in with widely accepted social norms. Indeed, laws and social norms work best when they coincide, because when they do there is little need to police the law.

The scientific community has sometimes helped in the creation of new social norms. For example, the banning of international trade in endangered species, the creation of an international regime for the protection of Antarctic marine life, and governance of pollution in the Mediterranean Sea all stem at least in part from scientific findings on the need for them. And as Gislason et al. (2000, p. 471) note, "Governments and stakeholders want scientists to provide their best advice on potential indicators that relate to broader conservation objectives of management (for fisheries as well as other ocean industries)".

In terms of game theory, enhanced scientific knowledge and the creation of new social norms can in theory turn a prisoners' dilemma game into a cooperation game, as shown in Figure 9.7.

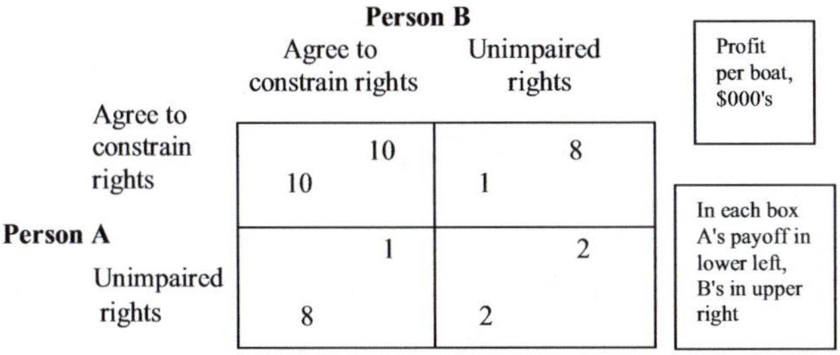

FIGURE 9.7 Cooperation game and constraining fishing rights

The only difference between the payoffs in Figures 9.6 and 9.7 is that the cheating payoff in the southwest and northeast boxes has been reduced from 14 to 8. This could be brought about by the realization that over-exploiting a resource is undesirable, perhaps because of its negative impact on marine ecosystems, for example the over-fishing for pollock in the Bering Sea in the 1980s severely reduced populations of marine mammals (Steller sea cows, Steller sea lions and Northern fur seals and Harbor seals) and sea birds (black legged and red legged kittiwakes).[4] If the social disutility of this negative externality is 6 (i.e. $6,000 in Figure 9.7), the cheating *net* payoff falls to only 8. As both players now see that constrained rights is the best outcome – 10, 10 is the highest either player can achieve – the remaining problem is just how quickly the players can draw up an agreement to manage a fishery with constrained rights.

13 Fisheries co-management: Some examples of private cooperative fishing agreements

There are examples of private sector solutions to the over-fishing problem. Fisheries community-based co-management is a set of methods used to resolve problems caused by the over-use of common property fisheries, especially access control and rent sharing. As an example, town mayors may agree that fishers resident in their towns will not fish in each other's waters. It amounts to power-sharing combining government and decentralized community-based fishers. An example of successful fisheries co-management is of Chilean abalone, that by the end of the 1980s was heavily over-exploited. Beginning with a mere two-mile stretch of coast, fishers agreed to share and limit their catches. A decade later, 2,500 miles of Chilean coast was similarly locally managed (Gutiérrez, Hilborn and Defeo, 2011).

Gutiérrez, Hilborn and Defeo (2011) collected data from 44 countries on 130 co-managed fisheries with the aim of discovering what conditions were essential for co-management to work. The main findings were that community leadership and clearly defined individual fish catches (shares in economic rents) in well-defined, protected areas were essential. Similarly, Pomeroy, Katon and Harkes (2001) identified 18 conditions related to successful artisanal fisheries co-management, including well-defined property rights (at least at the community level), homogeneous group identity, local leadership, adequate financial support, support from local government, clear objectives, and accountability in that violations are punished.

Establishment of fisheries co-management requires at the very least that government trusts local communities to execute agreed management plans, and this requires the establishment of locally based institutions where fishers meet to discuss and decide on fisheries matters such as who has access when and what types of fishing gear are permissible. According to Pomeroy and Berkes (1997), the establishment of such institutions has taken three to five years in the Philippines, and up to fifteen years in Turkey. At one level, top-down governance is largely retained, with government merely consulting fishers on possible new laws; but in a bottom-up arrangement fishers may design, implement and enforce new fisheries laws only in consultation with government, but requiring some sort of government involvement – for example, writing rules into municipal ordinances. The advantage of the latter is that fishers have a democratic say in management, while government benefits from having in place a management system that is regarded at the local level as being "legitimate". The latter is important because, typically, government provides the services of policing, enforcement and conflict resolution.

Proposition II: The social surplus and the assignment of property rights

The other matter concerning the Coase theorem is that with low transaction costs the social surplus will be maximized regardless of the assignment of property rights. An illustrative example of this is the Falkland Islands, which have the property right in a 200-mile exclusive economic zone. However, it is also the case that it has a virtually non-existent fishing industry. Nevertheless, this assignment of a property right to this high-cost (or, non-)producer does not reduce the social surplus to be gained from the resources. This is because the Falkland Islands, while retaining the property right, in exchange for a license fee sells a limited right to fish mainly for squid in its waters to low-cost distant water fleets from East Asia.[5] Another example of Coase's second proposition in action is the payment by US fishing boats and the US government of access fees and other economic benefits to fish for tuna in the EEZs of the members of the South Pacific Forum Fisheries Agency (Herrick, Rader and Squires, 1997). The implication of these two examples is that the assignment of property rights, while not necessarily affecting the size of the social surplus – because efficient fishers buy their way in – does influence its distribution of rents between players.

Notes

1 Indeed, there is some hope for economically rational fisheries management, as examples of effective fisheries management can found in countries such as Cyprus and the Philippines – where in the 1980s sustainable production of some fish doubled within

18 months – and in Norway's cod fisheries in the Northeast Atlantic and Barents Sea, with the biomass in the 1990s recovering from low levels to approximate those of the 1950s (FAO, 1997a).

2 European Commission, "Total Allowable Catches and Quotas", 2012, available online at http://ec.europa.eu/fisheries/cfp/fishing_rules/tacs/index_en.htm.

3 A completely different type of "high grading" is discussed in Chapter 23 on deep sea mining. It is anticipated that, if and when deep sea mining begins, commercial mining companies will have an incentive to take only the low cost, densely packed, polymetallic nodules. Rules operated by the International Seabed Authority are designed to prevent this.

4 "North Pacific Overfishing (Donut)", available online at www1.american.edu/ted/donut.htm.

5 *The Economist*, "The South Atlantic: A breezy, squid-rich paradise", May 28th, 2002.

PART V

Fisheries regime formation

10

IMPATIENCE, ECOLOGY AND FISHERIES REGIME FORMATION

1   Introduction

In this chapter we discuss the relationship between the ecology, specifically rates of reproduction of living marine resources, and regime formation to manage those resources. The main point to look for is that when the rate of reproduction is high, other things equal, there is a better chance of agreeing sensible management rules, compared with when the rate of reproduction is low. The key variable is the rent-maximizing harvest, H^*, compared with the environmental carrying capacity of a species, K – that is, H^*/K.

2   Payoffs: Biomass and harvest

To analyze the dynamics of reaching international agreements on living marine resources, here we will use the game theory approach. In this model two countries are exploiting a living ocean resource – or "biomass" – and they have to decide whether or not they should cooperate to conserve it. Figure 10.1 shows the payoffs.

K is the maximum biomass of a given environment or habitat;[1] H^* is the rent-maximizing sustainable annual harvest, and m is the "multiplicative factor" (explained in Box 10.1 and Table 10.1). Assuming that the price of fish is $1 per unit,

---

BOX 10.1 DISCOUNTING AND THE MULTIPLICATIVE FACTOR

Standard tables are available to calculate the present value of an annuity. An annuity is a constant annual income, or dollar value – of a sustainable harvest in our case. If the discount rate is 10 percent, $1 per year forever has a multiplicative factor of 10. This means that this stream of payments, at this discount rate, is worth $10 in today's money. If the discount rate is higher, say at 15 percent, the multiplicative factor is lower, at about 6.7. The discount rate can be thought of as representing people's impatience. The higher the discount rate (the greater is impatience), the lower the multiplicative factor and the lower is the present value of an annuity.

K and H* are both measured in either thousands of tons or thousands of dollars. The payoff to player 1 is in the lower left-hand corner of each box; that to player 2 is in the upper right-hand corner.

If there is no fishing agreement – both players following the "Deplete" strategy – the resource is exhausted in just one period, with each player sharing 1/2 of the biomass, viz.: K/2. However, if they decide to manage the resource under a rent-maximizing agreement they share equally in the sustainable annual harvest of H*. This annual harvest can be gathered year after year, and to find the present value of its annual payoff, the appropriate multiplicative factor, m, is used. The annual payoff from an agreement is, therefore, H*m/2.

Two other possible outcomes are that player 1 chooses to conserve while player 2 chooses the deplete strategy. In this case it is assumed that the resource is depleted in one time period, with player 2 collecting the whole of it, and player 1 none of it. This is the northeast box of Figure 10.1. Alternatively, if the two players switch strategies the symmetric outcome is shown in the southwest box of Figure 10.1.

	Player 2	
	Conserve	Deplete
Player 1 Conserve	H*m/2 H*m/2	K 0
Player 1 Deplete	0 K	K/2 K/2

FIGURE 10.1 International agreement payoff game

TABLE 10.1 Present value of a $1 annuity

Number of years	*Discount rates*			
	2%	*10%*	*15%*	*20%*
1	0.98	0.91	0.87	0.83
10	8.98	6.14	5.02	4.19
20	16.35	8.51	6.26	4.87
55	33.17	9.95	6.66	5.0

Numbers in the body of the table are the present values of the cash flow. For example, $1 for twenty years discounted at 10 percent has a present value of $8.51. 8.51 is the multiplicative factor, m, applied to the cash flow to find its present value.

3 Biomass and rates of reproduction

It is instructive to consider two contrasting combinations of rent-maximizing sustainable harvest and biomass.

Example A: The biomass is depleted

In example A the following conditions hold:

Carrying capacity, K = 3.0 (million metric tons or dollars)
Sustainable harvest, H* = 0.2 (million metric tons per annum or dollars)
Multiplicative factor = 10 (commensurate with a 10% discount rate)

From these numbers it is easy to calculate the present value of the sustainable rent-maximizing annual harvest collected by each player:

$$H^*m/2 = (0.2 \times 10)/2 = 2/2 = 1 \text{ (million metric tons or dollars)}$$

With this calculation completed, the payoff matrix in Figure 10.2 can be filled in. There is a dominant strategy in Figure 10.2 for both players, and the outcome is

	Player 2: Conserve	Player 2: Deplete
Player 1: Conserve	1, 1	0, 3
Player 1: Deplete	3, 0	1.5, 1.5

FIGURE 10.2 Example A: The biomass is depleted

for each to deplete the resource – the equilibrium is deplete–deplete. This is easily seen from the point of view of player 1. Thus, whether player 2 "plays" conserve or deplete the payoff to player 1 is always larger when choosing the deplete strategy. Similarly with player 2 as this game is symmetric.

Example B: The biomass is conserved

In Example B we retain the same multiplicative factor but make the sustainable harvest larger (due to as yet unspecified biological factors – see Sections 3 and 4 below) in relation to the biomass:

Carrying capacity, K = 3.0 (million metric tons or dollars)
Sustainable harvest, H* = 0.8 (million metric tons per annum or dollars)
Multiplicative factor = 10

From these numbers it is easy to calculate the present value of the sustainable annual harvest that can be collected by each of the two players:

$$H^*m/2 = (0.8 \times 10)/2 = 8/2 = 4 \text{ (million dollars or million metric tons)}$$

With this calculation we can fill in the payoff matrix in Figure 10.3.

In Figure 10.3 the payoff for each player is highest if they both follow a conservation strategy – a player loses income by following a deplete strategy if the other player conserves (3 earned by depleting is less than 4 earned conserving). Thus, player 1 thinks "player 2 will conserve because it knows that I will conserve because it is in my best interests". As this is true for both players, the outcome is that both want to conserve the biomass.

Example B in Figure 10.3 is a coordination game. There are two Nash equilibriums: deplete/deplete and conserve/conserve. Some form of coordination is needed to move the players from the "bad" equilibrium (deplete/deplete) to the

	Player 2	
	Conserve	Deplete
Conserve Player 1	4 4	3 0
Deplete	0 3	1.5 1.5

FIGURE 10.3 Example B: Conservation is optimal

good equilibrium. A coordinated move to the good equilibrium is achieved as long as each player believes the other player is a rational maximizer of the present value of the biomass.

The difference between Examples A and B is that in Example B the sustainable harvest, H*, is larger in relation to the maximum biomass, K, than in example A. Thus, in both examples, K = 3, but in example A, H* = 0.2, while in example B, H* = 0.8. This implies that the conserve strategy becomes viable as the sustainable harvest increases relative to the biomass, i.e. H*/K increases. As is discussed in the next section, ecological factors determine this ratio. For example, for animals with low rates of reproduction, such as whales and "trophy fish", the ratio is low because they cannot quickly replace themselves. Higher sustainable harvest/biomass ratios are possible with a biomass that can quickly reproduce itself.

4 Sustainable harvest in relation to the biomass

Recall that if fishers take only the growth in the biomass, the harvest is sustainable and the biomass will remain constant at the corresponding level. Figure 8.2 graphed the growth rate of the biomass as a function of the size of the biomass. At first, with a depleted biomass (in relation to the maximum biomass, K) the growth rate is slow, thereafter picking up, reaching a maximum and falling thereafter, eventually reaching zero when the carrying capacity is reached. Figure 10.4 shows the growth in the biomass for two fisheries with different rates of growth of the biomass. In fact, these curves are marked (TR for 'total revenue'), but if it is assumed that the unit price of fish is $1 they also give the growth biomass by weight.

The higher of the two curves shows the growth of the biomass for the species with the faster rate of reproduction, r, say, anchovy. The fact that this curve always lies above the lower curve simply means that anchovy reach the environmental

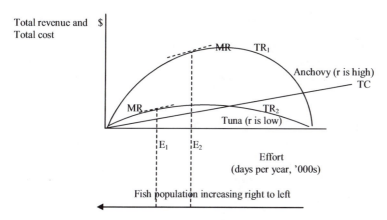

FIGURE 10.4 Optimal catches with different biological growth rates

carrying capacity, K, more quickly than does the species with the lower curve, say, tuna.

Adding a total cost function to Figure 10.4 allows us to find the rent-maximizing level of effort. Rent maximization for tuna occurs at E_1 and for anchovy at E_2, where in both cases marginal revenue = marginal cost; rent is also higher for anchovy than it is for tuna. More important for the present discussion is that the anchovy harvest is larger than is the tuna harvest – as measured by the height of the TR (= total catch) functions above the x-axis. Since we're assuming that each species has the same carrying capacity, K, this means that the ratio of harvest to biomass, H/K, is higher for anchovy than it is for tuna.

What we saw in Example A above was that, with a low sustainable harvest in relation to biomass, the stock is depleted because the prisoners' dilemma problem remains. However, in Example B, with a higher H^*/K ratio, the stock is conserved because the prisoners' dilemma is resolved by turning it into a coordination game – both players can see that they are better off conserving than depleting.

As the following variables are the same between Examples A and B – discount factor (m), environmental carrying capacity (K), unit price of fish, and marginal cost of fishing (the slope of the total cost function is constant) – the different outcomes ("not conserve", "conserve") are due to the different rates of biomass growth, r. It is the latter that allows a higher ratio of sustainable harvest to biomass in the case of anchovy and induces the players to enter into a fisheries agreement. For tuna the ratio of harvest to biomass is too low to interest the players in breaking the prisoners' dilemma.

5 Some ecology

The logistic curve illustrated in Figure 8.1 implies

$$\frac{dN}{dt} = \frac{rN(K-N)}{K} \tag{1}$$

where N is the biomass at any given time, K is the maximum possible biomass, given the carrying capacity of a specific environment, and r is the maximum rate of reproduction or growth of the biomass – which occurs at the inflection point of the logistic curve.

Ecologists refer to "r selected species" and "K selected species". The former tend to live in environments that fluctuate a lot – they are affected by changes in water temperature, say – and after population crashes they recover at high rates of growth largely because they have early maturity, short gestation, wide dispersal and, so, high fecundity. K selected species have low r-values, and live in populations that are at or near the environmental carrying capacity for extended periods of time. They are often competitive because of the lack of resources; they put little energy into reproduction – therefore have few offspring – but put a lot of energy into protecting the offspring they do have, and also tend to reproduce later in life. When perturbed by over-fishing, because of their slow rates of population growth, these species do not recover quickly (see Adam, 1980).

The variable we are interested in here is the ratio of sustainable harvest to biomass. Data on this is sparse, but there is, however, some suggestive evidence. Hutchings (2000) assessed the potential for recovery in over-fished marine fisheries. He examined 90 fish stocks that experienced fifteen-year declines of between 13 percent and 99 percent, followed by five-year changes in biomass after fishing for the target species had either stopped or was much reduced. Of these 90 stocks, 37 continued to decline after the fifteen-year period, 46 showed some recovery, and seven had fully recovered. However, overall, subsequent population size was negatively correlated with magnitude of population decline. He concluded that "there is very little evidence for rapid recovery from prolonged declines" (Hutchings, 2000, p. 882) including those among the commercially important species of cod, haddock and flat fish. And "although the effects of over-fishing on single species may generally be reversible, the actual time required for recovery appears to be considerable" (p. 883). He also found that "clupeids [e.g. herring] are more likely to recover to previously experienced population sizes and are more resilient than other marine fishes. Such an increased rate of recovery may be attributable to the younger age at which clupeids mature relative to gadids [e.g. cods and hake], scorpaenids [e.g. rock fish], scombrids [e.g. tuna, mackerel], sparids [e.g. sea bream] and pleuronectids [e.g. flounder], and the higher intrinsic rate of increase that earlier maturity generally effects" (p. 884).

Similarly, McClanahan et al. (2007) examined recovery time of fishes on some Kenyan coral reefs in the years after fishing there was prohibited. They found that "the two main herbivorous families displayed differing responses to protection, scarids (parrot fishes) recovering rapidly . . . while acanthurids (e.g. surgeon fishes) recovered more slowly". Relatedly, the marine biologists Minns et al. (2011) state that increasing habitat capacity, i.e. K, while increasing optimal stock size, leaves optimal harvest rate, H/K, unaffected for any given species.

6   Rational impatience

It is quite possible that people on very low levels of income, with little or no alternative to eating fish for their protein, are acting rationally when they deplete a biomass. The logic is simple: "better to eat and live today and die later, than to conserve and die now" (a high discount rate implies "living for today"). However, such logic hardly seems justifiable for individuals in high-income countries that do in fact have readily available alternative sources of income and protein.

It is not only income level that influences an individual's rate of discount (their rates of time preference). Becker and Mulligan (1997) argue that education itself affects time preference – more education seems to teach people to be more patient. Lawrence (1991), using a panel of data, does indeed find that time preference is stronger for poorer people. Among high-income, college-educated Americans the rate of time preference is calculated to be 12 percent; but among low-income Americans it is 19 percent. Equating "level of education" with "scientific and cultural understanding", it may be argued that the more that people know about a living marine organism (nice ones, anyway) the more they will treasure it.

Note

1 Mantzouni et al. (2010) give data on habitat size ("carrying capacity of the ecosystem") as defined by the juvenile feeding ground for various cod stocks. For example, at the specific dates they were estimated, it was about 85,000 km^2 on Georges Bank, 48,000 km^2 in the Gulf of Maine, and 235,000 km^2 off the Norwegian coast. However, the carrying capacity of these habitats can change – for example, getting smaller when water temperatures rise above 58°F.

11

INTERNATIONAL NEGOTIATIONS

Successes and failures

1   Introduction

We begin our discussion of the creation of international agreements to manage ocean resources – regime formation, in the vocabulary of political scientists – by considering the case of the *North Pacific Fur Seal Treaty*. This treaty was signed in 1911, after about two decades of on-off self-interest-seeking negotiations between the interested parties – the USA, Russia, Japan and the UK (for Canada) – and then only after fur seal stocks were recognized as having fallen to critically low levels. We will also discuss some cases where regime formation has largely failed, remarkably, even after agreements had been signed. The discussion points to difficulties that arise at either the negotiation or the implementation phases. Attention first turns to the fur seal treaty, the aim being to illustrate the sort of problems that must be resolved for an effective international governance regime to be formed.

2   The *North Pacific Fur Seal Treaty* and international cooperation

Mirovitskaya, Clark and Purver (1993) and Barrett (2003) describe the history of hunting for the North Pacific fur seal and the often futile international negotiations that eventually led to the *Fur Seal Treaty* of 1911 – but only after the fur seal, with rookeries on the Pribilof, Commander, Robben and Kurile islands, had come close to extinction just a few years earlier.

Here we outline the main phases of governance arrangements that are as relevant today as they were then. The main issues to look for are: monopoly as the conservationist's friend; rent-sharing between private companies and the sovereign; international conflict caused by divergent interests; the long, drawn-out and fractious nature of international negotiations; unilateral claims to regulate fur seals on the high seas; and free riders as spoilers.

Discovery of the breeding grounds and uncontrolled harvesting

In the early eighteenth century, Russians began hunting the North Pacific fur seal. In 1741 the Commander Islands – a main breading ground off the Kamchatka peninsula – were discovered. Following this, the herds were progressively, though not totally, exhausted. The Russians knew that there must be more breeding grounds north of the Aleutians, and in 1786 the Pribilof Islands (also known as the Seal Islands) were discovered just north of the Aleutian Island chain and about 400 miles west of Alaska. There followed a "gold rush" to the Pribilofs, with uncontrolled harvesting. Beginning with a herd of five million, it fell rapidly.

Private monopoly created

In 1799 Czar Paul I granted a monopoly to the Russian–American Company. Hunting was limited to "surplus" male seals and only on land; and a rent was paid to the Russian government, actually the family of the Czar, which was a major shareholder (Mirovitskaya, Clark and Purver, 1993). Over the next several decades, 2.5 million seals were taken without endangering the herd's survival.

Early signs of international conflict

With the objective of protecting the profits of the Russian–American Company, in 1821 a Russian decree was issued to keep foreign ships at least 100 miles away from the Pribilofs (Barrett, 2003). Ships caught poaching were subject to confiscation. However, Great Britain and the USA denounced the decree. In other words, it did not get international recognition, and Russian writ was not recognized as extending to the high seas.

USA purchases Alaska

In 1867 the US bought Alaska from the Russians, thereby acquiring the Pribilof Islands. Accordingly, the Russian–American Company's monopoly was eliminated and uncontrolled harvesting of seals immediately began. In the single year, 1868, 250,000 seals were taken. The following year, the USA imposed a temporary ban on sealing.

This was followed in 1870 by the US copying Russia's earlier solution to over-harvesting – the granting of a monopoly on sealing to a private company, the Alaska Commercial Company. Various conditions were imposed on the company – in particular, an annual limit on the harvest of 100,000 seals; only surplus males were to be taken and only on land; no firearms were to be used; natives were to be allowed to hunt; and the US government was to share in the rent through an annual fee payable to the US Treasury and a tax on skins and oil. One year later, the remaining Russian seal islands – Commander and Robben – were contracted by the Russians to the ACC.

During the next twenty years – to about 1890 – the ACC monopoly worked well, as harvesting did not threaten to eliminate the herds; about 135,000 seals per year were harvested.

The problem of pelagic sealing

Seals spend about one-half of the year (winter) in the open sea, and even during the rest of the year they may swim up to 150 miles from land: they could be found in international waters. Pelagic sealing off the Commander Islands in fact began soon after the Alaska purchase, especially by Japanese sealers. But pelagic sealing grew larger as time passed – especially by Canadian sealers. Unfortunately, pelagic sealing is a very inefficient harvesting method as it kills about four seals for every one captured – wounded seals die at sea and pregnant females lose their unborn pups. Moreover, pelagic sealing robbed the US Treasury of revenues.

As a result the USA claimed ownership of fur seals on the high seas, just as the Russians had done in 1821. In August 1886 the US seized three Canadian schooners 75 miles offshore, and a US court confiscated the schooners and imprisoned their captains. Great Britain, representing Canada, complained, with the result that both schooners and captains were released. As the arrests were made on the high seas, under customary international law the USA in fact did not have legal authority to make them. Even so, the following year fifteen more Canadian schooners were detained by the USA. In 1889, with the threat of further arrests on the high seas, Great Britain sent warships to protect the Canadian schooners. The upshot was that Great Britain and the USA agreed to negotiate a treaty banning pelagic sealing. But it was more than twenty years later that North Pacific sealing nations signed the *Fur Seal Treaty*.

Tribunal of Paris

At the 1892 Tribunal of Paris the USA claimed that it had property rights over Pribilof seals, even on the high seas. Great Britain countered that US writ ran only as far as its territorial sea. The Tribunal agreed with Great Britain. However, the Tribunal recommended a ban on harvesting for one year, later extended for two more years; thereafter there was to be no harvesting during May to July in either the Bering Sea or the North Pacific. There was to be no use of nets or explosives. The *Treaty of Paris* came into force in 1894 when the Americans and the British passed the necessary legislation. However, as neither Japan nor Russia did so, both with pelagic sealing fleets, pressure on the already diminished stocks, if anything, increased. In 1867 there had been about two million fur seals, falling to only about 150,000 by 1908 (Barrett, 2003).

Russo–Japanese War

When Japan won the Russo–Japanese war in 1905, it gained control of the previously Russian-owned Robben Island (Stejneger, 1925) and the game of international regime formation governing conservation of the North Pacific fur seal changed once again. Now, Japan had a herd of its own (the one it had had on the Kurile Islands had been hunted to extinction), and it too came to see the sense of an international treaty.

Multilateral success

Negotiations began in 1910, and led to the *North Pacific Fur Seal Treaty*, signed in 1911, banning pelagic sealing in the Bering, Okhotsk and Kamchatka seas. By 1917 the Pribilof herd had increased threefold. By 1940 there were again two million seals in the north Pacific – just like the old days. The 1911 *Treaty* ran to 1940, when Japan withdrew; but this was not of much significance as not much sealing was done during the Second World War or thereafter.[1]

In 1956 the 1911 *Treaty* was revived, but in 1987 the US failed to ratify an extension of it. However, by then commercial interest in sealing had passed. Even so, the Pribilof Islands herds have declined to about one million today – only one-half of their level in 1950. Why this is so is unclear, but it could be due to lack of food caused by over-fishing, which is an optimal yield issue – see Chapter 8. Thus, severe over-fishing for pollock in the Bering Sea has been implicated in the sharp fall in the number of Steller sea lions, fur seals and kittiwakes.[2]

3 Some lessons learned from the *Fur Seal Treaty* (1911)

As Mirovitskaya, Clark and Purver (1993) point out, that there was no hegemon (a preponderant actor) that could impose its will on a workable treaty to manage the fur seal. Rather, the four powers involved – the USA, Russia, the UK (for Canada) and Japan – were quite equally matched in diplomatic leverage.

Given this constraint, Mirovitskaya, Clark and Purver (1993) and Barrett (2003) point out that for a treaty to succeed it must restructure the relationship between countries. For this to happen it must achieve seven things.

First, it must create an aggregate gain so that all countries potentially gain by abiding by the treaty. In the terminology of Young (1989), there was no "veil of uncertainty" – all participants could see quite clearly how they could gain (or lose) from a treaty.[3] Proper management of fur seal stocks, especially ending pelagic sealing, would achieve this. The fact that fur seal stocks were near collapse just prior to agreement on the treaty in 1911 may have helped in reaching agreement because, according to Mirovitskaya, Clark and Purver (1993), there was a switch from "distributive bargaining" (concerning who gets how much) to "integrative bargaining" (how to increase the joint gains). We will see this again in Chapter 12 with two treaties on pollock fisheries, respectively, in the Bering and Okhotsk seas – a crisis focuses minds.

Second, all countries exploiting the resource need to be included in the treaty, otherwise the treaty is likely to be ineffective. Thus, the Paris arbitration between the UK (for Canada) and the USA was ineffective in curbing pelagic sealing because Japan, with its large pelagic fleet, was not also a signatory.

Third, an absence of linkage to other issues helps. According to Mirovitskaya, Clark and Purver (1993), when the Canadians linked the fur seal question to an Alaska–Canada boundary issue, progress on a fur seal treaty was slow. After agreement on that issue was accepted, the Canadians had no scope to use it as leverage in the fur seal context.

Fourth, there must be equity as well as efficiency; the aggregate gains must be distributed between the players such that abiding by the treaty makes all players better off. Allocation of side payments to the pelagic sealers – Canada and Japan – ensured this was the case with the *Fur Seal Treaty*; Articles 10 to 13 deal with this issue and, in fact, take up most space in the five-page treaty.

Fifth, compliance mechanisms must be in place to ensure that signatories abide by the rules of the treaty – that they do not cheat. For this, the *Fur Seal Treaty* signatories agreed to police the ocean and to impose penalties on sealers not in conformity with the *Treaty* (Article 7).

Sixth, entry by new players must be deterred. This was achieved by the four signatories banning imports of non-authenticated seal skins. As it happened, most seal skins were processed – dressed, dyed and marketed – in London because that was where the best dying processors were located. Thus, a seal skin could be authenticated as having been caught under the terms of the treaty if it had indeed passed through London. All that was necessary was for London to keep track of the source of uncured skins.

Finally, the treaty-makers must ensure that a player loses when dropping out of the treaty. This matter was not addressed in the 1911 *Treaty*, though conditions were stated for giving notice of intention of non-renewal beyond the initial fifteen-year period covered by the *Treaty*. It seems that either the signatories had not thought about this matter, or they had a high degree of trust between themselves. However, more generally, how might signatories ensure that abrogating a treaty would likely incur losses? One way is the "grim strategy": if one player drops out then they all do. Output would then fall from the cooperative solution back to the Nash, low-output equilibrium. According to Barrett (2003) this strategy was included in later versions of the fur seal treaty.

	Don't comply with treaty	Comply with treaty
Don't comply with treaty	0 0	10 0
Comply with treaty	0 10	1 1

FIGURE 11.1 Illustration of the grim strategy

More generally the *Vienna Convention on the Law of Treaties* provides a legal basis for the grim strategy. Thus, Article 60 on the termination or suspension of the operation of a treaty as a consequence of its breach in its paragraph 2(c) states that "A material breach of a multilateral treaty by one of the parties entitles: . . . any party other than the defaulting State to invoke the breach as a ground for suspending the operation of the treaty in whole or in part with respect to itself if the treaty is of such a character that a material breach of its provisions by one party radically changes the position of every party with respect to the further performance of its obligations under the treaty."

Thus, any signatory thinking of breaching a treaty has to take into account the possible reaction of the other signatories to a material breach of the terms of a treaty.

Here is how the grim strategy works. Figure 11.1 shows a prisoners' dilemma with the Nash equilibrium being 0, 0 and the Pareto optimum being 1, 1.

As the treaty game is played as a repeated game, a player has to compare the payoffs over time. Complying with the treaty gives a payoff of 1 each period into the distant future. But cheating on the treaty gives a one-time payoff of 10 followed by zero thereafter when the other player carries through with the grim strategy of also not complying with the treaty. Thus, the choice for a player is between 1, 1, 1, 1 . . . and 10, 0, 0, 0 . . .

If a player's discount rate is 15 percent, the present value of 1 forever is 6.7. This is less than the 10 available if a player immediately doesn't comply with the treaty. The treaty fails. But if the discount rate is 9 percent, the present value of 1 forever is 11. A player would be better off complying with the treaty. The grim strategy therefore works if the discount rate is low enough – the signatories are not too impatient. That is, the "don't comply" payoff is lower than the "comply payoff".

Folk theorem

The foregoing discussion of discount rates illustrates the "folk theorem": namely, that a Pareto optimal – best – solution is possible in a repeated game if the players are patient enough. In our example, "patience" is the 9 percent discount rate. "Impatience" is the 15 percent discount rate, because it discounts future benefits to a greater degree. As we have just seen, if the players are patient the Pareto superior outcome is the equilibrium outcome. However, if they are impatient, the game collapses to the Nash equilibrium of non-compliance by all players.

Number of players

The grim strategy has a better chance of "working", discouraging "don't comply" if the number of players is small. If the number of players is large, the grim strategy poses a less credible threat to a potential cheater and is, therefore, less likely to discourage cheating.

To illustrate, suppose there are 100 signatories to an agreement. Each gets $1 from complying with the agreement and $0 if nobody complies. However, a cheater gets $10 if it cheats, reducing the payoffs to each of the other 99 signatories to $0.91 (i.e. ($100 − $10)/99). But $0.91 is better than $0, and a potential cheater knows this – so the threat of the other 99 players withdrawing from a treaty is non-credible. But if potential signatories know that they do not have a credible threat to discipline cheaters the treaty is unlikely to be signed in the first place.

The *Fur Seal Treaty* is a treaty that worked, with all parties committed to making it work. In the next section we will discuss some modern cases where countries sign treaties, though do not necessarily commit to rules making them work. This is a strange phenomenon that we will discuss in more detail in Chapter 14.

4 Some examples of the causes of weak international agreements

International ocean resource management agreements have often been rendered weak and ineffective at either the negotiation or operation stages. Some examples of each will illustrate.

Negotiation stage

When it has a mind to, even a signatory nation can render a fishing agreement ineffective (Swanson, 1991). It has the scope to do this under international public law – both customary and treaty (the latter as codified under the *Vienna Convention on Treaties* – see Chapter 1). Techniques to do this used at the negotiation stage include:

1 Massaging scientific results on sustainable yields, claiming that they are larger than otherwise would be safe. A case in point occurred with Norwegian cod in 1975, when the USSR claimed that the sustainable catch was much larger than what other members of the North East Atlantic Fisheries Commission (NEAFC) thought it to be.

2 Making inflexible claims for overly large quota-shares – often on the basis of "historical rights" and "industry problems". In several cases the NEAFC dealt with this by allowing quota shares to sum to more than 100 percent.

3 Rendering monitoring ineffective or not including a monitoring system in an agreement. For example, safety standards at sea adopted in UNCLOS 1982 but ignored by flag of convenience states.

4   Adoption of ineffective sanctions against offenders, should they be caught.
    An example is low fines for oil spills under the *International Convention for
    the Prevention of Pollution of the Sea by Oil* (OilPol), 1954 – see Chapter 20.
    Sumaila, Alder and Keith (2006) list many cases of high seas fisheries where
    expected fines are low in relation to expected revenues, including fishing for
    the Patagonian tooth fish, Greenland halibut, cod, haddock and Alaska pollock.
    From tonnages of fish recorded on fishing boats arrested for illegal, unreported
    and unregulated fishing (IUU), as well as fish prices, actual fines paid and an
    assumption about the probability of arrest, they calculate that expected fines are
    insufficient (i.e. are less than revenues) to deter illegal activity. They also argue
    that the problem of IUU fishing is likely to get worse if and when more high
    seas fisheries agreements are concluded that further restrict legal fishing with
    measures such as quotas and closed seasons.

Operation stage

There are also four broad problems that can render an international agreement ineffective, or less effective than it could be, even *after* it has come into force:

1   Signatories take "reservations", meaning that they choose not to agree to a
    given article of a treaty, which is allowed under international law. For example,
    a reservation may be taken on a fishing quota limitation, so a country does not
    then have to reduce its catch. For example, in the NEAFC in 1974, two signa-
    tories opted out of quotas, with the result that herring stocks collapsed.
2   Signatories do not implement the agreement. An example of this is safety at sea
    under International Maritime Organization rules: flags of convenience (FOC)
    states often do not enforce regulations. For example, Alderton and Winchester
    (2002) report that in the 1990s, while FOC accounted for only 47 percent of
    vessel tonnage, they also accounted for 66 percent of tonnage lost at sea; they
    did find, however, that some FOC states now more diligently enforce IMO
    safety rules.
3   Deliberate ambiguity in an agreement's wording, rendering it dubious. An
    example of this could be said to be Japan and the International Whaling Com-
    mission. While it is true that Japan has ceased "commercial" whaling – see
    Chapter 15 – it still takes whales for "scientific purposes", which is allowed.
    The effect, however, is that this fudge allows Japan to continue whaling, when
    most other members of the IWC have stopped.
4   The free rider problem occurs when some countries do not join an agreement
    that would otherwise affect their hunting efforts. Pintassilgo (2003) identifies
    it as a critical problem preventing efficient high seas fisheries management.
    An example, as we have seen, is the various attempts over several decades to
    regulate fur sealing prior to the signing of the comprehensive treaty in 1911.
    Similarly, the International Pacific Halibut Commission formed by the USA

and Canada in the 1920s enabled stocks in the northeast Pacific to recover until the 1960s, when non-signatory distant water fishing nations entered (Clark and Hare, 2006, p. 8).

5   Conclusions

This chapter has demonstrated that reaching an effective international agreement to manage ocean resources through international negotiation is difficult to achieve. Without a global, or shared, social norm to the effect that the commercially valuable living resources in the oceans should be managed to the benefit of the global community, both living and yet to be born, there are many ways that countries can prevent effective management. Many of these were discussed in this chapter, but three deserve repeating. One method is to simply not turn up, choosing to be a free rider. Another is to write rules into international agreements that render them largely ineffective – such as insisting on absurdly inflated "scientific" estimates of sustainable yields. Or, a country may simply take a "reservation" – meaning it chooses not to abide by what otherwise might have been an effective rule governing management of an ocean resource. This chapter has also described how tortuous it can be to arrive at an effective international agreement – the 1911 *Fur Seal Treaty* being a case in point.

Notes

1   For example, in 1968 about 13,000 seals were harvested on the Pribilof Islands (Table 3, Roppel, A.Y. (1984) "Management of Northern Fur Seals on the Pribilof Islands, Alaska, 1786–1981", US Department of Commerce).
2   See "North Pacific Overfishing (Donut)", available online at www1.american.edu/ted/donut.htm.
3   See Chapter 12 for a discussion of treaty formation and the veil of uncertainty.

12

PREPONDERANT ACTORS AND THE BARGAINING GAME

1   Introduction

One way to develop rules for the management and efficient exploitation of high seas resources is for a preponderant actor – a hegemon – to impose them on the other actors. Both the US and Russia at different times tried to nationalize the fur seal in the north Pacific high seas with the aim of efficiently managing the stock (see Chapter 11). They didn't succeed. However, as discussed in Section 2, the Russian Federation in the early 1990s *de facto* nationalized the pollock stock in the high seas area of the Sea of Okhotsk known as the "peanut hole", giving itself powers over the setting of total allowable catch and access by distant water fishing nations. Section 3 looks at the role afforded to the USA under the *Convention* to manage pollock stocks in the Bering Sea "doughnut hole" – also an area of high seas – which, while not amounting to *de facto* nationalization did give the USA extra bargaining leverage compared with that of the other signatories.

In Section 4 a bargaining game is presented that shows that "fair shares" in economic rents can be achieved even if there is a preponderant actor that has more power over outcomes than do other fishing nations. The final two sections of this chapter discuss some further complications involved in the "games" that countries can and do play to reach international environmental agreements.

2   The Sea of Okhotsk "peanut hole"

The strongest claim by a coastal state unilaterally to manage a high seas fishery is that made in the early 1990s by the Russian Federation in the case of the Sea of Okhotsk "peanut hole" – an area that is completely surrounded by the Russian EEZ between Kamchatka and Sakhalin Island. Distant water fishing fleets entered the fishery in 1991 following the collapse of the Bering Sea pollock fishery. The biomass in the Sea of Okhostsk was also to collapse, though, as it turned out, not to the same extent. In April 1993 the Supreme Soviet of the Russian Federation resolved to take sole responsibility for conserving the "peanut hole" pollock stock. Its legal argument for sole control of the fishery was that UNCLOS did not apply to high seas completely surrounded by a single coastal state's EEZ (Elferink, 2001). However, the distant water fishing nations – China, Japan, Korea and Poland – objected, arguing correctly that it had no basis in international law. Russia then took three further measures: warning that it would engage in prolonged naval maneuvers in the area, banning distant water fleets that fished in the peanut hole from having fishing quotas in its EEZ, and also banning these fleets from docking at its ports. All of these measures were revoked in 1995 following agreement by all parties temporarily to cease fishing in the peanut hole.

Under the *Sea of Okhotsk Agreement*, according to Elferink (2001), the Russian Federation has powers that go beyond the *Fish Stocks Agreement* of 1995 that deals with the management of straddling stocks, as in the peanut hole. Thus, while the *Agreement* says that distant water fishing nations shall *take into consideration* the rights, duties and interests of coastal states (Article 16 (1)), the *Sea of Okhotsk Agreement* drops the phrase "take into consideration", so "any fishing for straddling stocks in the central Sea of Okhotsk is subject to the rights, duties and interests of the Russian Federation" (Article 1). This implies that that the Russian Federation has the last say.[1] Elferink draws the conclusion that the *Sea of Okhotsk Agreement* indeed amounts to a *de facto* extension of the coastal state's powers over fisheries management. As Vicuna (1999) observed, in 1993 "Russia took on the responsibility for the conservation of the living resources in the high seas area concerned, established a temporary moratorium for Russian and foreign fishing vessels until international agreements could be reached" (p. 94).

3   The Bering Sea "doughnut hole"

The Bering Sea "doughnut hole" is similar to the Sea of Okhotsk "peanut hole" in that it is completely surrounded by EEZ waters, but, in this case, those of two countries, the USA and the Russian Federation (the Soviet Union before 1991). In 1983 the pollock catch in the doughnut hole was about 100,000 tons, rising to 1.4 million tons in 1989, and thereafter collapsing – with only 300,000 tons taken in 1991 and zero tons in 1992.

As early as mid-1988, the Reagan–Gorbachev summit declared an "over-fishing problem"; two years later Bush–Gorbachev called for urgent conservation measures to be negotiated by the coastal states and the distant water fishing nations – China, Korea, Japan and Poland. In the meantime an Alaskan US Congressman called for the USA and the Soviet Union to work together to extend coastal state fishing jurisdiction to the doughnut hole so as to exclude distant water fishing fleets. Also, the Soviet Union urged the USA to consider managing the doughnut hole bilaterally, without the distant water fishing nations necessarily agreeing to the measures taken (Balton, 2001). In March 1988 the US Senate passed a resolution calling for a moratorium on fishing in the doughnut hole, though it did not call for an extension of coastal state jurisdiction – largely because it did not want to set a precedent that could be to the disadvantage of its own fishing fleets. It was, however, the precursor of ten rounds of diplomatic conferences held between the two coastal states and the four distant water fishing nations (Balton, 2001).

Vicuna (1999) points to the immediacy of the threat to "doughnut hole" marine resources and the last-resort action taken by the USA: "In the 'doughnut hole' case a voluntary moratorium came to be accepted by distant water fleets at a very late point in time and only after a threatened unilateral action by the United States in the high seas had been explicitly made in terms of a proposed functional extension of fisheries jurisdiction beyond 200 miles" (pp. 91–92).

This threat eventually led to the signing of the *Convention on the Conservation and Management of Pollock Resources in the Central Bering Sea* in 1994 by Japan, China, Korea, Poland, Russia and the US.[2] The main management measures are:

1   The setting of an "allowable harvest level" (i.e. a total allowable catch) and allocation of national quotas at annual conferences between the parties.
2   Should one of the annual conferences not reach agreement on TAC, determination would be by Russia and the US.
3   Failing agreement between the latter pair of countries, determination of TAC would be by the USA alone.
4   Fishing boats of each country have to be authorized by the respective home governments.
5   All fishing boats are required to use position-fixing transmitters.
6   Any signatory government can board and inspect any fishing boat in the area.
7   The flag state of an offending fishing vessel enforces penalties.

It appears that the initial threat by the USA effectively to enclose the doughnut hole at least in part led to the drawing up of the international agreement. However, contrary to the Russian Federation's position in the Sea of Okhotsk peanut hole, the US has not gained *de facto* control over the doughnut hole, though it retains influence over the size of the TAC. Whether this control could be leveraged to affect quota allocations remains to be seen, though conceivably it could; for example, the US might refuse to increase the TAC unless quotas were reallocated in some specified way.

4 The bargaining game

We can analyze the economics of a coastal state distant water fishing nation dispute where the coastal state claims a right to extend its fisheries jurisdiction to the high seas. This is more applicable to the Sea of Okhotsk peanut hole than the Bering Sea doughnut hole because, in the former case, the opinion has been stated that the coastal state did *de facto* extend its jurisdiction to the high seas, while in the latter case this did not happen. Even so, the complaints of the coastal states about over-fishing in the doughnut hole did lead to ten rounds of diplomatic negotiations between the countries concerned. As we shall shortly see, somewhat surprisingly, even if a coastal state does threaten to exclude distant water fishing nations from an area of high seas, the parties concerned can, through a series of negotiations, reach an agreement to share a fish stock.

To see how the bargaining game works, consider the following simplified model. The coastal state, country A, announces that unless an international agreement is reached after ten rounds of negotiations it will nationalize the high seas fishery. That is, it will manage the resource its own way and reserve the economic rent created for its own citizens. Assuming that this threat is credible justifies describing country A as a "preponderant actor". The other interested party, country B, a distant water fishing nation, has to respond to this threat.

Bargaining is over the shares of economic rent allocated to countries A and B under an international agreement. The response depends on the "rules of the game", which are as follows:

1 For diplomatic reasons country A allows ten rounds of negotiation over the allocation of economic rent.
2 Country A gets to choose its share last, on round 10.
3 Beginning in round 1, round by round the countries take it in turns to make offers to each other.
4 There are no bargaining costs.
5 Country A, the coastal state whose straddling stocks are in danger of being fished-out, wants an agreement to manage the stocks on the high seas more urgently than does the distant water fishing nation, country B. To reflect its greater sense of urgency, country A's discount factor, α, is 0.8, while country B's discount factor, β, is 0.87.[3]
6 The economic rent derivable from efficient management of the high seas resource is \$1. You can add as many zeros as you like to this.

At stake are shares in the maximum economic rent of \$1. The payoffs in each round of negotiation are shown in Table 12.1.

The game has to be solved backwards in order to see how shares are ultimately determined. Thus begin by considering round 10, the last round.

TABLE 12.1 Payoffs in the preponderant actor game

Round	Country choosing	Country A's share α = 0.8	Country B's share β = 0.87
10	A	1.0	0.00
9	B	0.8	0.20
8	A	0.83	0.17
7	B	0.66	0.34
6	A	0.705	0.295
5	B	0.56	0.44
4	A	0.62	0.38
3	B	0.50	0.50
2	A	0.56	0.44
1	B	0.45	0.55

In round 10 country A awards itself $1 and zero to country B.

In round 9, B realizes that A would accept 0.8 of $1 this round because $0.80 this round is equivalent to $1 next round – given A's discount factor of 0.8. B makes this offer, gaining a share of $0.20 for itself. Country A accepts this offer.

In round 8 it is A's turn to make an offer. Country A realizes that B will accept 0.87 of $0.20 – or $0.17 – this round instead of waiting until the next round (round 9) to obtain $0.20. So A makes this offer to B, retaining $0.83 for itself. B accepts this offer.

In round 7 it is B's turn to make an offer, and B realizes that A will accept 0.8 of $0.83 = $0.66. B makes this offer, retaining $0.34 for itself.

In round 6 it is A's turn to make an offer. A realizes that B will accept 0.87 of $0.34. Thus, A gets $0.705 and B $0.295.

In round 5, B offers A 0.8 of $0.705 = $0.56, retaining $0.44 for itself.

In the first round B realizes that A will accept 0.87 of $0.56 = $0.45. Country B makes this offer, retaining $0.55 for itself.

Thus, in this bargaining game A ends up with a 45-percent share of the economic rent in the high seas portion of the straddling stock's range, with B garnering the remaining 55 percent.

It is worth asking why the preponderant actor's share – country A – falls, getting lower the further away are negotiations from the final round. This is because the present value of $1 falls as the bargaining period is extended, i.e. the longer A has to wait for its payoff. Also, why does country B – the distant water fishing nation – accept only $0.55 in round 1? This is because this is the best it can do given the structure of the game – which is determined by the values of the discount factors, α and β, the number of rounds of negotiation, and the fact that the preponderant actor, country A, chooses last.

An odd thing is that in this game there would be no need actually to go through 10 rounds of negotiation to reach a definitive agreement. Assuming that the players are far-sighted, at the first negotiation each player can see how the bargaining will work out round by round. To avoid wasting time – perhaps the negotiators would rather be out on the golf course than holed up in some lousy five-star hotel, as international diplomats tend to be – they will immediately agree the 45–55 split.

Probably the negotiators will not be so perfectly far-sighted and some rounds of negotiation will be needed while they feel each other out: working out approximately what each other's discount factors are, and how determined the preponderant actor is to impose its will in round 10. That international agreements on the Sea of Okhotsk "peanut hole" and Bering Sea "doughnut hole" were negotiated quickly (compared with, say, the long, drawn-out negotiations leading to the *Fur Seal Treaty* in 1911), though not instantaneously, tends to bear out the idea that the negotiators needed some time to feel each other out.

5 Young's institutional bargaining: Not hegemonic leadership, not utilitarian game theory

The approach of analyzing regime formation through a hegemon, or preponderant actor – as in the bargaining game – Young dubs "the political scientists' method of analysis". According to Young, political scientists look to the distribution of power as key to understanding the origination of collective international agreements: the most powerful country in a negotiation being the most likely to get its way, or something close. Moreover, in this view a hegemon is needed to force negotiations along, which is what Russia, and, perhaps, the USA, did in the two cases just discussed.

Young, however, rejects the view that a preponderant actor is needed for regime formation. He gives several examples of regime formation without a preponderant actor. The list includes: i) the *Fur Seal Treaty* (1911); ii) the 16 countries, including two superpowers, that negotiated the Antarctic regime governing marine wildlife and minerals; iii) Mediterranean Sea pollution control – no superpower was involved, and it had virtual enemies agreeing to it (Arabs/Israel); iv) some regimes that were formed through intergovernmental organizations, and even non-governmental organizations (for example, the regime governing trade in endangered species – the *Convention on International Trade in Endangered Species* – which was motivated by the International Union of Nature and Natural Resources. Besides these, the power of a preponderant actor can be balanced by coalitions of opposing states, which raises the opportunity cost of exercising power. The bargaining game would be nullified if the other players refused to join in.

Young contrasts the political scientists' approach with the economists', which he calls the "utilitarian approach". The prisoners' dilemma game is a case in point. As we know, important elements in game theory are the existence of known alternative strategies, self-interest and the search for equilibrium outcomes.

Young criticizes the economists' game theory approach to analyzing international regime formation for resource conservation. He points out that utilitarian models assume a defined number of players who have full information on what they are trying to achieve and are perfectly clear as to what the payoffs are. Young argues that in real international negotiations things are much murkier. Thus,

1   Gains may be forgone due to disagreement on how to share them. That is, a move to Pareto optimality may not occur because of disagreement on how to share the gains. The deep sea mining treaty is a case in point: this treaty was held up for about two decades because third-world and developed countries could not agree on how to share the gains (see Chapter 23).
2   The existence of intra-state bargaining problems may mean that the strategy of any given player changes while the game is in motion. For example, the US has vacillated between supporting and not supporting measures aimed at reducing carbon emission to reduce the threat of global warming. Thus, it supported such measures when American environmentalists had influence over the Clinton administration, only later not supporting them when oil and coal interests gained influence during the Bush administration.
3   Linkage issues to other areas may complicate a game in any given area. For example, the British linked signing the *Fur Seal Treaty* to settlement of the Alaska–Canada border. Third-world countries used the *common heritage of mankind* concept to try to shape the outcome of the UNCLOS, but this was rejected by the "North" because it was viewed there as a step on the way to a New International Economic Order – something that they had resolved to block (see Chapter 23).
4   Progress to regime formation may be blocked by problems of policing and verification – for example, attempts to reduce oil pollution at sea during the first several decades of the twentieth century (see Chapter 20).

6   Institutional bargaining and the veil of uncertainty

It is Young's view that international resource-conservation regime-formation is, for want of a better word, more "touchy feely" than is suggested by the hard calculations of the analytical models of either political scientists or economists. Thus, "Leadership in connection with the formation of international regimes is a matter of entrepreneurship. It involves a combination of imagination in inventing, institutional options and skill in brokering the interests of various actors" (Young, 1989, p. 355). Note the emphasis on "entrepreneurship" and what entrepreneurs have to do to manage uncertainty.[4]

Young argues that international negotiations aimed at regime formation should be seen as a process in which "entrepreneurs" strive to create efficient outcomes. Distributional bargaining – how to share out the gains – is not so important, or turns out not to have been in negotiations that do reach successful conclusions. Negotiators try to find institutional solutions that can be passed unanimously and, if necessary, possible spoilers may be excluded – as in the case of the resistance of the sixteen members of the "Antarctic club" to shift negotiations to the UN. Why distributional issues are not necessarily important is that negotiators often don't know how the agreement, once reached, will in practice work out for themselves.

There is a *veil of uncertainty*.[5] This veil of uncertainty actually improves the chances of reaching agreement because countries can concentrate on developing rules that seem to be fair, as opposed to promoting this or that country's self interests. Thus, "The parties endeavoring to form international regimes seldom, if ever, make a sustained effort to perfect their information regarding the full range of outcomes and the dimensions of contract zones before getting down to serious bargaining. Instead, they typically zero in a on a few key problems, articulate several approaches to the treatment of these problems and seek to reconcile differences among these approaches in the course of their negotiations" (Young, 1989, pp. 262–63).

In these circumstances, negotiators tend to concentrate on a few key problems. Young cites the *Antarctic Treaty* as an example of institutional bargaining: rather than individual national issues, what was mainly debated was whether to take an ecosystem approach (pressed by the USA), or a species by species approach, as advocated by some other countries. Interestingly, intra-state splits may occur (e.g. business versus environmentalists) that, in the context of institutional bargaining, can allow cross-country alliances (e.g. of scientists) to push negotiations along. The Mediterranean Sea pollution control treaty is said to have benefited from this process, similarly the treaty governing international trade in endangered species.

What is most interesting in Young's analysis of international regime formation is his emphasis on it being an entrepreneurial process operating in a milieu of less-than-complete information. This is certainly an advance on the ideas of simple game theory. However, he "tests" his theory of institutional bargaining, citing only cases of successfully concluded agreements (a biased sample, as it were). Such agreements may well have benefited from a veil of uncertainty clouding the calculations of self-interested bargainers.

But what of international environmental agreements that never came to fruition? Was self-interest a factor? For example, it is certainly no accident that the USA withdrew from the Kyoto Protocol, as it would have carried a great burden in reducing greenhouse gas emissions to targeted levels. Moreover, it can be questioned whether there really is much of a difference between political scientists' and economists' approaches to regime formation. After all, the bargaining game model of hegemonic leadership discussed earlier – in which an international regime resource-sharing agreement was reached – used the economists' chosen tool of game theory.

Notes

1 Article 16 (1) of the *Fish Stocks Agreement* reads, "Measures taken in respect of the high seas *shall take into account* the rights, duties and interests of the coastal State under the Convention" (italics added). Article 1 of the *Sea of Okhotsk Agreement* reads, "The parties recognize that the conservation of the stocks and management of fishing in the central Sea of Okhotsk must be based upon the best scientific evidence available and on the application of the precautionary approach, and that any fishing for straddling stocks in the central Sea of Okhotsk is subject to the rights, duties and interests of the Russian Federation."

2 The main objectives of the convention are: (1) To establish an international regime for conservation, management, and optimum utilization of pollock resources in the Convention Area; (2) to restore and maintain the pollock resources in the Bering Sea at levels which will permit their maximum sustainable yield; (3) to cooperate in the gathering and examining of factual information concerning pollock and other living marine resources in the Bering Sea; and (4) to provide, if the Parties agree, a forum in which to consider the establishment of necessary conservation and management measures for living marine resources other than pollock in the Convention Area, as may be required in the future (Article II). For full text of the agreement see www.jus.uio.no/english/services/library/treaties/06/6–05/pollock-resources-bering.xml.

3 In the Bering Sea case, as a matter of historical record, the bargaining rounds were more frequent than once per year; these are rather low discount factors, implying high discount rates and rates of high time preference. These numbers can be justified given the urgency of the need to reach agreement as fish stocks were under severe pressure in the peanut hole and, especially so, in the doughnut hole.

4 Even within the field of economics there is a minority view that an economic system should be analyzed as a *process* driven by decision makers, rather than as a system either in equilibrium, or automatically tending toward some inevitable equilibrium. Thus, in the well-known theory of the firm, revenue and cost determine price and quantity, with the entrepreneur playing a minor, if any, role in the operation of the firm. Models such as these are surely over-simplified. Any entrepreneur will tell you that what they do is manage change in an environment of much less than complete information on the universe they inhabit, and even without a very clear idea of what they are trying to achieve from one decision to the next.

5 The veil of uncertainty is not unlike Rawls's "veil of ignorance", which Rawls used in the context of answering the question "what is equitable?"

13

MANAGING HIGH SEAS FISHERIES

1   Introduction

In this chapter we discuss the transformation of high seas fisheries from open access (*res communis*) to managed access "in the common interest of the international community" – concepts discussed in Chapter 1. Today, straddling stocks – fish that move between EEZs and the high seas – and high seas fisheries (especially tuna) come under the management of regional fisheries management organizations (RFMOs) that have powers defined in the UN Fish Stocks *Agreement* (1995). It is widely believed, however, that RFMOs have failed to conserve fish stocks that amount to about one-third of all marine species.[1] The chapter is mainly descriptive in that we look at the international legal framework governing RFMO and the members' obligations. The next chapter asks why things are the way they are and is the more analytical of these two chapters on international fisheries management.

2 The *Convention* and the *Agreement*

In Chapter 1 it was pointed out that international public law is formed as either customary law or as treaty law, and that in either case countries have considerable latitude as to what they will agree to and how they will behave. The two main treaties governing high seas fisheries are the 1982 United Nations *Convention on the Law of the Sea* and the 1995 *Agreement on Straddling Fish Stocks and Highly Migratory Fish Stocks*. The *Convention* came into force in November 1994 and by 2013 had 165 ratifications (the USA has neither signed nor ratified it). The *Agreement* came into force in December 2001 and has 80 ratifications (including by the USA).[2] There is no linkage between the *Convention* and the *Agreement* as a country can ratify one without being bound by the other.

As they feature prominently in this and the next chapter it is worth noting that about 90 percent of high seas fishing is done by just six countries: Japan, Spain, Poland, South Korea, Russian Federation and Taiwan. All but the latter have ratified both the *Convention* and the *Agreement*; Taiwan hasn't because it is not a member of the UN.

3 Some relevant articles of the 1982 *Convention*

Section II of the *Convention* sets out the rights and obligations of states with respect to high seas fisheries. States are required to "cooperate", but the word "cooperate" is not given a binding legal definition (see Chapter 1).[3] The *Convention* also did not define the decision-making authority of the regional fish management organizations (RFMOs), the very bodies in which coastal states and distant water fishing nations are supposed to cooperate.

Several Articles pursue a *"common interest of the international community"* doctrine (as defined in Chapter 1), under which high seas fishing rights are qualified.[4] Thus, Articles 61 to 66 deal with straddling stocks and highly migratory species. In particular, coastal states should responsibly manage fisheries within their EEZs ("shall ensure through proper conservation and management measures"), and they are required to cooperate with the relevant RFMOs to this end; likewise, distant water fishing nations are to cooperate with coastal states. Article 66 deals with anadromous stocks such as salmon. Fishing for these stocks is only allowed in the EEZ and not on the high seas, *except* where this would result in economic dislocation for a state that had previously been fishing for such a stock on the high seas. Enforcement of regulations beyond the EEZ is to be by agreement through the regional organization.

Article 116 says that all states have a right to fish on the high seas but should take account of their treaty obligations and rights of the coastal states. Article 117 says that all states have a duty to cooperate with other states in conservation of the living resources of the high seas, and Article 118 says that such cooperation will be through regional fishing organizations. Article 119 details how states shall cooperate – they should use best scientific advice including that on both restoration of stocks and ecosystem interaction between fish species; total allowable catches should be set and enforced. However, while maximum sustainable yield is an objective, the *Convention* says that this *may be set aside* if it would, somehow, be harmful to the special requirements of a state – such as interfering with its established fishing patterns. Finally, Article 87 makes freedom of high seas fishing subject to the interests of other states, as defined in Articles 63 to 67. How these Articles are to work in practice, however, is not spelt out in the *Convention*. For instance, in an RFMO whose interests are to prevail – coastal states or distant water fishing nations? Or, how can an RFMO exert authority when its members can choose *not* to follow specific rules by stating objections?[5] What also of non-signatories to the *Convention*?

Details of how to cooperate are contained in the 1995 *Agreement*.

4   The 1995 *Agreement*

The 1995 *Agreement* on high seas straddling and highly migratory fish stocks is aimed at giving teeth to the 1982 *Convention*. Whether it did so is quite another matter. Part II of the *Agreement* sets out general principles: signatories should aim for "long-term sustainability" at maximum sustainable yield, using a "precautionary approach" together with an "ecosystem approach" so as "to protect biodiversity". Each of these is to be based on the best scientific evidence, taking account of the interdependence of fish stocks and using data collected by fishers in a timely manner. Also, by-catches (discards) should be minimized through using selective fishing gear, and excess fishing capacity should be eliminated. Fine words indeed.

The "precautionary approach" is an important concept because lags in data collection and scientific analysis can mean that the characteristics of a fish stock at a given point in time are not clearly known, hence it is better to be on the safe side when determining catch size. Juda (1997), however, says that the precautionary approach is not sufficiently well defined – for example, how much precaution should there be and who will bear the cost of reduced catches? Ecosystem management is also an important concept because it is meant to take into consideration the effect of fishing on non-targeted dependent stocks and to protect biodiversity.

Article 5h of the *Agreement* requires signatories to eliminate over-fishing; while Article 5k requires signatories to "develop appropriate technologies in support of fishery conservation and management; and implement and enforce conservation and management measures through effective monitoring, control and surveillance". The latter would seem to empower RFMO to monitor and enforce effective management systems.

However, Article 5b creates a giant loophole in the objective of responsible high seas fisheries management aimed at conservation, as other goals are also specified – in particular, "economic factors" and "established fishing patterns". In practice these have been used to justify fishing effort by DWFN that runs quite contrary to fisheries conservation, ecosystem management and the precautionary management of high seas fisheries. They reduce the effectiveness of RFMOs to manage high seas fisheries.

Article 8 (para. 4) of the *Agreement* restricts fishing in an RFMO's area, specifying that "only those States which are members of such an organization or participants in such an arrangement, or which agree to apply the conservation and management measures established by such organization or arrangement, shall have access to the fishery resources to which those measures apply". The objective of this clause is to restrict free riding by fishers that ignore the RFMOs and the rules they set down. However, whether Article 8 is strictly enforceable under customary international law or treaty law as expressed in the *Vienna Convention on the Law of Treaties* is another matter. As stated in Chapter 1, no country has to be bound unless it wishes to be. Besides, as the *Agreement* does not list any penalties for free riding, it is hard to see what the disincentive effect is. Moreover, even if Article 8 is enforceable this does not mean that fish stocks are "safe", because rules set by the RFMO are often ineffective – a matter discussed at some length in the next chapter.

In summary, members of RFMOs are required to agree on conservation measures aimed at long-term sustainability, to set and allocate total allowable catches, to collect data (the flag states being responsible here), to impose effective monitoring, control, surveillance and enforcement, to consider how new members can be allowed into an RFMO, and to promote peaceful disputes settlement through the establishment of dispute settlement machinery.

5 Neither the *Convention* nor the *Agreement* settles the coastal state vs. DWFNs game

As is discussed in the next chapter, there is a kind of game going on between coastal states and distant water fishing nations. Both the *Convention* and, especially, the *Agreement*, have tried to balance their differing interests and have not come down on one side or the other. Coastal states want straddling stocks rules consistent with their own EEZ management. However, DWFNs want a say in the management of straddling stocks, especially to ensure access. Juda (1997) questions how the two sides can be compatible with each other; if one has to give in, which one? Do DWFNs have to fit in with coastal state management, or do coastal states have to modify their EEZ management to suit the DWFNs? Whatever the balance, negotiation of agreements between these parties is to be accomplished in the RFMOs, or through direct negotiations; and both fisheries-biological issues and socioeconomic factors are to be addressed in these agreements.

6 Enforcement

According to customary international law only a flag state can police its flagged boats on the high seas. By allowing a coastal state or any other member of an RFMO to perform policing on the high seas the *Agreement* represents a large deviation from historical practices. However, flag state policing still takes precedence over that by coastal states or other RFMO members. Flag state obligations are to act quickly against violators and to impose penalties strong enough to deter future violations. Other members of an RFMO are allowed to board a flag state's boat if there is reasonable suspicion of illegal activity. Such evidence, if it exists, is to be secured and the flag state is to be notified within three days. The flag state then has a further three days in which to respond, either to take the case over itself or to authorize the inspecting state to do so. If the flag state fails to respond, the inspecting state retains policing power over the vessel and it can take it to one of its ports. However, the flag state can take the case over at any time.

7   Types of regional fisheries management organizations

Sydnes (2001) identifies three classes of RFMO: *Scientific research organizations* that are mainly concerned with collection of scientific information and provision of advice to member countries. Here there "is little substantive conflict of interest among the states parties" (Sydnes, 2001, p. 354). *Regional policy cooperation and development organizations* are mainly concerned with "establishing regulations coordinating joint efforts regarding harmonization of national policies and through programmatic tasks related to the development of the fishing sector" (Sydnes, 2001, p. 354). Expression of common interests tends to prevail in these organizations. *Regional fisheries management organizations* are institutions whose "functions may include collecting and assessing scientific information, setting regulatory measures, including determination of quotas, and the adoption of enforcement mechanisms" (Sydnes, 2001, p. 354). Expressions of common and, especially, conflicting interests prevail in these organizations. Sometimes the objection procedure is used, whereby the country using it does not have to be bound by the rule objected to. There are eight RMFOs using this mechanism.

The use of an "objection" in an RFMO is similar to the taking of a "reservation" under the *Vienna Convention on the Law of Treaties* (discussed in Chapter 1). Here is an example taken from the basic text of the *International Commission for the Conservation of Atlantic Tuna*: "the Commission may, on the basis of scientific evidence, make recommendations designed to maintain the populations of tuna and tuna-like fishes that may be taken in the Convention area at levels which will permit the maximum sustainable catch. These recommendations shall be applicable to the Contracting Parties under the conditions laid down in paragraphs 2 and 3 of this Article" (Article 8 para. 1(a)). However, paragraph 3(c) says that a "recommendation shall become effective . . . *except for those Contracting Parties that have presented an objection*" (italics added).[6] In other words, a country can join as a member of an RFMO yet choose to stand outside rules laid down to move fish stocks toward the biomass that would support the maximum sustainable yield. Over a forty-year period in ICCAT, six contracting parties have presented and confirmed reservations. This may not seem to be very many; however, the preferred method of decision-making is by consensus.[7]

Table 13.1 lists 24 RFMOs together with which of the three categories they fall into, year established, their decision-making authority and whether objection procedures exist.[8]

TABLE 13.1 Regional fishery organizations

	Category (based on Sydnes, 2001)	Year set up	Decision-making authority
Asia-Pacific Fisheries Commission	3	1948	Advisory
Commission for the Conservation of Atlantic Marine Living Resources	3	1980	By consensus, binding
Commission for the Conservation of Southern Bluefin Tuna	3	1994	By consensus, binding
Committee for the Eastern Central Atlantic Fisheries	2	1967	None
General Fisheries Council for the Mediterranean	3	1949	Binding, dispute settlement procedures, objections
Indian Ocean Tuna Commission	3	1993	Binding, dispute settlement procedures, objections
Inter-American Tropical Tuna Commission	3	1949	By consensus
International Baltic Sea Fisheries Commission	3	1973	Binding, dispute settlement procedures, objections
International Commission for the Conservation of Atlantic Tuna	3	1966	Binding, dispute settlement procedures, objections
International Council for the Exploration of the Sea	1	1902	Advisory
International Pacific Halibut Commission	3	1923	By consensus, binding
Latin American Organization for the Development of Fisheries	2	1984	Advisory
North Atlantic Marine Mammal Commission	3	1992	By consensus
North Atlantic Salmon Conservation Organization	3	1982	Advisory, dispute settlement procedures, objections
North East Atlantic Fisheries Commission	3	1980	Binding, dispute settlement procedures, objections
North Pacific Anadromous Fish Commission	3	1993	By consensus
North Pacific Marine Science Organization	1	1992	None
Northwest Atlantic Fisheries Organization	3	1978	Binding, dispute settlement procedures, objections
Pacific Salmon Commission	3	1985	By consensus, binding
Permanent Commission for the South Pacific	3	1952	By consensus, binding, dispute settlement procedures, objections
Regional Convention on Fisheries Cooperation among African States Bordering the Atlantic Ocean	2	1995	None
South Pacific Forum Fisheries Agency	2	1979	Advisory
Sub-Regional Commission on Fisheries	2	1985	None
Western Central Atlantic Fisheries Commission	2	1973	None

Five RFMOs have no decision-making authority; eight make decisions by consensus; eleven can make decisions that are binding on States Parties; and the remainder play only an advisory role.[9] The RFMOs with dispute settlement procedures are mainly those that make decisions by majority vote. Other dispute handling procedures are made by the technical disputes settlement board of the Pacific Salmon Commission; and the use of the International Court of Justice or an arbitration tribunal by the Commission for the Conservation of Atlantic Marine Living Resources and the Commission for the Conservation of Southern Bluefin Tuna are used when interpretation of agreements is in question. The International Court of Justice can also be used in the agreements covering four other RFMOs.

However, Sydnes (2001) comments that "disputes settlement mechanisms have had limited impact on regional fisheries cooperation so far" (p. 358), largely owing to the reluctance of states to surrender sovereignty. The mechanisms of decision-making by consensus, and making decisions only advisory, allow a member of an RFMO to abide by only what it wants to abide by; and if decision-making is by majority vote a country can always make an objection to any clauses not to its liking. These features of RFMO are entirely in keeping with the nature of customary and treaty law discussed in Chapter 1: abiding by international public law is a voluntary act that need not inconvenience any signatory nation.

What all of this amounts to is that while using the rhetoric of "responsible fisheries conservation", RFMOs really operate as forums for the expression of states' interests. Or, as Sydnes (2001) argues: "there appears to be a disconnect between the emphasis placed on RFMOs to solve or achieve sustainable fisheries management and knowledge about and understanding of the existing RFMOs and their operations" (p. 350).

This leads to the question of why countries choose to play non-cooperative when they have signed international agreements that on the surface commit them to act cooperatively. This is discussed in the next chapter.

8 RFMO performance

Cullis-Suzuki and Pauly (2010) examine the performance of 18 RFMOs with management powers, scoring each of them out of 10 on 26 different measures of effectiveness. The average score across all questions was 5.7, which meant, for example, that on one of the measures RFMOs did not typically get as far as "executing performance reviews" – which, of course, meant that it was near impossible to implement "tangible, positive changes" in policy. It is not surprising, therefore, that using the example of the International Commission for the Conservation of Atlantic Tuna (ICCAT), established in 1969, biomass in all eight tuna biomasses was down – in six cases by about 70 percent. They also found that biomass trend was downward for most species under RFMO "management" in all geographic areas.

Turning to the Northwest Atlantic Fisheries Organization (NAFO), since the mid-1990s violations have steadily increased. Non-compliance includes intentional fishing for species under moratoria, exceeding quotas, misreporting catches (by area and by species), improper use of fishing gear (e.g. inappropriate mesh sizes), fishing in areas closed to fishing, failure to employ independent and impartial fisheries observers, and interference with NAFO inspectors, observers or evidence (Churchill, 2001). The Canadians were disappointed with flag state enforcement, saying that flag state follow-up was "ineffective and inadequate". The EU, for example, was not even using observer data to back up legal charges.

Here are some opinions stated in the Canadian Parliament's *Report of the Standing Senate Committee on Fisheries and Oceans* (2003): "Despite at least 25 years of NAFO involvement, we have truly failed to develop and to implement an adequate conservation resource management regime for waters outside the 200-mile limit".[10] "NAFO has existed for 24, 25 years, and the stocks outside 200-miles have been decimated. There can be no argument about that".[11] And "Everything we ever achieved in NAFO was achieved by offering carrots. Nothing was ever achieved on the point of being a conservation measure. It was achieved because we offered them extra turbot, redfish or some other species. We have now run out of carrots".[12]

The Parliamentary Report concluded that "the evidence placed before us clearly shows that NAFO still does not adequately fulfil its role: noncompliance is on the increase; flag states seldom follow up and take action against their vessels found to have contravened NAFO rules; and NAFO does not always adopt the scientific advice of its Scientific Council when setting catch limits outside the 200-mile zone." But despite these failures witnesses thought that Canada would *not* be better off withdrawing from NAFO. Here are two representative statements: "No matter how bad things are, it is probably better to be in (NAFO) than to have nothing" (Art May); "At least NAFO is a forum by which we are able to speak to people in the fishing industry" (Gus Etchegary).

9 A success story: The Northeast Atlantic "Banana Hole"

Churchill (2001) offers an analysis of the herring fishery in the Northeast Atlantic Fisheries Commission (NEAFC) area.[13] Although coastal state and DWFN interests are again juxtaposed, especially with respect to quota allocations, it turns out that management of this fishery, in contrast to the NAFO on the other side of the North Atlantic, is a success story.[14] Beginning in 1995, coastal states (CSs) in the herring fishery initially wanted quotas in a TAC to be set in proportion to the geographic prevalence of stocks in their EEZs. The Russians, as the main DWFN, wanted them set by historic catch levels. A compromise formula was agreed, and the herring stock appears subsequently to have been managed in a sustainable manner.[15] Churchill (2001) puts this success down to the unusual nature of this fishery. First, the fishery had been all but destroyed by over-fishing from the 1950s to the 1970s, and neither CSs nor DWFNs wanted a repeat performance (only Norway's nurturing of the remaining tiny biomass had caused the fishery to recover). Second, the migratory pattern of the herring stock meant that several CSs have jurisdiction over parts of the fishery for some of the time. Third, the high seas segment of the fishery is quite small in relation to the combined EEZs of CSs, being restricted to the so-called Banana Hole, with only about 10 percent of the catch being on the high seas.[16] Fourth, fishing by other DWFNs in this fishery is quite small, as too is fishing by flags of convenience. Thus, the success of NEAFC management of this fishery might be characterized as stemming from the fact that it is more like an agreement between CSs than between CSs and DWFNs.[17]

10 Some conclusions

International law on high seas fisheries has so far proven to be largely ineffective in creating efficient fisheries management in the sense that stocks are allowed to recover and fisheries are then managed with high levels of fish stocks. The 1982 *Convention* created a duty to cooperate but did not operationalize the concept. The 1995 *Agreement*, while aimed at the operationalization of cooperation, also failed to achieve this, thereby leaving RFMOs as arenas for the expression of states' interests, with many loopholes that allow states not to cooperate in high seas fisheries management.

Notes

1 See, for example, Cullis-Suzuki and Pauly (2010) and Bailey, Sumaila and Lindroos (2010).
2 www.un.org/Depts/los/convention_agreements/convention_overview_fish_stocks. htm.
3 For example, in Articles 61, 62, 64 and 118 states are asked only to "cooperate".
4 Articles 62(2), 64, 66, 116, 117, 118 and 119.
5 RFMOs such as ICCAT, NAFO, CCAMLR, NEAFC and SEAFO allow a member to submit an objection to a conservation or management decision (Lodge et al., 2007, p. 75).
6 The *Vienna Convention* defines a reservation in the following way: "'reservation' means a unilateral statement, however phrased or named, made by a State, when signing, ratifying, accepting, approving or acceding to a treaty, whereby it purports to exclude or to modify the legal effect of certain provisions of the treaty in their application to that State" (Article 2(d)).
7 UN, *Oceans and Law of the Sea*, available online at www.un.org/Depts/los/convention_ agreements/reviewconf/ICCAT_submission.pdf.
8 See also the FAO's list at www.fao.org/fishery/rfb/search/en.
9 Sydnes (2001) comments that there are no significant differences in authority powers between RFMOs established before or after the *Law of the Sea Convention*, 1982.
10 Alastair O'Rielly, member of the Newfoundland Provincial Advisory Council on Foreign Overfishing, Committee Proceedings, February 25th, 2003.
11 Dr. Art May, member of the Newfoundland Provincial Advisory Council on Foreign Overfishing, Committee Proceedings, February 25th, 2003.
12 Fred Woodman, Chair of the Fisheries Resource Conservation Council, Committee Proceedings, May 6th, 2003.
13 The NEAFC can make recommendations on TAC, quotas, fishing gear, closed areas and seasons. In aiming for optimum management of fish stocks in its area it seeks to ensure consistency between its measures and those of the coastal states. All Northeast Atlantic CSs are members, as are the DWFNs Russia and Poland. All countries are parties to the

Convention on the *Law of the Sea*, except Denmark, but Churchill remarks that this is not a problem as most fisheries provisions of the *Convention* have passed into customary law (Churchill, 2001, p. 237). Also, three states have ratified the 1995 fish stocks *Agreement* – Iceland, Norway and Russia – and the EC has signed but not ratified it.

14 Churchill (2001) notes that the NEAFC is "clearly a regional fisheries organization of the kind referred to in the Fish Stocks Agreement" (p. 238) aimed at efficient management of straddling stocks, and that it was modeled on the Northwest Atlantic Fisheries Organization (NAFO). Moreover, "NAFO in turn served to a considerable extent as a model for the provisions of the Fish Stocks Agreement dealing with regional fisheries organizations" (p. 238).

15 Japan and Poland are small-scale DWFNs in this fishery. The coastal states are Greenland, Iceland, the Faroes and Norway.

16 The Banana Hole is bounded by four CSs – Greenland, Iceland, the Faroes and Norway.

17 Churchill's analysis of management of the redfish fishery by the NEAFC is also characterized as a game between CSs and DWFNs. However, he is not so sanguine about this fishery, arguing that the acceptance of allocated quotas was possible largely because the TAC was set at what is probably an unsustainable level.

14

HOW AND WHY TO MAKE A FISHERY TREATY INEFFECTIVE

1   Introduction

Even with the Law of the Sea *Convention* and Fish Stocks *Agreement* in force we know that management of fish stocks on the high seas (including straddling stocks) is largely ineffective, with stocks in many fisheries being "depleted" or "severely depleted". The management agencies are the Regional Fish Management Organizations, but of these a Canadian report said, "the secretariats running the various RFMOs were described to Committee members as weak and having essentially no authority. With respect to NAFO, one suggestion was for impartial, professional staff to be brought from the UN Food and Agriculture Organization or other global organisations."[1] In other words, RFMOs would be better run by somebody other than the representatives selected by member countries.

That member countries of RFMOs are choosing not to run them effectively raises two questions. First, how do the members make them ineffective while still appearing to cooperate in the spirit of the *Convention* and the *Agreement*? Second, why do countries sign treaties even though they know the agreements will be ineffective in practice? The answer to the first question is reasonably straightforward; the answer to the second is less clear, though we will make some suggestions. Among other things, what is emphasized is the common interests of all coastal states in extending sovereign rights to exclusive economic zones; the clashing of interests between coastal states and distant water fishing nations in certain fisheries following the creation of these EEZs; the reluctance of distant water fishing nations to submit to management measures that would significantly limit their high seas fishing activity; and the necessity for patience on the part of coastal states in developing effective high seas management rules and institutions. Additionally, in Section 8 it is suggested that sometimes at least coastal states and distant water fishing nations are playing a game of chicken with dwindling fish stocks.

2   How to make an RFMO ineffective

Possible answers to the first question of *how* signatories render a treaty ineffective while appearing to cooperate with each other include: a) insignificant penalties written into the agreement; b) inadequate policing of the ocean space covered by the agreement; c) significant probability built into a treaty that even if cheating is detected fines or other punishments will be small or not imposed at all.[2]

Any one of these three features can turn an apparent cooperative game, aimed at maximizing the social surplus, into a non-cooperative game in the sense that individual countries are left free to choose their own actions regardless of the spirit of treaty commitments and regardless of the social interest. In other words, even signing a treaty does not change state behavior; the signatories continue to play non-cooperatively. A strong-enough treaty will cause the signatories effectively to cooperate with each other. To make it effective they also have to agree on enforcement and penalty mechanisms – policing and punishments. When such a "strong" treaty is in force, signatories' behaviors will be modified, but only if the punishment incurred when illegal behavior is detected is greater than the expected gain from cheating.

3   Treaty formation, cooperative and non-cooperative games

Here we discuss the matter of the importance of effective policing and the need to impose effectively large penalties if signatories are to be encouraged to move from the non-cooperative (bad) to the cooperative (good) equilibrium.

In a prisoners' dilemma game the idea of a treaty is to move the players from the Nash, cheat/cheat, equilibrium to the comply/comply, Pareto optimal, payoffs in Figure 14.1.[3]

A treaty does this by making the return to cheating less than the return to complying – as in Figure 14.2. The latter is achieved through a "fine", F (or, more generally, "punishments", upon which monetary values can be put).

	COMPLY	CHEAT
COMPLY	2, 2	0, 3
CHEAT	3, 0	1, 1

FIGURE 14.1 Prisoners' dilemma

	COMPLY	CHEAT
COMPLY	2, 2	0, 1.5
CHEAT	1.5, 0	1, 1

FIGURE 14.2 Payoffs with a fine for cheating

	COMPLY	CHEAT
COMPLY	2, 2	1.5, 1.5
CHEAT	1.5, 1.5	1, 1

FIGURE 14.3 Payoffs with a fine for cheating and compensation for the complier

The fine must be large enough to reduce the payoff to cheating from 3 to less than 2. In the payoff matrix of Figure 14.2, comply/comply is the better of what are now two Nash equilibriums. A treaty is used to make the socially superior (comply/comply) the one that is chosen.

In Figure 14.2 the fine for cheating is 1.5. But as there is some probability that cheating will not be detected it is the expected fine, $E(F)$, that must equal 1.5. Notice that if one player cheats, the other player has an incentive to cheat too; a payoff of 1 with cheating is better than a payoff of zero if one complies and the other cheats. If the complier did not also switch to cheating on the rules, it would be a "sucker".

However, it is theoretically possible to change the structure of the payoffs in Figure 14.2 to those in Figure 14.3.

The payoffs in Figure 14.3 are the same as in Figure 14.2 except for the change that the payoff from complying while the other cheats has been increased from 0 to 1.5. In this case, even if the other player cheats, the payoff to complying remains greater than from cheating (1.5 > 1) – the sucker problem is done away with.

How such a change in payoffs could be accomplished is by transferring the fine, of 1.5, paid by the cheater, to the complier. Thus, a fine-with-compensation system could get over the "sucker" problem, so inducing compliers to continue playing comply even in the face of cheating. Notice that under the 1982 *Convention* and the Straddling Stocks *Agreement* of 1995, it is the flag state that levies any fines. Hence, even if fines are large and are paid by a vessel caught cheating, the return to cheating is retained by the flag state. Moreover, a fine in a roundabout way may be returned to the company that paid the fine through subsidies on the cost of vessels or labor.

What is crucial here is the size of the *expected* fine, E(F), rather than the fine itself. A large fine that has low probability of being imposed is likely to have little impact on cheating behavior. Fines need to be larger the smaller is the probability of being detected.

Begin with the simplest model:

$$E(F) = Pr_{DETECT} \cdot F$$

where Pr_{DETECT} is the probability of being detected cheating, and F is the monetary value of the fine imposed.[4]

Countries that prefer the cheating option will argue for a treaty with low Pr_{DETECT} and/or a low fine. That is, they intend to operate non-cooperatively even after they have signed an agreement to cooperate. More generally, countries that wish for some reason to sign a treaty – an agreement to cooperate – while retaining their freedom of action (that is, to continue playing non-cooperatively) will argue for rules that create low values for the expected fine.

In a study of 16 cases of high seas fishing violations that led to actual fining of violators, Sumaila, Alder and Keith (2006) found that in all but one case the notional expected fine (actual fine imposed multiplied by a 0.2 notional probability of being caught illegally fishing) was less than the catch value that could have been earned by selling the fish the fishers were caught with. Taking into account estimates of variable costs and adding them to the expected fines, 12 of the 16 cases were still found to have expected revenues in excess of these aggregated costs.

4 A broader model of E(F)

In practice the expected fine depends on more than just the probability of detection, Pr_{DETECT}, and the size of the fine, F. Other determinants include: a) the probability that a fine will be levied after cheating has been detected. Here the results of bargaining over the disciplinary system of a treaty matter – for example, whether coastal state or distant water fishing nation courts impose the fines; whether there is voluntary or compulsory arbitration of disputes; whether the International Court of Justice can be used; and whether reservations can be used extensively or not. Also, b) the size of a fine may depend on who is levying it – a court in a coastal state or one in a DWFN.

An extended model of E(F) is:

$$E(F) = Pr_{DETECT} \times Pr_{FINE\ IMPOSED} \times [\alpha(F^{HIGH} + (1 - \alpha)F^{LOW}]$$

where "α" is the probability of a high fine given that a fine is imposed – which probably depends on who is imposing it. According to the Report of the Standing Committee (2003), disciplinary action through flag state countries (DWFNs) is weak, implying either low $Pr_{FINE\ IMPOSED}$ or low α, or both.

International bargaining covers all of the elements in the last equation. For example: Pr_{DETECT} relates to whether a coastal state has the right to board, to inspect below decks, or to arrest with or without the permission of the flag state. According to the *Agreement*, it does, but the flag state can intervene to take over the case at any time. Also, the ease of detection depends on such things as licensing being in place (rendering detection of the legality of fishing boats easier), and requirements to broadcast positions.

A possible method increasing the E(F) is through the extra-territorial application of domestic law and sanctions. For example, shipmasters could be licensed by their home state and they would be required to report upon which vessels they are working (Erceg, 2006). Licenses could be withdrawn in the event that a shipmaster was caught illegally fishing. Gallic and Cox (2006) favor "long arm" approaches which would allow for prosecutions of nationals for breaking foreign laws wherever they are committed.[5] These types of sanction are aimed at raising the E(F), especially $Pr_{FINE\ IMPOSED}$. However, Erceg (2006) says that lack of cooperation from flag states could well render the system largely ineffective. A problem with the *Convention* is that coastal states are not allowed to imprison fishers caught illegally fishing on foreign flagged vessels; indeed, as already mentioned, the flag state can take over legal prosecutions at any time. A possible way around this problem is the use of bilateral agreements between countries allowing coastal state prosecutions.

Erceg (2006) and Gallic and Cox (2006) discuss a number of other measures that if implemented could raise the E(F) – such as better surveillance, increasing sanctions and enhanced collaboration between states. However, discussion of these matters, while valuable, does not get to the heart of the matter. The prevalence of illegal fishing due to low E(F) exists not because it is beyond the wit of fishing authorities or economists to think of ways to reduce it – rather, E(F) is low because it results from bargaining between signatories to an agreement. The first step toward reducing illegal fishing is to get the signatories to accept rules that when applied increase the E(F).

5 Optimal spending on policing

Here, "expenditure on policing", E, means all expenditures related to policing: monitoring, surveillance, data collection and management, cost of positional devices, cost of licensing systems, and cost of running quota systems – in fact, all things that relate to the governance of a high seas/straddling stocks fishery. Use:

$$E(F) = Pr_{DETECT}(E) \times F$$

where $Pr_{DETECT}(E)$ means that Pr_{DETECT} is a positive function of E, expenditure on policing.

The gross gain from cheating in Figure 14.4 is the payoff from cheating while others comply. The E(F) rises as expenditure on policing rises.

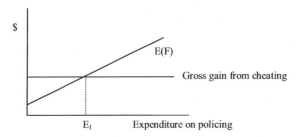

FIGURE 14.4 Necessary minimum expenditure on policing

E_1 is the necessary minimum expenditure on policing to encourage compliance with a treaty. If policing expenditure is less than E_1, the gross gain from cheating exceeds the expected fine and policing is not a deterrent to cheating.

The treaty formation game is one of devising rules that will achieve at least E_1 through sufficient surveillance and policing, and sufficiently large fines.

6   Policing cost versus legitimacy

It has been theorized that there is an inverse relationship between policing cost and the perceived legitimacy of an institution. Thus, North (1981) states:

> The costs of maintenance of an existing order are inversely related to the per-ceived legitimacy of the existing system. To the extent that the participants believe the system fair, the costs of enforcing the rules and property rights are enormously reduced by the simple fact that the individuals will not disobey the rules or violate property rights even when a private cost/benefit calculus would make such action worthwhile.
>
> (p. 53)

This is the point raised by Honneland (2001) when he argues that if new insti-tutional arrangements for fishing for straddling stocks are viewed as "legitimate" by DWFNs as well as coastal states, policing costs will thereby be reduced. The argu-ment certainly applies to the coastal state *versus* DWFN game outlined above – all the more so if straddling fish stocks were allowed to recover to their historic biomasses.

North also observes that:

> The premium necessary to induce people to become free riders is positively correlated with the perceived legitimacy of the existing institutions.
>
> (1981, p. 54)

In other words, in the straddling stocks context, the more legitimate the fishing regime, the more difficult it becomes to induce operatives, such as shipmasters, knowingly to break the law and, therefore, the more effective is the regime.

However, the fundamental problem is to settle on rules that both DWFNs and shipmasters and other significant operatives would find legitimate. Unfortunately, both the *Convention* and the *Agreement* built in loopholes as a matter of compromise. Examples are the right to use the objection, thereby freeing the objecting state from abiding by the measures objected to, and historical fishing rights, that have been used to justify DWFNs taking straddling stocks that thwart coastal state management of them within their EEZs.[6] From the beginning, both the *Convention* and the *Agreement* were written with weak rules, or rules that would be enforced ineffectively – rendering low values of expected "fines" – largely because at least some fishing nations did not think that a regime with tough rules, high E(F), was legitimate.

Compromise may well have encouraged the acceptance by DWFNs of qualified rights to high seas fishing (as claimed by Vicuna (1999)), but the compromise is such that they are enabled to continue playing non-cooperatively, with the result that the conservation objective – efficient management of straddling fish stocks – is by and large thwarted. In short, the *Agreement* created only the illusion of a cooperative game.

A justifiable supposition is that a flag state has a lesser incentive to impose stiff "fines" on violators than does a coastal state. The latter has an incentive to impose stiff penalties as a deterrent against future violations, but a flag state has a lesser incentive both because its citizens benefit from illegal fishing on the high seas (profits, employment, etc.) and, if it is a flag-of-convenience state, it collects registration fees.

7   Why sign ineffective treaties?

One may wonder why a country that wants to play non-cooperatively would sign a treaty to cooperate in the first place. I had the opportunity to ask an Ivy League Professor who had taught for several decades a "legendary" course in Diplomacy this very question; his off-the-cuff answer was, "So they can cheat!" That much is clear, but there is still the puzzle of why a country that does not want to cheat, and does not want the other signatories to cheat, signs such a treaty in the first place. We know, of course, that signing a treaty but taking reservation can make the treaty largely ineffective and that this is entirely legal under international public law (Chapter 1); perhaps this is why countries sign on to RFMOs – they might be useful, and if not, what is the alternative?

In terms of high seas fishing the answer to the question "why sign ineffective treaties?" has an historical origin. The high seas fishing games discussed above are in effect played between coastal states and DWFNs. Broadly speaking it is the DWFNs that are reluctant to manage high seas fish stocks effectively. Yet they have agreed to do so. Coastal states are more likely to press for effective high seas governance because open access on the high seas can severely degrade their own management efforts within their EEZs. The reason why both groups of countries signed the 1982 *Convention* is that both groups benefited from the *Convention* through the creation of 200-mile EEZs. But the creation of EEZs left open the matter of fish stocks that straddle the high seas (as well as the management of highly migratory fish stocks). Even though at least some coastal states saw that distant water fishing of straddling stocks could complicate their own management of fish stocks in their EEZs, they were willing to sign the *Convention* even with weak rules governing straddling stocks.

Knowing that coastal states put greater weight on obtaining an agreement on the EEZ than on reaching agreement on straddling stocks, DWFNs argued for and got weak rules governing straddling stocks. That coastal states signed-on to the *Convention* did not mean that they did not want to reform it in subsequent rounds of negotiation – the negotiations leading to the 1995 fish stocks *Agreement* being a case in point, and so too the continuing negotiations in RFMOs. However, having got what they wanted in the *Convention*, DWFNs continue to insist on maintaining weak high seas governance regimes.[7]

Coastal states looking at the payoffs from agreement to the *Convention* in the early 1980s may well have thought that they received net benefits from it. However, in more recent years it has become apparent that DWFNs fishing for straddling stocks can render fisheries management within the EEZ ineffective or at least severely defective. An issue worthy of consideration is, therefore, the question of why coastal states didn't foresee this and insist on tougher rules before finalizing the *Convention*. Similarly, why didn't coastal states foresee the intransigence of DWFNs in amending the rules in later years? Perhaps it was because coastal states could not see that far into the future. Indeed, Bjorndal and Munro (2002) argue that many coastal states thought that DWFNs would not harvest straddling stocks unless they were granted access to the adjacent EEZs (p. 7). Besides, while some coastal states are intent on fisheries conservation in their EEZs, others are not strongly motivated – as is evidenced by the collapse of many non-straddling fish stocks around the world.

Three situations can arise between coastal states and DWFNs.

1   A coastal state responsibly manages a fishery that happens to straddle the high seas. If a distant water fishing nation cheats, the coastal state will not revert to cheating – as in Figure 14.3.[8] Because it wishes to continue playing a non-cooperative game, the DWFN argues for low Pr_{DETECT} and/or a low fine. However, the CS wants sufficiently high values of these to deter cheating. Why, then, does the coastal state settle on a treaty with insufficiently high values of Pr_{DETECT} or F? The answer, as hinted at above, could be because the treaty is viewed as a first step in a series of treaties – the *Convention* of 1982, the *Agreement* of 1995 – bargaining in regional fisheries management organizations after that. Coastal states hope for a rising Pr_{DETECT} and/or F through a series of steps.

2   DWFNs responsibly manage straddling stocks but a coastal state does not. The situation in situation 1 is reversed. Pintassilgo (2003, p. 192) argues that as DWFNs have to be members of a relevant RFMO and to obey its rules, it is

adjacent costal states that are responsible for free riding behavior since the rules they set for fishing in their exclusive economic zones do not have to be consistent with those of the RFMO. "This can be a reliable scenario if the main fisheries of the coastal state occur within their EEZ's, since under international law they cannot be prevented from fishing in their own territorial waters." However, this argument seems to miss the point that RFMOs are largely ineffective in managing their straddling stocks and/or high seas fisheries and that this is no accident; the members, or at least some of them, want it this way. As the case of Canada in NAFO – discussed in the last chapter – makes clear, it is the DWFNs that are thwarting the Canadian desire for more efficient straddling stocks management and not the other way around.

3   Neither responsibly manages, so both want low Pr_{DETECT}. F. Why, then, does either bother to sign a treaty that they want to be ineffective? As mentioned above, there must be other payoffs outside of the immediate game, e.g. to placate environmentalist lobbies whose governments hope to fool with "fine words". Balton (1996) and Stokke (2001) are of the view that environmentalist lobbies were a factor pushing the USA to sign the 1995 *Agreement*.

Once a coastal state realizes that year after year an RFMO is ineffective, why doesn't it withdraw from it? Canada and its relationship with the Northwest Atlantic Fisheries Organization is a case in point, as Canada has become disillusioned over the ineffectiveness of NAFO.[9] Thus, extracting from the *Report of the Standing Senate Committee on Fisheries and Oceans* (2003):

> There have been calls for Canada to withdraw from NAFO, an option usually made in conjunction with another proposal: the establishment of a new "Canadian custodial management" regime outside the 200-mile limit . . . The two are typically linked because, with nothing else to replace NAFO, simply leaving would be self-defeating, and the consequences unacceptable. Indeed, witnesses strongly opposed the option for a number of reasons. For example, the problem of non-compliance would [be] more widespread because there would be less enforcement. Canada would no longer benefit from information obtained from the observer program, the inspections and surveillance scheme, and vessel monitoring. There would no longer be an international forum for discussion of issues with the other countries. The remaining countries would be unlikely to offset Canada's large financial contributions to NAFO's budget, which could lead to the dismantling of NAFO and an unregulated fishery . . . . The very strong consensus in our deliberations was that it is much better for Canada to have an imperfect, internationally agreed upon regime, such as NAFO, than no regime at all.

The Committee identified several instruments that could in the future be used to improve the effectiveness of NAFO management on the Grand Banks, including modifying the objection procedure, thereby increasing the power of the scientific council or countries with greater conservation preferences; incorporating the precautionary and ecosystem approaches into the NAFO *Convention*; using a "ships of shame policy" by publishing lists of violators; harmonizing the sanctions regime between members; and adopting a disputes settlement system. However, it was recognized that adopting measures such as these required the political will to do so – something that was at that time lacking.

This Canadian position can be characterized as "looking to the future with hope". It suggests a repeated game through institutional development. At some point a new institution may be created, or the fundamental rules of an existing one modified, shaping effective fisheries management. Indeed, Canada is already on this course of supporting successive international instruments: the *Convention*, the *Agreement*, the 1993 FAO *Compliance Agreement* to prevent re-flagging as a means of avoiding conservation measures, the 1995 FAO *Code of Conduct for Responsible Fisheries*, and further FAO management plans in 1999 and 2001.[10] This succession of international efforts in high seas fisheries comes about because of the voluntary nature of international public law (see Chapter 1), and is similar to the succession of efforts to devise more effective international law to reduce free riding in the enforcement of laws against maritime piracy on the high seas – see Chapters 3 and 4. The theme is "try and try and try again".

8   A speculation: International fisheries management as a game of chicken

Failure to manage fisheries stocks straddling the waters of a coastal state and the high seas can be analyzed as the outcome of a game of chicken, and this framework offers insights beyond those offered by the prisoners' dilemma and cooperation games.[11] The fact that both the *Fur Seal Treaty* and the new rules to manage herring stocks in the Banana Hole were only introduced when both stocks were on the edge of extinction is suggestive of a game of chicken – the players only choosing to "swerve" away from excessive exploitation at the last moment.

There are four possible outcomes to a game of chicken. The worst is that neither swerves and they are both wiped out – the southeast box in Figure 14.5; the best outcome from a given player's point of view that he/she drives straight on while the other swerves – respectively, the southwest and northeast boxes. The fourth outcome is that both swerve – each loses face, but at least they are still alive; this, the second best outcome for both players, is indicated in the northwest box.

Some numbers (economic rents) illustrate the game of chicken as it is played between coastal states and distant water fishing nations (DWFNs) over the international management of straddling stocks in an RFMO – we will illustrate with the case of NAFO. In Figure 14.6 Canada chooses the rows and the EU the columns. Each has two choices: not to cooperate in effectively managing straddling stocks (equivalent to dangerously driving straight on), or to cooperate with the other party (equivalent to swerving to avoid a crash).

	Swerve	Straight on
Swerve	Second best, Second best	Third best, Best
Straight on	Best, Third best	Worst, Worst

FIGURE 14.5 A game of chicken

EU

Canada		Cooperate	Don't cooperate
	Cooperate	6, 6	2, 8
	Don't cooperate	8, 2	-2, -2

FIGURE 14.6 Canada–EU chicken game

If neither cooperates to manage straddling stocks (that is, neither side attempts to reduce fishing effort toward MSY or MEY) each receives a payoff of –2: no economic rent earned from the fishery, and extra costs are incurred in retraining redundant fishermen and women. However, if Canada "cooperates" – reducing its fishing effort so that there is some recovery of straddling stocks), while the EU chooses the "don't cooperate" option (the northeast box) – the EU gathers 8 units of economic rent and Canada only 2 units. The payoffs are reversed in the southeast box. Finally, if both Canada and the EU cooperate in managing straddling stocks, the fisheries recover to the greatest extent possible and each player obtains an economic rent of 6 units.

Notice that in Figure 14.6, while there is no dominant strategy, history has dictated that the outcome is the northeast box – with Canada choosing to manage straddling stocks while the EU refuses to do so. That is, the EU persistently rebuts Canadian efforts to introduce effective straddling stock fisheries management through the NAFO. How has this come about? The reason is in the history of negotiations over the *Convention* (1982). First, the signatories rejected a *common heritage of mankind* approach to fisheries management – which could have allowed for unified rational management of high seas fisheries. Second, the *Convention* recognizes 200-mile EEZs, which all coastal states, including Canada, were willing to accept as it extended their sovereign rights well beyond their territorial waters. However, third, in the Northwest Atlantic, the Canadian continental shelf – the area of most productive fisheries – extends beyond Canada's EEZ to the so-called "nose" and "tail" areas. As a result Canadian fisheries management in its EEZ also benefits high seas fisheries by the EU on the nose and tail. Finally, while the Canadians claim that they foresaw the problems that this latter fact could lead to – that is, other countries benefiting from their fisheries management – they hoped that these could be sorted out in the NAFO. Surely reasonable countries would accept "reasonable" fisheries management?

Unfortunately, faith in the reasonableness of the other side to see things your way is misguided in a game of chicken. Observe that the northeast box of Figure 14.6 is a Nash equilibrium. Neither the EU nor Canada would want to change their strategies. The EU's payoff would fall from 8 to 6 if it chose "cooperate", and Canada's would fall from 2 to −2 if it were to move from "cooperate" to "don't cooperate". History had dealt Canada a bad hand – it is stuck practicing management of straddling stocks while the EU runs away with its fruits (the increased economic rents). In this equilibrium, each time Canada argues in the NAFO for improved fisheries management – reduced fishing effort by both itself and the EU – the EU's (own rent-maximizing) answer is to say no. Each side is committed to a given strategy, which when combined do not maximize the fisheries' economic rent and, indeed, leave fishing effort at dangerously high levels.

The game of chicken is not like the prisoners' dilemma. In the latter game *both* sides have an incentive to find ways to move from the equilibrium of the game (the bad outcome – which is "Worst, Worst") to reach the "Cooperate, Cooperate" outcome (which is second best for both players). The issues of how to solve a prisoners' dilemma are mainly concerned with finding institutional solutions (indeed, such as "let's set up an RFMO") and how to police them. But in the game of chicken, in equilibrium one side has no incentive to seek means of moving from that (beneficial for it) equilibrium. Given this, the NAFO is an empty vessel. While it was set up with the stated objective of improving high seas fishing, one side has no incentive to do so.

9 A side-payment solution?

However, a possible way out of the northeast box stalemate, where combined economic rent is only 10 units, to the Pareto optimal (socially best) solution in the northwest box – with total economic rent equal to 12 units – is for Canada to bribe the EU into effective fisheries management. For example, Canada could offer a side payment to the EU of 2.1 units of economic rent if it would also play "cooperate". In this case, the EU's payoff would rise to 6 + 2.1 = 8.1 > 8, and Canada's payoff would also increase from 2 to 6 − 2.1 = 3.9 > 2. In practice this would mean Canada allowing a sufficiently large share of the increased fisheries biomass. In fact, we can reason that Canada has attempted this very gambit, or, at least, this is what can be read into the following statement by a senior Canadian fisheries management executive that we have already quoted in the last chapter:

> Everything we ever achieved in NAFO was achieved by offering carrots. Nothing was ever achieved on the point of being a conservation measure. It was achieved because we offered them extra turbot, redfish or some other species. We have now run out of carrots.[12]

Why, though, has the EU largely rebuffed these Canadian offers to engage in responsible fisheries management in the NAFO region? There may be several possible answers, but one of them is that Canada might not have been offering enough incentive. Thus, in Figure 14.6, if the side payment is less than 2 units, the equilibrium play for the EU remains "don't cooperate". The offer of "extra turbot, redfish or some other species" is simply pocketed by the other side, with only token fisheries management measures offered in return.

There is a "Catch 22". Given that fish stocks are depleted, the Canadians are not able to offer the EU very many fish by way of a side payment. However, if the EU would first cut its fishing effort enough to move the game to the cooperate/cooperate position, then the Canadians could indeed offer a large enough side payment out of the larger biomass. Both time preference and uncertainty over biomass recovery are involved in resolving the dilemma. For one thing the EU's rate of time preference may be so high that they would rather persist without interruption in taking a small catch, rather than cutting the size of the catch in the short-run and later enjoying a larger catch. Moreover, there is uncertainty over how long it would take for the biomass to recover from its depleted level and then to what size. The example of the cod biomass on Georges Bank shared by Canada and the US is not encouraging, as recovery has not occurred despite many years of reduced fishing effort.

10 Conclusions

A question asked in this chapter is: why do countries sign ineffective agreements? Two answers were provided: DWFNs want ineffective management of straddling stocks so that they can continue to play a non-cooperative game in which they are concerned only for their own payoffs rather than for the social interest. Coastal states sign ineffective agreements because parts of them are, in fact, effective – the claiming of EEZs under the *Convention* being a case in point; the ineffective part of the *Convention* concerned with straddling stocks they see only as a first step in a repeated game.

All coastal states gained EEZs through the 1982 *Convention*, but problems of straddling and highly migratory fish stocks, while recognized, were not adequately dealt with. The underlying problem was that, while countries engaged in distant water fishing wanted EEZs – which they got – they did not want to give up fishing rights on the high seas beyond the 200-mile limits. Coastal states such as Canada have joined a game with DWFNs with rules that favor the interests of the latter. Why Canada joined such a game in the first place is an open question, but part of the answer would appear to be that Canada went along with the *Convention* because a half-a-loaf was better than none. The evidence seems to be that Canada sees itself in a repeated game with DWFNs – as is evidenced by the statements of Canadian fisheries officials and others (as discussed in Chapter 13). Finally, DWFNs have agreed to the *Convention* and the *Agreement* with their weak conservation rules, similarly with RFMOs, because it allows them to play a non-cooperative game. This operates on two levels: a) rules don't have to be agreed to in the first place; and

b) even if rules are agreed, monitoring and enforcement is so weak that expected punishments are small in relation to the value of fish illegally caught. The signing of an international agreement, one would think, would create a cooperative game in which the "best" overall outcome would be achieved. However, the ineffectiveness of these agreements allows DWFNs, in effect, to play non-cooperative games in which they pursue their own private, rather than social, interests.

Notes

1 *Canadian Report of the Standing Senate Committee on Fisheries and Oceans* (2003).
2 McDorman (2005) has a good discussion of the internal workings of many RFMOs, pointing to their shortcomings and emphasizing the lack of political will to make them work more effectively.
3 The numbers in the payoff matrix could be either monetary values (in millions of dollars) or ordinal utility values.
4 This is the basic structure of many policing models that are based on the assumption that crime is deterred if the expected cost of crime is less than the expected benefit. Non-economic factors – such as loss of moral or social standing in a community – should also be taken into account as deterrence factors (see, for example, Sumaila, Alder and Keith (2006) and Honneland (2001)). However, if in principle it is possible to place pecuniary values on these "non-economic" factors, these too may be subsumed under "F" in the preceding equation.
5 The US *Lacey Act* allows for this with respect to US nationals.
6 Canada as the coastal state has often faced this problem in the NAFO.
7 An extra consideration is that there was another player at the table prior to the 1982 *Convention*: the *common heritage of mankind* doctrine, largely supported by low-income and landlocked countries. However, they had a weak hand. Enclosure and the creation of sovereign rights over ocean space had by the mid-1970s pretty much won out over the *common heritage* doctrine (Eckert, 1979). However, had the *common heritage* doctrine been robust, it is possible that a more rational high seas fishing management regime would have been put in place.
8 This situation is like a law-abiding household suffering crime – it does not turn to crime itself.
9 Non-compliance with NAFO rules includes: directed or intentional fishing for species under moratoria; exceeding quotas; misreporting catches, by area and species; improper use of fishing gear (e.g. inappropriate mesh sizes); fishing in areas closed to fishing; failure to maintain independent and impartial fisheries observers; and interference with NAFO inspectors, observers or evidence (Report of the Standing Senate Committee on Fisheries and Oceans, 2003).
10 For a fuller discussion of these see Rayfuse (2003).
11 The classic example of this game is where two cool dudes accept a challenge to drive their cars as fast as possible straight at each other: the loser is the one that swerves to avoid a crash and is the chicken, the winner is the one that doesn't. Taylor and Ward (1982) offer an excellent discussion of the use of the game of chicken in the analysis of fisheries and whale management.
12 Fred Woodman, Chair, *Canadian Fisheries Resource Conservation Council*, Committee Proceedings, May 6th, 2003.

PART VI
Marine mammals

15

WHALES – CRASHING NUMBERS, CLASHING VALUES

1   Introduction

Whale numbers have crashed from what they once were, and while there is a moratorium on commercial whaling, whales are still harvested for "scientific research".[1] On the international governing body, the International Whaling Commission, there are clashing values between pro- and anti-whaling countries, which has led to policy-deadlock but at an historically low level of capture. Whether deadlock is a viable whale-management non-system in the long-term is an open question. A replacement that potentially could satisfy at least some whaling and anti-whaling factions is that of trading in a yet-to-be-created instrument, the whale quota unit (WQU). In theory this would move quotas to countries that value them the most highly. Under such a system, anti-whaling countries, or entities such as non-government organizations, could end up owning all WQUs; if so, commercial whaling would end, but with compensation paid to commercial whalers. However, as discussed in this chapter, a lot of questions need to be answered about the practical efficacy of such a trading system.

Commercial whaling has passed through a sequence similar to that of commercial fishing – over-hunting crashing the numbers of a targeted stock, moving on and crashing the numbers of the next target. Thus, the annual catch of blue whales peaked at about 30,000 in the early 1930s, thereafter collapsing, and stocks of the next targets, humpbacks, fin and sei whales, collapsed in the 1960s.

The need to manage whale stocks internationally was recognized even before World War II, following the collapse of stocks due to over-hunting in the previous century (Oberthur, 1999). The *International Whaling Commission* was set up in 1948 under the *International Convention for the Regulation of Whaling* (1946) to manage whaling, with the aim of increasing stocks and sustainable harvests. The original idea behind the IWC was therefore to increase direct use values – consumption of whale meat and oil. This was no different from fisheries management, also aimed at increasing stocks and sustainable yield – see Chapters 8 and 9.

However, for about the last forty years the general public has seen whales and whaling differently to fish and fishing, in the sense that whales have significant non-use values (existence, option and bequest, as well as non-consumptive use values) – whale watching in particular. These non-use and non-consumptive values are typically lacking with respect to most fish, though reef fish also have non-consumptive values upon which coral reef tourism is based – see Chapter 16. Whales therefore fall into the category of mixed goods combining private and public good values (Bulte and Van Kooten, 1999; Mazzanti, 2001). Private good values are realized through capture; but non-use values are a public good – as long as whales continue to exist the non-use and non-consumptive values they offer are neither depletable nor excludable.

We will assess how this movement away from whales being just private goods to being mixed goods has complicated whale-stock management at the International Whaling Commission. Also examined are the pros and cons of a WQU trading system, the main question being: could WQU trading maximize the social value of whales?

2   Trend toward reduced whaling

Under the IWC regime quotas and closed seasons have been set, scientific whaling allowed, super-majorities required for rule changes, and commercial whaling, when allowed, restricted to the North Pacific and the North Atlantic – Antarctica was made off-limits in 1994. Hanging over proceedings is that under international law any IWC member can file an "objection", so as not to have to obey specific rules set by the majority. Thus, without a preponderant actor (see Chapter 12) to impose its will, progress has to be sanctioned not only by a super-majority but also by each member of the minority.

Initially, quotas were set in terms of "blue whale units" (bwus), each unit being worth one blue whale, or two fin whales, or 2.5 humpback whales, or six sei whales.

In the 1950s the overall quota was set at 14,500–16,000 bwus, which turned out to be too large to stabilize various whale populations. The quota acted as a total allowable catch (TAC) with no individual country quotas. This, like other TAC schemes, led to a race to "fish" before the quota was filled and the season closed – see Chapter 9 on the economics of TACs. Until 1971 each country was responsible for counting its own catch, but flagrant under-counting was strongly suspected. An international observer system was set up in 1971 with whaling nations observing each other's catches.

Over time, quotas were slowly reduced, with a major reduction in the 1964/65 season and another in 1970. In addition to blue whales and humpbacks that had been protected in 1966, a moratorium on catching fin and sei whales was put into effect in the 1970s. Already, the UK, Norway and the Netherlands had stopped commercial pelagic whaling because it was unprofitable. Today, only Russia and Japan appear to be still interested in it, though reports suggest that Norway could rejoin the industry if it again became profitable.

In 1972 the bwu system was abolished, and in 1974 new regulations to protect severely depleted whale populations were introduced. In 1982, by majority vote, a moratorium on all commercial whaling, starting in 1986, was agreed. Following this moratorium commercial pelagic whaling came to an end, with Norway and the USSR not using objections; Japan even withdrew its right to object. No quotas have been allocated since then. In 1994 a Revised Management Procedure was discussed to establish acceptable commercial catch limits; however, discussions led nowhere and in 2006 the IWC recognized that it had reached an impasse – among other things, there was disagreement on appropriate procedures for monitoring and enforcement, and the USA demanded a perfect monitoring system before agreeing to any resumption of commercial whaling. In 2010 new efforts to revive commercial whaling also failed.

Even without commercial quotas whaling continues; on an annual basis Japan takes about 1,000 whales for "scientific purposes", Norway and Iceland together take about 600 and indigenous people about 350.[2] Also, some whales die from being entangled in fishing gear, are hit by ships, and some may suffer from human-generated low-frequency noise (for example, respectively, Waring et al., 1990; Laist et al., 2001; Natural Resources Defense Council, 2008).

3   Reasons for trend toward protection

There are at least six reasons for this trend toward protecting whales.

1   From 1962 the scientific consensus was that whales were indeed endangered; hence, the 1964 agreement sharply to reduce quotas.
2   Over time, the IWC became packed with non-whaling nations who threatened never to allow the reintroduction of quotas if whaling nations used their

objection rights. Thus, what was once a "whalers club" managing commercial whaling became packed with non-whaling countries; in 1972 the IWC had only 14 members – ten years later when the crucial vote against commercial whaling was taken it had 39.

3   There was an "explosion" of worldwide opinion in favor of "save the whales" – particularly expressed in IWC forums by non-government organizations (NGOs). There were only six NGOs at the 1972 IWC convention, but there were more than 50 by the 1980s.

4   Whaling nations themselves desired *not* to be seen acting in conflict with international opinion.

5   Whale products became of much reduced importance in both protein supply and employment.

6   In a weak reflection of a true preponderant actor, the US tried to exert pressure under 1971 and 1979 laws that ban fish imports and fishing in the US EEZ from and by nations that are not in compliance with international fishery (including whaling) laws. Likewise, under the *Endangered Species Act*, 1973, the US listed many whale species as "endangered" – see Table 15.1; and in 2000, to show its displeasure with Japan's expansion of "scientific" whaling, the US boycotted two Japanese environmental conferences.

TABLE 15.1 Pre-exploitation and recent whales stocks

	Pre-exploitation[f]	Early 2000s[c]	Status[d,e]
Blue whale	More than 200,000	2,300	Endangered[b]
Humpback whale	More than 150,000	141,000	Endangered/depleted
Fin whale	More than 500,000	26,500	Endangered
Sei whale	More than 200,000	50,000	
Sperm whale	2,500,000	850,000[a]	Endangered
Minke whale	Fewer than 500,000 (?)	700,000	Protected
Bowhead whale	More than 50,000	13,500	Endangered
Grey whale	More than 20,000	20,000	Endangered/depleted
Southern right whale	100,000	23,900	Endangered
Northern right whale	More than 45,000	400	Endangered

Notes:

a   Mid-point of estimate in National Marine Fisheries Service (2010);

b   endangered throughout its range, US *Endangered Species Act*;

c   column data from IWC; downloaded May 23rd, 2013, http://iwc.int/status;

d   all cetaceans are protected under the US *Marine Mammal Protection Act* (MMPA); some may be designated as "depleted" under the MMPA. Endangered and threatened cetaceans are further protected under the *Endangered Species Act* (ESA); www.nmfs.noaa.gov/pr/species/mammals/cetaceans/;

e   also named under *The Convention on the International Trade in Endangered Species of Wild Fauna and Flora* (CITES);

f   Oberthur (1999).

4   International law

It is useful briefly to review international law regarding whaling. Article 64 of the *Law of the Sea* applies to highly migratory species including whales and ocean dolphins; it reads as follows:

> The coastal State and other States whose nationals fish in the region for the highly migratory species listed in Annex I[3] shall cooperate directly or through appropriate international organizations with a view to ensuring conservation and promoting the objective of optimum utilization of such species throughout the region, both within and beyond the exclusive economic zone.

Then Article 65 says:

> Nothing in this Part restricts the right of a coastal State or the competence of an international organization, as appropriate, to prohibit, limit or regulate the exploitation of marine mammals more strictly than provided for in this Part. States shall cooperate with a view to the conservation of marine mammals and in the case of cetaceans shall in particular work through the appropriate international organizations for their conservation, management and study.

The main points to stress about these Articles are:

1   As the word "cooperate" is not defined, a signatory country can, within wide bounds, define whatever it is doing with respect to whaling and whale conservation as "cooperation". This point is discussed in some detail in Chapter 1, where it is argued that the signing of a treaty does not necessarily change state behavior – because states agree only to what they want to; moreover, if there are parts of a treaty a state does not like it can make an objection so as not to have to abide by those parts.
2   No property rights in whales are defined; whales remain a common pool resource to be managed under agreement by the members of the IWC.

5   Moving toward maximizing the value of a mixed good

Open access whaling evidently maximizes neither whale capture (use value), witness collapsed whale stocks, nor non-use values (option, existence, bequest). At the same time, some countries, NGOs and people concerned with the public good value of whales see a sharp tradeoff between the consumptive and non-consumptive values of whales. The tradeoff is especially acute at the presently low stock levels – some of which are less than 10 percent of historic levels – see Table 15.1.

A result of clashing values between whaling countries wishing to extract use value, and conservationists wishing to augment the non-use value of whales, is paralysis on the IWC. In 1982 zero commercial quotas were voted at the IWC, but the vote was peculiar in that the anti-whaling vote was increased through the expedient of adding new members pre-committed to voting that way. Three responses from the pro-whaling nations are notable. They, too, recruit new members pre-committed to voting in favor of a resumption of commercial whaling. Second, some, Japan in particular, continue to capture whales for the purpose of selling whale meat under a loophole in the IWC code that allows whaling for the recovery of scientific knowledge. However, the annual harvest is widely recognized as being far beyond what would be a reasonable size for this purpose (Tinch and Phang, 2009). Third, some whaling countries – Norway, Iceland – simply ignore the IWC's zero quotas.

Maximizing the value of a mixed good is problematic, requiring the development of a legal framework to make it possible. It is instructive, therefore, briefly to review the case of another mixed good – historic shipwrecks, where US law had to be reinterpreted to take account of the trade-off (or externality) between use value (treasure that can be monetized) and non-use values (historical knowledge that is difficult to monetize). The case of historic shipwrecks is discussed at length in Chapter 2.

In the USA, admiralty law was initially aimed at recovering only private use values from wrecks with no protection for historical (public good) values other than the treasure. At one time this made sense because the diving technology and the science of underwater archaeology did not exist. All that admiralty law aimed for was to return lost cargoes back to the stream of commerce with suitable rewards for salvagers for their risk-taking.

However, as the science of underwater archaeology progressed, US admiralty courts reinterpreted existing laws with the aim of promoting the recovery of historic knowledge as well as treasure values. Specifically, the courts award larger percentages of the value of treasure recovered the better, in their estimation, the quality of the archaeological work done by salvagers. In other words, the courts moved in the direction of maximizing the value of a mixed good with its two components: use and non-use values.

Similarly, international whaling law was initially designed for the purpose of recovering private use values (whale meat and oil). Then things changed; whales came to have significant non-use values in the minds of many people. The legal framework designed over sixty years ago to maximize private use values is not necessarily sufficient to maximize the combined use and non-use values of a mixed good.

There are two significant differences between the cases of historic shipwrecks and whales as a mixed good. First, while under English common law US admiralty courts have the scope to reinterpret the law in an economically rational direction, the IWC has no such scope. Rather, it has to abide by its constitution, and changes in that constitution have to be voted on by its fractious membership. Second, unlike American admiralty courts, the IWC lacks police powers. So even if the membership voted to move in the direction of maximizing the value of whales as a mixed good, any single member could take a reservation and not abide by the new laws. Both of these considerations make changing international law in the direction of maximizing the value of whales problematic at best.

A possible way to maximize the economic value (use and non-use values taken together) of a common pool mixed good – such as whales – is to create property rights in it, and arrange for the transfer of these rights to those countries, people, firms or institutions that value them most highly. Restricting ourselves to the level of countries, either countries in favor of whale conservation could buy out the rights of whaling countries, or whaling nations could buy the right to continue whaling – or some mixture of the two. Such a legal contract would be enforceable in civil courts if countries chose to write them into national laws, though this would have to be tested. Ultimately, whether whale populations would be (mainly) managed by whaling or conservationist countries would depend on preferences and the willingness of countries to monetize those preferences.

6   Economic analysis of whale quota units (WQUs)

In fact, a system has been suggested to set an overall whale-catch quota and to distribute tradable shares – whale quota units (WQUs) – in it to members of the IWC (Costello, Gaines and Gerber, 2012; Clark and Lamberson, 1982).

These WQUs could either be given away to each member country of the IWC, though non-member countries could well object to giving away a scarce resource to favored countries, or, in the first instance, WQUs could be sold to whomever wanted to buy them – in which case countries currently with (restricted) common pool access to whales might protest.

Leaving initial allocation issues aside, the foregoing proposal has the attractive feature of trade leading to property rights in whales, ending up with those people that value them the most highly. A major stumbling block however is, yet again, that there is no basis in the *Law of the Sea* for such a system.

Also, as Costello, Gaines and Gerber (2012) point out, some non-whaling countries could object because they are fundamentally opposed to any form of commercial whaling. For some people the international whaling regime needs to be changed not in order to maximize the economic value of a mixed good, but to put an end to animal cruelty (see, for example, Verissimo and Metcalfe, 2009).[4] Moreover, whales appear to possess certain human characteristics – high intelligence, self-awareness and, like humans, a spindle cell associated with abstract reasoning.[5] Some people therefore see a moral obligation toward whales and they don't see them as a resource to be hunted and quotas in them traded. Even so, the economics of a tradable WQU system deserves attention.

Supposing international law was amended to award tradable property rights in whales, the outcome would depend on how those rights ended up being allocated between whalers and conservationists. In measuring environmental benefits, values can be ascertained by an individual's willingness to pay to maintain an existing environmental amenity or their willingness to accept compensation for the loss of an amenity (see the Appendix Benefit–Cost Analysis).

If rights to hunt reside with the whalers, the starting point with a common pool resource, then the minimum value of a WQU is determined by hunters' willingness to accept (WTA) compensation for giving up the right to hunt. If the willingness to pay (WTP) of people wanting to protect whales is greater than this WTA a bargain can be struck in which those wanting to protect whales can buy the rights to hunt them from whalers. However, if rights in whales were to reside with those that would protect the species, the economic benefit of a WQU is measured by the WTA of the conservationists. As this could be a very large sum it is problematic that the WTP of whale hunters could be large enough to buy the right to hunt. Indeed, according to Tinch and Phang (2009), in Japan whalers do not cover economic costs even without having to buy WQUs.

7 The Coase theorem and the efficiency of a WQU market

The foregoing discussion is based on the Coase theorem that has been discussed in Chapter 9. It says that as long as property rights exist in a good with some public good characteristics, trade can move ownership to those people that value it the most highly (Coase, 1960). However, there are a number of restrictive assumptions: first, that WTP and WTA can be accurately calculated; second, that the cost of making transactions is low enough to make exchange of property rights practicable; third, that the quality of the good – WQUs – transferred is easily ascertained and is sustainable over time; and fourth, that payments are actually made from buyers to the sellers. If these assumptions hold, there is some presumption that whales will go to those entities that value them most.[6]

The most critical assumption is that the quality of WQUs is easily ascertained. This requires adequate policing of the oceans against pirate whaling, otherwise a conservationist has no guarantee that a WQU bought will in fact lead to less whaling. Without some sort of quality assurance the value of a WQU to conservationists is probably not very much, and they would place only low bids, so leaving the field to whale hunters. To create credibly high-quality WQUs, whale-hunting nations such as Japan, Norway and Iceland, and perhaps Denmark, Russia and the USA, who permit whale-hunting by indigenous people, might have to commit to closing whaling support facilities on their territories *and* not to reopening them in the future. Without this latter commitment the present value of a whale quota unit would be lower than it would otherwise be. This is because its value depends on the flow of expected benefits – the non-use and non-consumptive values – that would be uncertain, and so subjected to higher discount rates.

A related problem is that of credible commitment, on the part of all countries, not to increase the quantity of WQUs once auctioning had finished. Without this assurance the value of a WQU would again be lowered because of uncertainty about future supply. Indeed, according to Cooke, Leaper and Papastavrou (2012), there is some presumption that if whale stocks recovered larger quotas would be allowed, or at least they would if the Revised Management Procedure was adopted.

What these quality control and credibility of commitment assumptions suggest is that for a transferable WQU market system to work properly it needs to be water-tight from the beginning – especially that policing will be adequate, and that the future supply of WQUs is predictable. Realizing this, whaling nations may see that it is in their interests to spread uncertainty about the future development of the system – because uncertainty would lower the price that whale conservationists would be willing to pay (or to accept) for a WQU.

Calculation and funding of WTP and WTA also raises issues. First, who will own the WQUs? Is it the governments of whaling and conservationist countries, or is it entities at the decentralized level of whaling firms and individual people (or their aggregation in NGOs), that believe in whale conservation? If at the government level, how much is offered (WTP) or set as a reservation price (WTA) is essentially a political decision that might not reflect "true" values. For example, a government might feel pressured to bid high (or set a high reservation price) for political rather than economic reasons. Or, perhaps a government at the time WQUs are auctioned happens to face a more severe budget constraint than is normally the case, and therefore bids low.

If, rather, funding was to be decentralized to whaling firms and conservationists, a free rider problem could be encountered, especially on the side of conservationists. With many conservationists, especially as they are scattered around the world, there is an obvious question for each one of them regarding whether their financial contribution to the "pot" will really make any difference. On the side of whaling firms free riding is probably a lesser problem as there are so few of them.

The other two assumptions pertaining to a WQU system – low transfer costs and actually making financial transactions – are not quite so problematic. However, some sort of institutional device would be necessary to keep track of WQU ownership and to affect payments between the parties when WQUs were transferred. Moreover, an accessible registry of WQU ownership would be necessary so as to promote efficacy in policing.

While whalers selling WQUs would lose the right to hunt for those units, they must have been adequately compensated because the transaction would have been voluntary.[7] However, there is another aspect to the question of to whom payments for WQUs should be made. Thus far it has been considered natural that whalers would receive these payments because they have the right to hunt, albeit a constrained right in the IWC. A different approach would be to recognize that the *common heritage of mankind* doctrine has some bearing on who should receive payments made for WQUs. The *common heritage* doctrine influences the *Law of the Sea* in just one place – deep sea mining; and here the benefits of a common pool resource – sea floor polymetallic nodules – are to be shared with the wider international community (see Chapter 23).

It is problematic that the *common heritage* doctrine could be inserted into the whale management debate because, if payments for WQUs were made to, say, the

UN for distribution to all member states, this would be a disincentive for whaling nations to sell WQUs in the first place. However, this point about whales and the *common heritage* doctrine does point to the fact that a WQU trading arrangement – with payments made to sellers, favors a self-selecting small group of countries that have erstwhile laid claim to a high seas common pool resource for their own benefit to the exclusion of the *common heritage* aspect of whales.[8]

8 Conclusions

A fair assessment of the IWC is that it has been quite successful in protecting whale stocks – not through the full agreement of all of its members, but rather through gridlock caused by the need for super-majorities to reintroduce commercial pelagic whaling quotas.[9] This gridlock has come about because whales are widely viewed as mixed goods with both use and non-use values. Because of this the "field" is no longer left to whaling nations. Conservationists also want a say, and indeed have it on the International Whaling Commission, where they easily have a blocking vote.

However, whether gridlock is a sustainable system is open to question. At any point in time whaling nations could exercise their rights under international public law and simply ignore the gridlock and resume commercial whaling. This possibility is the main reason why the regime governing whaling needs to be modified. A system of tradable whale quota units would at least compensate whalers according to their own valuations – their willingness to accept, should they choose to exit, or to reduce their whaling activity. However, we have argued that even a tradable quota system has pitfalls; the sad situation is that no obviously workable system exists to manage pelagic whaling.

Notes

1 Whale meat is first sold by the whalers to the Japanese government under their "scientific" research program; the government on-sells to wholesalers who distribute it to retailers and restaurants (*Economist*, "The politics of whaling", September 7th, 2000).

2 The *Economist*, "Good whale hunting", March 14th, 2012.

3 Annex 1 lists cetaceans as "highly migratory".

4 According to Breach Marine Protection UK (1998) in Norwegian data, once harpooned, about 20 percent of whales take ten minutes or more to die and 2.5 percent escape when the harpoon comes out or with it and the attached rope still attached to them.

5 See *New Scientist*, "Whales boast the brain cells that make us human", November 27th, 2006; and *Economist*, "A declaration of the rights of cetaceans", February 25th, 2012.

6 Freeman (1991) also argues that the value of a resource depends not only on its biological characteristics but also on institutional considerations.

7 Kuronuma and Tisdell (1994) point out that the current ban on commercial whaling is not Hicks-Kaldor welfare efficient – in the sense that whalers are worse off because they have not been compensated for their loss of access. A WQU market system could automatically compensate whalers for loss of access.

8 There is also the matter of to whom payments by whalers should be made if they buy WQU. "To the conservationists" would presumably not be possible as there are so many of them. However, "to the UN" would seem to fit with the *common heritage* notion.

9 See Hurd (2012), who similarly refers to stalemate on the IWC as both a successful and proven stable outcome that has reduced the overall level of annul whale capture.

PART VII

Coral reefs, marine protected areas, wetlands

16

CORAL REEF ECONOMICS

1 Introduction

The tragedy of the commons largely accounts for the declining condition of the world's coral reefs, as in most areas of the world there is little to prevent over-harvesting and habitat destruction. Coral bleaching caused by global warming is also a problem. We might wonder why a large reef fish is worth more alive on the reef than served up on a plate in an expensive hotel: older fish lay disproportion-ately more eggs, so helping to increase reef biomass.[1] Reef fish also perform various ecological services, helping to maintain the ecosystem of a reef by eating algae and seaweed and preventing the corals from being over-grown. Can coral reefs be managed to better health? The device of the marine park discussed in this chapter is useful; the "classic" example is Australia's Great Barrier Reef Marine Park. Even "traditional" social organizations can be used to reduce over-harvesting: in Fiji a Chieftain exercised the right to manage reef fish stocks, withdrew commercial fish-ing licenses, established no-take zones and used scientific knowledge of fish breeding habits and life cycles to set closed seasons. The results were impressive – labor productivity quickly doubled with the same quantity of fish being caught in half the time. Scientific evidence suggests that biomass inside no-take zones doubles in three to five years, and that this also benefits nearby areas.[2]

2 Goods and ecological services of coral reef ecosystems

The four types of coral reef are listed in Box 16.1. While coral reefs cover only 0.1–0.5 percent (255,000 km^2) of ocean floor they supply about one-third of its marine fish species and 10 percent of fish consumed; more than 100 countries have coral reefs and at least 10 million people, mainly living in small island states, depend on them for their livelihoods and/or protein supply.[3] One square km of healthy coral reef can support 300 people (Moberg and Folk, 1999). The same authors point out that "coral reefs are among the most productive and biologically diverse ecosystems on Earth. They supply vast numbers of people with goods and services such as seafood, recreational amenities, coastal protection and aesthetic and cultural benefits" (p. 215).

Renewable goods supplied by coral reefs include seafood, raw materials for medicines, other raw materials such as seaweed for agar and manure, curio and jewelry, live fish, and coral for the aquarium trade. *Non-renewable goods* derive from reef mining mainly for building materials – blocks, rubble and sand.

Ecological services of coral reefs fall into four categories:

1 Physical structure services such as shoreline protection, the promotion of mangroves and seagrass beds, and the generation of coral sand (see Box 16.2).
2 Biotic services within a coral reef ecosystem, especially maintenance of habitats and biodiversity, regulation of ecosystem processes and functions, and biological maintenance of resilience – including for spawning, nursery, breeding, and feeding areas. Coral reefs also offer a large genetic "library".

BOX 16.1 TYPES OF CORAL REEF

- *Platform reefs*: found in lagoons created by barrier and atoll reefs; examples include the Great Barrier Reef lagoon, and areas in the Red Sea, the Bahamas and Belize.
- *Fringing reefs*: follow shorelines; examples include areas in the Red Sea, off East Africa, in the Caribbean and off many Indo-Pacific islands.
- *Barrier reefs*: separated from land by a wide lagoon; examples include the GBR, areas off Belize and Mayotte, and areas in the western Indian Ocean.
- *Atolls*: horseshoe-shaped islands with a central lagoon; 95 percent of them are in the Indo-Pacific.

BOX 16.2   INTERACTIONS OF CORAL REEFS WITH MAN-GROVES AND SEAGRASS BEDS

- Interactions between these are such that damage to one causes damage to the others.
- Coral reefs buffer waves and currents, export landward fish and invertebrate larvae to seagrass beds and mangroves, and seaward supply organic material and nutrients supporting the pelagic (or marine) food web.
- Seagrass beds bind sediments – important because coral reefs need clear water, absorb nutrients (corals need nutrient poor water) and export maturing fish to the coral reefs.
- Mangroves prevent erosion (clear water, again) export fish and crustaceans, absorb nutrients, and interrupt fresh water flow.

---

3   Biotic services between ecosystems – of "mobile" links such as the export of organic matter, and plankton to pelagic food webs (on this see especially Chapter 17). Herbivorous fish and sea urchins move from reefs to seagrass beds, beneficially influencing their plant structures; reefs supply organisms that serve as food for fish caught by commercial fishing, and they support pelagic food webs with export of mucus, wax esters and dissolved organic matter.

4   Biochemical services: nitrogen fixation (important where eutrophication is a problem); sinks for CO_2 over geological time; managing world calcium balance – they precipitate about one-half of calcium delivered to the sea; and waste assimilation, especially of oil.

Near heavily populated or agricultural areas coral reefs suffer from pollution runoff – oil, sewerage, sediment and nutrient loads. Moreover, reefs are very often over-harvested, sometimes by destructive fishing methods using explosives or poisons. Uncontrolled tourism can damage coral reefs – through, for example, trampling and anchor damage. A World Resources Institute study claims that 60 percent of the world's coral reefs are "threatened" by local activities – combined over-fishing and destructive fishing, watershed-based pollution, coastal urban development and marine-based pollution and damage (Burke, 2011). Local threats are most prevalent in South East Asia and the Caribbean, and least prevalent in Australia and the Pacific. As coral reefs are also being damaged by global warming and ocean acidification, coral resilience is being lost and recovery from environmental and human impacts is weakened. About 75 percent of all coral reefs are under pressure from these local or global causes (Burke, 2011). Bellwood et al. (2004) point to a marked loss in the resilience of coral reefs, defined as "their ability to absorb shocks, resist phase shifts and regenerate after natural and human-induced disturbances"

(p. 827). In their view, a critical problem is over-fishing – indeed, removal of preda-tor fishes, such as groupers, and species that "clean" the reefs (scrapping grazers) has unbalanced reef ecosystems by allowing them to be taken over by algae, seaweeds or crown of thorns star fish.

3 Measuring the economic value of coral reefs

The Appendix to this book discusses some theoretical aspects of benefit–cost analy-sis that are relevant to the rest of this chapter.

Economists look at coral reefs as a natural resource offering both use and non-use values. There are two types of *direct use value*: direct consumption value (as with the consumption of reef fish) and extraction values (as with collectable corals). Market prices and quantities can be used to measure these values. Direct non-consumption values, such as eco-tourism, can be measured in various ways: if available, by market prices and quantities, and if not, willingness to pay (WTP) can be estimated by travel cost, contingent valuation, or hedonic price index methods.

Non-use values are values placed on a resource independent of current use. There are three non-use values: a) option value, or the value of having a resource available for future use: "I don't want to dive on a reef this year but sometime in the next five years there is a good chance that I will"; b) existence value – "I may never visit a coral reef but I do value the continued existence of coral reefs in good condition"; c) bequest value – "I place a value on coral reefs as I want future generations to be able to enjoy them". Bequest value comes close to the idea of sustainable development. Sustainable development is the idea that use should not deplete a renewable resource so much that it will be unavailable to future generations. Technically, this asserts that very low or zero discount rates should be applied to future expected benefits.

A problem with calculating non-use values is discovering how much and how many people would actually pay when, in fact, they don't have to. The travel cost method values a resource by collecting data on visitors' travel costs to a given desti-nation – a coral reef, say. Travel costs proxy for willingness to pay and, given a large enough sample of visitors, a demand curve can be traced out. Contingent valuation can be used to ascertain non-market prices as well as option, existence and bequest values. CV uses the method of the questionnaire to inquire into values placed by individuals on a given resource. It may be possible to calculate a hedonic price index in the case of multi-attribute goods. For example, a beachfront house sup-plies various goods, such as living space, closeness to schools, quality of ocean water and quality of ocean view. If data is available on houses from districts that combine these in different amounts, statistical methods can be used to value each variable – how much is a view of clean ocean water worth? Such a valuation could be used to calculate benefits of reducing sediment runoff into the ocean. As an example, the non-use value of Solomon Island reefs, which was calculated from respondents' willingness to contribute time, money or food to maintain coral reef health, lies between \$1,200–\$7,700 per km^2 reef per year (Research Program, 2012).

4 Some economic valuations of coral reefs

Here are some values that have been put on coral reefs by various researchers. Cesar, Burke and Pet-Soede (2003) put the worldwide annual value of coral reef tourism and recreation at $10 billion, out of a total valuation of $29 billion (not including non-use values).

The recreational value of the two million people visiting Australia's Great Barrier Reef each year is estimated to be between $700 million and $1.6 billion (Carr and Mendelsohn, 2003).

In Belize the annual economic contribution of coral reefs in 2007 is put at between $270 million and $370 million, mainly in the form of tourism and recreation and shoreline protection, with fisheries making a smaller contribution (Burke, 2011).

Tourist spending in South Pacific Forum countries amounts to over $700 million per annum and on some islands (e.g. Cook and Fiji) tourism is the main component of GDP (Lal, 2005).

Arin and Kramer (2002) asked visitors to three reef areas in the Philippines how much they would be willing to pay as access fees in excess of their existing costs – such as international travel and hotels. On Mactan Island potential revenues were estimated to lie between $850,000 and $1 million. If collected, these revenues could be used for reef management purposes.

Values of coral reefs as coastal defense have been calculated as the cost of building beach defenses to replace reef lost to coral mining. Thus, a hotel in West Lombok spent $880,000 to replace 250 meters of mined reef; and the average cost of building beach defenses in Sri Lanka made necessary because of coral mining was up to $836,000 per km of coast line (Cesar and Chiew Kieok Chong, 2005).

Pham Khanh Nam and Tran Vo Hung Son (2005) performed a benefit–cost analysis (BCA) of the effect of a nearby port expansion on coral reefs in the Hon Mun Islands in Vietnam. The benefits of the port-expansion were measured as the expected increase in the port's annual revenues of $3.1 million. Costs were assessed as the loss of expenditures by tourists visiting the islands. To find these values, both travel cost and contingent valuation methods were used. They found that total tourist expenditure in the islands was between $8.7 and $17.9 million. The authors conclude that even a 20 percent fall in tourist revenues would outweigh their estimate of the benefit of the port expansion and that "the port expansion proposal needs to be reconsidered".

Brown et al. (2001) involved major stakeholders in a "multi-criteria analysis" (economic, social and ecological) to set management objectives for the use of the Buccoo Reef Marine Park, Tobago, in the Caribbean. They claimed that this approach, previously applied to land-use analysis, had the advantage of recognizing non-pecuniary values that can be overlooked in BCA. 1,000 visitors and residents were interviewed using a contingent valuation methodology to estimate WTP to prevent loss in water-, coral- and fish viewing quality. The key finding was that reef valuation was highest (as measured by the size of consumers' surplus) if "complementary environmental management" was combined with maintenance of the then level of tourists. Across stakeholder groups – informal sector workers, recreational users and regulatory agency officials – there was consistency in this view. This finding suggests that management aimed at this object may be broadly accepted as "legitimate", so increasing stakeholder support for the objective. Unrestrained tourism development with no environment management was given the lowest ranking.

Hanauma Bay coral reef

Cesar et al. (2004) performed a benefit–cost analysis on an investment to protect the Hanauma Bay coral reef, O'ahu, Hawaii. The over one million visitors per year were damaging the reef through feeding the fish (thereby changing the natural balance of fishes), trampling the corals, stirring up sediment, dropping trash, and creating a suntan oil slick. Educating visitors was seen as a way to reduce these externalities, requiring spending $13.5 million on an education center with a $500,000 per annum operating expense. Over a fifty-year time horizon and 4 percent discount rate the present value of these costs was $29 million. But was this expenditure worth it?

Expert opinion was that, without the education center, coral cover would slowly decline from 27 percent to 19 percent of the reef, but would remain constant with it. Keeping the coral cover as it was would maintain the quality of the diving experience, allow more visitors for the same stress level, create positive fisheries spillover, increase biodiversity, and create an educational spillover to other reefs when divers visited them.

Annual benefits of the with-education versus without-education scenarios were calculated through a questionnaire designed to elicit increases in WTP and taking the form of acceptable increases in hypothetical user-fees. The present value of these benefits, calculated on the same basis as the present value of costs, was $100 million – indicating a 3.5 benefit–cost ratio. At a 1 percent discount rate this ratio increased to 7. Either ratio justified investment in the education project, which was, in fact, built in 2002.

5 The Montego Bay study

The 43-hectare coral reef in Montego Bay, Jamaica, has been adversely affected by runoff pollution. A World Bank (1999) study inquired into the value of its benefits and the cost of restoration.

The study found that the reef's use value (tourism, fishing and coastal protection) had a net present value (or social surplus) of $381 million, calculated as the sum of the values of tourism and recreation ($315 million), fisheries ($1.31 million) and coastal protection ($65 million). A further $19.6 million was added for the value of

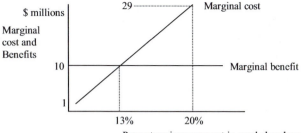

FIGURE 16.1 Calculating optimal coral reef improvement – Montego Bay

biodiversity. Altogether, the total net present value of the reef came to $401 million, translating into $893,000 per hectare of reef per year.

The study also found that the value of a 1 percent *improvement* in coral abundance was about $10 million. This is the *marginal benefit* of improvement – as shown in Figure 16.1. Moreover, marine scientists estimated that it was biologically feasible to increase coral abundance by 20 percent.

The present value of the cost of improving coral abundance by the full 20 percent was estimated at $153 million. This cost included expenditures on installation of sewage outfall, improved household solid waste treatment and better waste management by the tourist hotel industry. *Marginal cost* per 1 percent improvement in coral abundance increased from about $1 million to $29 million as coral abundance increased.[4]

Equating the marginal cost and marginal benefits of increasing coral abundance in Montego Bay indicated that a 13 percent increase in abundance was optimal.[5]

The value of biodiversity per species was estimated to be $8,000. The same World Bank (1999) study also inquired into the value of the reef for bio-prospecting by pharmaceutical companies, finding that this was about $225,000 per 1 percent improvement in coral abundance. However, the study concluded that adding this benefit to the other benefits already reported left the optimal improvement at 13 percent.

6 Marine parks

Though the size of a marine protected area is often determined as a political bargain between stakeholders, it is more appropriate to take into account biological factors. Concentrating on biological factors, Kenchington (1990) and Boersma and Parrish (1999) say that the appropriate size of an MPA depends on either or both site fidelity (how attached an adult animal is to a given site) and site dispersal. Marine protected areas are appropriate for three classes of marine animals: 1) animals that have both a restricted territorial adult phase and reproduction that does not use plank-tonic larvae; 2) animals that have a restricted territorial phase but with a planktonic phase (e.g. corals, shore crabs, lobsters); or the reverse, 3) a widely disbursed adult phase but restricted breeding grounds – e.g. turtles, sea birds, seals (for some parts of the year), whales (needing calving areas) and fish (needing spawning areas, such as salt marshes – see Chapter 18). Not suited for protection by a marine park are high seas species such as tuna. As to fisheries, according to some experts biological factors suggest that marine protected areas need to be between 20 and 70 percent of a fishing ground.[6] Finally, in the bioeconomic model of Holland and Brazee (1996) optimal reserve size is simply stated as that which maximizes the present value of the harvests.

As the following discussion of the Great Barrier Reef Marine Park shows, man-aging coral reef resources through the device of the marine park can be successful. It is estimated, however, that only about 25 percent of the world's coral reefs are included in marine parks, and that only a minority of these are managed effectively (Burke, 2011). Australia and the USA account for over two-thirds of the world's coral reef protected areas (Bellwood et al., 2004).

The Great Barrier Reef Marine Park

Off the Queensland coast in northeastern Australia, the GBRMP, at 345,000 km^2, is almost the size of California. It spans 14 degrees of latitude from the Queensland coast to up to 300 km out. It is a mix of 2,900 reefs and 940 islands and coral cays. Reef size varies from less than one hectare to 100 km^2. It includes coral reefs, mangrove estuaries, seagrass beds, algal and "sponge" gardens, sandy and muddy bottoms, continental slope, and deep ocean troughs – each of these offering differ-ent types of ecosystems for marine life.

Governance

The *Great Barrier Reef Marine Park Act 1975* set up the GBRMP Authority, which was created to provide for the protection, wise use, understanding and enjoyment of the GBR in perpetuity. In 1979 the Commonwealth (Federal) and Queensland state governments agreed to share governance. In 1981 the first GBR Zoning Plan was devised as the "cornerstone" of GBR management. The main objectives set out in the legislation were: conservation of the GBR; regulation to allow reason-able human use and protection; minimization of the effect of resource exploitation on the GBR; preservation of some areas undisturbed by humans; and field based, day-to-day management, funded by the two governments, with various agencies involved in day-to-day operations – the Queensland Boating and Fishery Patrol, Queensland Water Police, the Australian Customs Service, and the Australian Mari-time Safety Authority.

The zones

New zones were drawn in 2004 and permitted activities are shown in Table 16.1.[7] One of the most significant features of this rezoning was to increase the area of no-take zones from about 5 percent to 33 percent of the marine park. For illustrative purposes Box 16.3 shows the boundaries of the zone around Lady Elliot Island in the southern part of the GBR.

TABLE 16.1 GBRMP Zones and restrictions on use*

	Zone 1	Zone 2	Zone 3	Zone 4	Zone 5	Zone 6	Zone 7
Aquaculture	No	No	No	No	Permit	Permit	Permit
Bait netting	No	No	No	No	Yes	Yes	Yes
Boating, diving, photography	No	Yes	Yes	Yes	Yes	Yes	Yes
Crabbing (trapping)	No	No	No	No	Limited	Yes	Yes
Harvest fishing for aquarium fish, coral and beachworm	No	No	No	No	Permit	Permit	Permit
Harvest fishing for sea cucumber, trochus, tropical rock lobster	No	No	No	No	No	Permit	Permit
Limited collecting	No	No	No	No	Yes	Yes	Yes
Limited impact research	Permit	Yes	Yes	Yes	Yes	Yes	Yes
Limited spearfishing (snorkel only)	No	No	No	No	Yes	Yes	Yes
Line fishing	No	No	No	No	Limited	Yes	Yes
Netting (other than bait netting)	No	No	No	No	No	Yes	Yes
Research (other than limited impact)	Permit	Permit	Permit	Permit	Permit	Permit	Permit
Shipping (other than a designated shipping area)	No	Permit	Permit	Permit	Permit	Permit	Yes
Tourism program	No	Permit	Permit	Permit	Permit	Permit	Permit
Traditional use of marine resources	No	Permit	Permit	Permit	Permit	Permit	Permit
Trawling	No	No	No	No	No	No	Yes
Trolling	No	No	No	Yes	Yes	Yes	Yes

*The zones are: 1 Preservation Zone; 2 Marine National Park Zone – e.g. Lady Elliot Island;
3 Scientific Research Zone; 4 Buffer Zone; 5 Conservation Park Zone; 6 Habitat Protection Zone –
e.g. Lady Musgrave Island; 7 General Use Zone.

BOX 16.3   MARINE NATIONAL PARK ZONE

6.157 [MNP-23-1169] Lady Elliot Island Reef (24-008)
   The area bounded by a line commencing at 23° 55.200′ S, 152° 35.999′ E
then running progressively:

 1   southeasterly along the geodesic to 24° 04.800′ S, 152° 48.000′ E;
 2   south along the meridian to its intersection with latitude 24° 10.800′ S;
 3   west along the parallel to its intersection with longitude 152° 37.800′ E;
 4   south along the meridian to its intersection with latitude 24° 13.798′ S;
 5   south along the meridian to its intersection with latitude 24° 19.984′ S;
 6   west along the parallel to its intersection with longitude 152° 12.000′ E;
 7   north along the meridian to its intersection with latitude 24° 07.965′ S;
 8   east along the parallel to its intersection with longitude 152° 22.800′ E;
 9   north along the meridian to its intersection with latitude 23° 55.593′ S;
10   easterly along the geodesic to the point of commencement.

There are seven types of zone; in order of strictness of conservation they are:

1   *Preservation Zone* (0.2 percent of GBRMP area): a "no–go", no extraction area; scientific research is allowed with a permit. Provides high-level protection for unique places, habitats, plants and animals within the Marine Park and provides an undisturbed "baseline" for comparison with other zones.

2   *Marine National Park Zone* (33 percent): a "no–take" area; extractive activities (fishing, collecting) only with written permission; swimming is allowed. The aim is to protect biodiversity, important breeding and nursery areas such as seagrass beds, mangrove communities, deepwater shoals and reefs.

3   *Scientific Research Zone* (0.05 percent): similar to a Marine National Park zone; public access is allowed and scientific research is allowed with a permit.

4   *Buffer Zone* (2.9 percent): for the protection and conservation of areas of the Marine Parks in their natural state by limiting accidental incursions; trolling for pelagic fish species is allowed, but all other forms of fishing such as bottom and spear-fishing are prohibited.

5   *Conservation Park Zone* (1.5 percent): limited extractive use – line, trolling, spear, bait-netting, crabbing and limited collecting (excludes taking of coral dead or alive).

6   *Habitat Protection Zone* (28.2 percent): zoned to be free of damaging activities, especially trawling, but allows "reasonable activities".

7   *General Use Zone* (33.8 percent): reasonable use but still aiming at conservation.

Zone markings

An important aspect of any zoning layout is that zones are clearly marked – to prevent accidental intrusions and to reduce the cost of policing. However, boundary marking is difficult in the ocean, where permanent features are usually unavailable. To make the zones easier to identify a Great Barrier Reef Zoning SD Memory Card has been developed that carries colored-zone charts to aid navigators. Individual zone names are displayed in the information panel on the map screen where the present position is also recorded; as a ship moves a cursor moves across that area of the chart.[8]

Policing costs

From a conservationist's point of view, the more zones there are, the more fine-grained the ecological targets can be. However, high policing costs argue against too fine-grained zoning. The next chapter looks at the policing cost issue in detail.

7 Improvement in biomass

There is good evidence that zoning around Australian coral reefs is effective: coral trout (grouper) numbers rebounded by 31 to 75 percent on a majority of reefs which have been closed to fishing for as little as 1.5 to two years. Also, closed inshore reefs in the Palm and Whitsunday Islands off the coast of North Queensland showed increases in coral trout population densities of 65 and 75 percent respectively, compared with paired reefs left open to fishing.[9]

A detailed survey of research by McCook et al. (2010) found that zoning had significant positive effects on the biomass of reef fish. Thus,

1   One study found that there was a two-fold increase in coral trout biomass appearing within two years of the implementation of the 2004 rezoning on sampled protected reefs, and fish were found to be larger.
2   Three surveys of deep coral reef-based habitats found that coral trout, red emperor and red throat emperor were all more abundant on no-take reefs compared with open access reefs.
3   A large-scale study of offshore reefs found that no-take reefs had more, larger, and older fish than did reefs open to fishing. A different study of reef sharks found the same thing with respect to whitetip and gray reef sharks, where shark abundance increased by between four and thirty times.
4   A study compared pre-2004 fished, no-take, and no-entry zones and confirmed the benefits of no-take zones. However, the study also showed that coral trout, the red throat emperor, and tropical snappers were markedly more abundant and coral trout were larger in no-entry zones than in no-take zones. McCook et al. (2010) suggest that these findings indicate that illegal fishing was probably

occurring in no-take zones but was less prevalent in no-entry zones. The reason, they suggest, is that policing of no-take take zones is more difficult than no-entry zones – wrongdoers are easier spot in the latter.

McCook et al. (2010) conclude that their "comprehensive review of available evidence [on large-scale networks of marine reserves] shows major, rapid benefits of no-take areas for targeted fish and sharks, in both reef and non-reef habitats, with potential benefits for fisheries as well as biodiversity conservation".[10]

In a different area Polunin and Roberts (1993) found on two coral reef protected sites, one in the Netherlands Antilles and the other in Belize, that four years after commercial fishing was stopped the stock of visible demersal target fishes was 1.9 to 2.0 times greater in biomass and 2.2 to 3.5 times greater in commercial value than in fished sites.

8 Marine protected areas in the USA

In June 2006 President Bush by executive order created the Northwestern Hawaiian Islands National Marine Monument. It is the largest marine park in the world at 140,000 square miles around ten islands to the northwest of the main Hawaiian group. Included is 4,500 square miles of coral reef – 69 percent of the US total – and protected from fishing and oil drilling are 7,000 marine species. Eighty percent of commercial fishing had to be stopped immediately and the rest over five years.[11] In August 2010 the World Heritage Committee of the United Nations Educational, Scientific and Cultural Organization designated the Monument a World Heritage site.

The Executive order side-stepped the *National Marine Sanctuaries Act* (1972). This had created 13 very small marine sanctuaries (0.5 percent of US territorial waters), and is anyway largely ineffective because, to satisfy commercial fishing interests, commercial fishing is in fact allowed virtually throughout the 13 sanctuaries. As Bellwood et al. (2004) observe, "In the United States . . . there are . . . modest plans to increase [no-take zones] to incorporate 20 percent of reefs . . . a clear case of too little, too late" (p. 831).

9 How big should a protected zone be?

Bellwood and Hughes (2001) argue that the species-habitat targeting typical of many marine parks is too narrowly focused. On the basis of their study of coral reefs across the Indo-Pacific Oceans they find that small marine protected areas are only a good first step and that protection for coral reefs should be more holistic. They find that coral reef size is a predictor of coral reef biodiversity, and that unless a whole reef is protected there is a risk that the biodiversity of the entire reef could suffer. Moreover, their evidence suggests that that coral reef biodiversity across the whole Indo-Pacific Ocean is interconnected – especially by organisms such as plankton and sponge pieces that float between them. Thus, destruction of even one coral reef may cause reduction in the biodiversity of other reefs.

One implication of this analysis is that coral reef management at the national level may not be on a sufficiently large scale. As Bellwood and Hughes (2001) put it, "even the largest [no-take zones] in the world are not self-sustaining, because they are too small relative to the scale of natural and human disturbances, and to the dispersal distances of many larvae and migrating adults". The implication is that international agreement on the management of coral reefs is needed and this, of course, raises a fresh set of challenges – as we have repeatedly argued, the record of international cooperation in the face of external diseconomies is not particularly good.

Notes

1 See McCook et al. (2010), p. 18279.
2 Data from The *Economist*, November 2nd, 2000.
3 Burke (2011) estimates that about 275 million live within 30 km of coral reefs.
4 World Bank (1999), Table 3.1a.
5 World Bank (1999), p. 148.
6 See Sumaila (2002) and Ward, Heinemann and Evans (2001).
7 Australian Government (2003) "Great Barrier Reef Marine Park ZONING PLAN 2003", Great Barrier Reef Marine Park Authority; available at www.gbrmpa.gov.au/__data/assets/pdf_file/0016/10591/Zoning_Plan.pdf.
8 For more information see www.magellan.com.au.
9 GBRMP Authority, July 2008; available at www.icriforum.org/secretariat/ICRSGM/pdf/GM_ICRS_MR_GBRMPA.pdf.
10 McCook et al. (2010).
11 *The Economist*, "George Bush makes a surprising stand for marine wildlife", June 22nd, 2006.

17

MARINE PROTECTED AREAS, OPTIMAL POLICING AND OPTIMAL RENT DISSIPATION[1]

1   Introduction
2   The basic economic model
3   Zoning
4   Modeling a rent profile
5   Policing activity
6   The effect of some exogenous events on the equilibrium solution
7   Conclusions

1   Introduction

Many marine scientists think that enough is known about marine biology for the scientific positioning of marine protected areas (MPAs) to protect marine environments, so creating associated biological and economic values.[2] To select from a large literature, Ward, Heinemann and Evans (2001) review 89 research papers and claim this for "high topographic" areas such as coral reefs. Auster and Shackell (2000) claim it for "low topography" areas, as, for example, in the Gulf of Maine. Ward, Heinemann and Evans (2001) point to scientific evidence on a "reserve effect", a "spillover effect" and an "export effect" of MPAs. The "reserve effect" occurs within an MPA. The improved habitat offered by protection from invasive fishing activity has been recorded to cause greater spawning, settlement, and larval and juvenile survival; lower fish mortality; and greater mean age, density, biomass and reproductive potential. Resulting from these is also a "stability effect" that takes the form of reduced yield variability and chances of population crashes.

Translating these biological-physical effects into economic terms, economic values within an MPA are known to increase in "before–after" comparisons. The "spillover effect" is in the form of a net movement of larvae, young fish and adults out of an MPA that causes increased local fish density and local fish catches. The export effect is the scientific basis of the "source-sink" model developed below. The "export effect" refers to the net outward movement of larvae such that there is increased regional recruitment and increased regional catch. As both the spillover and export effects potentially increase economic values outside of an MPA there is an external economy from one geographic area to another. Bellwood and Hughes's (2001) research on coral reefs describes the large scale of the export effect. They find that the most important predictor of diversity in coral and fish species on the coral reefs researched by them was the incidence of suitable reef habitats within 600 km of the site – biological spatial inter-connectedness being maintained by the movement of fish and plankton. See also Knowlton (2001, and references therein). Auster and Shackell (2000) survey research on temperate and boreal low topography demersal fish assemblages in the Northwest Atlantic. They conclude that these zoological assemblages can be stable in both ocean space and over time – though they do note that assemblage boundaries can change if the taxa are disturbed by exogenous events such as over-fishing or changes in ocean conditions such as water temperature. Nevertheless, these authors claim that "fish assemblage boundaries can serve as the primary filter for selection of MPA sites" (p. 423). They also identify other site selection markers. Thus, sites should be chosen as far as possible with mixed ocean floors (sand, rock, gravel, cohesive sediments) with the aim of maximizing both the number of species included and species interactions – so promoting the development of a wider ecosystem than just one or a few target species. Moreover, Auster and Shackell (2000) say that there is a case for setting some MPAs over spawning areas and where juveniles congregate.

Recently, several bioeconomic models of MPAs have been developed that are largely concerned with simulating effects of MPAs on biomass inside a no-take zone, and whether aggregate harvests will increase or diminish following the introduction of a closed zone – see Beattie et al. (2002); Boncoeur et al. (2002); Hannesson (1998); Holland (2000); Holland and Brazee (1996); Pezzey, Roberts and Urdal (2000); Polacheck (1990); Rodwell et al. (2002); Sanchirico and Wilen (1999, 2001, 2002); and Smith and Wilen (2003). It is acknowledged in this literature that a desirable objective of an MPA is to maximize economic rent in a fishery in the ocean space adjacent to a closed zone – i.e. to attain maximum economic yield (MEY) in the remaining "open" areas.

Several economic studies acknowledge that MPAs need to be policed and that enforcement costs will be incurred (Hall, Hall and Murray, 2002; Milon, 2000; National Research Council, 2001; Pezzey, Roberts and Urdal, 2000; and Polacheck, 1990). Acknowledgement of policing costs changes the objective function from straightforward maximization of economic rent, to maximization of economic rent net of policing cost. This chapter offers what I think is the first model of an MPA in which the objective function is to maximize this latter function. As Homans and Wilen (1997) observe, to understand fisheries management it is important not only to consider the underlying marine biology, but also to examine the dynamics that may exist between a fishery and other economic values that may be contained in an MPA, and the regulatory apparatus. This chapter is an attempt to do so.

Given the vastness of ocean space that may have to be policed – the Great Barrier Reef Marine Park is approximately the size of California – policing costs are not necessarily trivial. Policing can also be presumed to become more complicated and costly when an MPA encompasses more than just two zones. Indeed, NMFS (2003) points out that policing costs may even depend on the shape of an MPA – straight line boundaries being easiest to police. Policing costs as a positive function of the number of zones that a larger area is divided into is assumed in Demsetz (1967) – a seminal paper on zoned property rights – and Field (1989). Farrow (1996) and Sanchirico and Wilen (2002) discuss the idea of the equalization of social costs of invasive human activities between defined areas of ocean space within a "greater" MPA.[3] It is also worthwhile mentioning that policing costs have featured in the *International Whaling Agreement* to the effect that it was deemed so costly to place monitors on each whaling boat that effective monitoring of catch was difficult or impossible to achieve. In other words, policing costs are known to influence choices over ocean governance arrangements.

As mentioned above, it is an open question whether the introduction of a no-take zone increases or reduces aggregate harvests: even as harvests in the open zone increase, they may not increase enough to offset harvests lost to the closed zone. In this chapter it is simply assumed that economic rent in the open zone (or zones) increases at some point in time following the creation of an MPA, and that the objective is the maximization of this economic rent subject to policing cost.[4] However, the aggregate harvest issue is an interesting one for the policing cost issue in a broader context than the one investigated in this chapter. Thus, if one sets an objective of maximizing economic rent net of policing cost from the entirety of ocean space (say, out to a sovereign's 200-mile exclusive economic zone – where it has the right to police), the matter of choice *between* governance regimes becomes the central issue. Such an analysis might show that an individual, transferable quota-cum-policing model yields higher social value than does an MPA-cum-policing model. However, this type of evaluation is much more ambitious than is attempted here, where our attention is focused on understanding how policing costs may affect social returns from an MPA.

Consideration of the economic value of ocean policing activity must distinguish between rent dissipation through legal and illegal activities. The well-documented practices of capital stuffing, high grading and Derby fishing that are associated with management practices such as the use of shortened fishing seasons and fishing quotas are legal ways in which economic rents are known to be dissipated – see Chapter 9. Policing against such legal activities does not arise. However, economic rents may be protected, and perhaps should be protected, through institutional arrangements that if properly policed are not necessarily subjected to rent dissipation. Included among these are zoning prohibitions and the creation of property rights in ocean resources.[5]

In the following discussion, what is optimized is policing expenditure against *illegal* rent dissipation activities – "poaching" for short. Thus, a critical assumption in the following analysis is prior to (or, at least, simultaneous with) the introduction of rent-sustaining institutional devices that – with effective policing – actually sustain marine resource economic rents. A theoretical result derived in the following analysis is that in the presence of positive marginal policing costs maximization of economic yield (MEY) is not the correct objective. Rather the correct objective is to maximize sustainable economic rent net of policing cost.

2   The basic economic model

The following examination of MPAs is concerned with several factors – namely, the case for no-take zones and spatially graduated admission of human activities, the effect of zoning on sustainable economic rents, and the optimal policing of an MPA. To analyze these factors a simple model is developed based upon the following equation:

$$V = f(x, h) \quad f_x < 0, f_h < 0 \tag{1}$$

where V is the monetary value of sustainable economic rent available from a well-sited and well-managed MPA. The term x signifies distance from the center of a no-take zone, which is itself sited in the center of the MPA, and h is the rate of a pre-defined human activity – say, fishing using a given technique.

The negative signs on the partial derivatives, f_x and f_h, indicate, respectively, that sustainable rent falls as distance from the center of an MPA increases, and that higher rates of human activity degrade economic rent. The first of these assumptions is consistent with the biological studies cited earlier, in that biological spillovers from a no-take zone decline with distance. Also, it is a matter of common observation that $f_h < 0$ – namely that over-fishing degrades economic rent.[6]

The economic analysis of the features described by equation (1) proceeds sequentially, beginning with how the impact of human activity, in combination with ocean biological conditions, makes restricted zoned access rational economic policy.

3   Zoning

The economic case for zoning activities – banning some or all human activities from specific areas – follows from non-convexity in the production possibility frontier (Helfand and Rubin, 1994). Thus, a pair of activities is incompatible when the opportunity cost of one, measured in terms of what is given up of the other, falls. An example is trawling and the richness of an ocean floor habitat. Even one pass of a trawler can so substantially destroy a rich habitat as to render it almost worthless from an ecological point of view (Auster and Shackell, 2000). A similar non-convexity can also exist between coral reef habitat and tourism, since the constant dropping of anchors and taking of specimens can substantially degrade a reef.

Given declining marginal social cost of an activity, the job of a zoning board, using some sort of estimate of willingness to pay, is to determine the appropriate allocation of a given tract between incompatible activities. A corner solution would be to separate incompatible activities to different zones. This is exactly what has happened in the ocean zoning of the Great Barrier Reef Marine Park (Day, 2002), where there is a fine separation of human activities into seven distinct zones. It is also the case with many other MPAs around the world where, for example, all fishing activity is banned within a defined zone, with regulated fishing, or even open access, allowed outside of that zone.

Using equation (1) the case for zoning can be modeled as an attempt by policymakers to equate the marginal social cost of a given human activity across ocean space. As mentioned before, $f_h < 0$ signifies that a given human activity destroys sustainable rent. Therefore, dV/dh measures the marginal social cost of the given human activity. Marginal social cost can be supposed to vary according to spatial variations in ocean conditions. For example, trawling will have a higher social cost in an area with a rich ocean floor habitat than in one where natural habitat conditions are not so rich.[7] Thus, in *absolute* terms, according to ocean conditions:

$$\frac{dV^1}{dh} > \frac{dV^2}{dh} > \frac{dV^3}{dh} > \cdots > \frac{dV^n}{dh} \tag{2}$$

where the superscript designates a numbered zone. If the objective is to minimize the total social cost of a human activity, or to accept some given amount of sustainable rent degradation, maintenance of the inequalities in equation (2) is not rational policy.[8] Rather, the human activity should be shunted out of those zones where its marginal social cost, measured by dV^i/dh, is relatively high to where it is lower, so reducing the total social cost of the activity. Such a policy of regulated access requires monitoring and policing and, presumably, the greater is the number of different types of zones that have to be policed, the greater will be policing costs. This is especially so when different types of human activities are allowed/disallowed in different zones.

4 Modeling a rent profile

In this section attention turns to the modeling of sustainable economic rent and the economic consequences of biological spillovers. There are several ways to model the economic consequence of an MPA with associated biological and economic spillovers. A simple source-sink model is used here to illustrate the main points.

In Figure 17.1 distance from the center of a closed zone is measured on the x-axis, and rent per square unit area (say, per acre) of ocean floor is measured in dollars on the y-axis. The function f(x) measures sustainable economic rent per

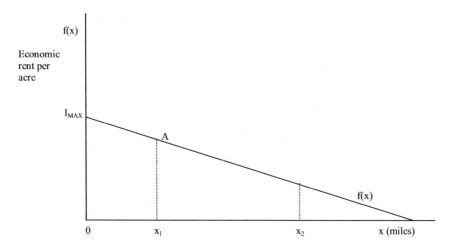

FIGURE 17.1 Potential sustainable economic benefits of a closed zone

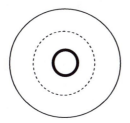

The inner circle in bold represents a closed zone. The inner broken-line circle
marks the outer boundary of a restricted zone. The remainder of the area is un-zoned.

FIGURE 17.2 A designated area with a central closed zone

unit area as depending on absolute distance from the center of the closed zone.
This declining function is consistent with the assumption that the value of positive
spillovers from the closed zone declines with distance. In equation (1), $f_x < 0$. It
should be emphasized that Figure 17.1 represents a cross-section through the center
of a "designated geographic area" shown in Figure 17.2 – which is drawn circular
only to simplify the calculations below. The function $f(x)$ can be thought of as the
outer edge of a profile (or side elevation) of sustainable economic rent that exists in
three-dimensional space with its highest point centered over the origin.

The rate of economic rent, $f(x)$, is sustainable in the sense that human users can
obtain it period after period. For example, rent is sustainable if fishers take only
the annual growth in biomass, or if hobbyist divers do not interfere with the ocean
objects that they view.

As the baseline case, suppose that the designated geographic area in Figure 17.2 is initially inefficiently managed to the extent that fishers and other human users of it reduce economic rent everywhere to zero. This assumption is consistent with the theory of the open access fishery as discussed in Chapter 8, and is assumed in many of the bioeconomic models cited earlier. It is also approximately consistent with the analysis of fisheries that use a total allowable catch in combination with fishing restrictions such as of type of gear, number of boats, or number of workers per boat. Thus, in order to capture the increased economic rents afforded by the catch limit, fishers engage in rent-destroying practices such as capital stuffing and Derby fishing (Chapter 9).

In order to increase economic rent from the baseline (zero) level a closed zone is introduced over a biologically productive area chosen on the basis of the considerations discussed earlier. In Figure 17.1 the distance $0x_1$ indicates the closed zone. It is assumed that, with time, the biological productivity of the closed zone increases – ultimately to its maximum monetary level, I_{MAX}. Such an assumption is consistent with the relevant field studies discussed, for example, by Ward, Heinemann and Evans (2001).

An observed problem with closed zones that are not accompanied with other zoning measures is that fishers will fish intensively right up to the edge of the closed zone. This is an example of "fishery displacement" by fishers excluded from the no-take zone, and is a familiar assumption in bioeconomic models. Such intensive fishing effort (and possibly other human activities such as diving and anchor damage) destroys the potential sustainable economic rent beyond x_1. If this is the case the rent profile becomes $I_{MAX}Ax_1x_2$ – which is obviously less than it could be along $f(x)$.

While the managers of some fisheries appear to be content with this state of affairs, others are not. Thus, US authorities governing the Gulf of Maine off the northeastern US coast allow fishing right up to the boundary of the closed zones, but in Australia's Great Barrier Reef Marine Park closed zones may be further protected by adjacent restricted zones (Day, 2002). Such a restricted zone is shown in Figure 17.1 as the distance x_1 to x_2. As a matter of policy, the objective of the restricted zone is taken to be to preserve as much of the sustainable economic rent as possible, subject to a policing cost constraint – as is discussed later. Accordingly, some human activities are allowed in the restricted zone, but not others. Such zoning restrictions are consistent with equation (2).

We are interested in the maximum amount of sustainable economic rent – i.e. maximum economic yield – created in the restricted zone through biological and associated economic spillovers from the closed zone. To find this we need to calculate the volume, V, which is a monetary measure of sustainable economic rent, created under $f(x)$ between x_1 and x_2 rotated around the y-axis.[9]

The necessary integration exercise yields:

$$V = 2\pi \int_{x1}^{x2} xf(x)dx \qquad (3)$$

To evaluate this equation the function f(x) needs to be defined. Thus, for illustrative purposes assume that $y = I_{MAX} - x/4$. The intercept here is the maximum amount of sustainable economic rent that can be created in the water column above the richest square unit area measured on the ocean floor. This maximum is assumed to be in the center of the closed zone – which is probably a biologically reasonable assumption if the closed zone is properly situated.

In this particular numerical illustration, the economic rent that can be created in the restricted zone is given by:

$$V = 2\pi \int_{x1}^{x2} xf(x)dx \qquad (4)$$

and

$$V = 2\pi \int_{x1}^{x2} x(I_{MAX} - \frac{x}{4})dx \qquad (5)$$

This economic rent, V, is the maximum sustainable rent that can be created through biological spillovers, assuming fishers and other human users of the restricted zone abide by the rules of the restricted zone. That is, they don't partake in illegal activities that reduce economic rent below f(x).

5 Policing activity

It is reasonable to assume that, without policing activity, fishers and other human users of the restricted zone will engage in illegal activities, so reducing the level of sustainable economic rent. Support for this proposition is widespread – for example, see Kuperan and Sutinen (1998); Charles, Mazany and Cross (1999); Nielsen (2003); and Nielsen and Mathiesen (2003). We are now interested in the benefits of policing activity in the restricted zone. If illegal activity does occur, rent is reduced below f(x) in Figure 17.1.[10] This cost is modeled on the simplifying assumption that the *actual* intercept, I, of f(x) is below I_{MAX} – the whole f(x) function shifting downward.

The cost of illegal activity in the restricted zone is calculated in two steps. First, evaluation of the previous equation yields:

$$V = 2\pi I_{MAX}(\frac{x_2^2 - x_1^2}{2}) - \frac{\pi}{2}(\frac{x_2^3 - x_1^2}{3}) \qquad (6)$$

Second, the change in economic rent for an effective downward shift in the intercept caused by illegal activity is:

$$\Delta V = 2\pi(\frac{x_2^2 - x_1^2}{2})\Delta I \qquad (7)$$

where ΔI has been substituted for ΔI_{MAX}, since the latter is a fixed quantity, but the actual intercept will be lower than this if illegal activity occurs. On rearrangement,

$$\frac{\Delta V}{\Delta I} = 2\pi(\frac{x_2^2 - x_1^2}{2}) > 0 \qquad (8)$$

In other words, a reduction in the intercept has a direct negative effect on the value of sustainable economic rent.

The optimum expenditure on policing effort depends on its respective benefits and costs. The benefit of policing effort is the containment of the actual intercept, I, as close as is possible to I_{MAX}, subject to the constraint of policing cost. Letting the number of police boats be the measure of policing effort, the total benefit of policing is:

TB = economic rent saved per police boat × number of police boats (9)

A TB function reflecting diminishing returns to policing is shown in Figure 17.3. Notice that policing effort POL_X coincides with V_{MAX} – the maximum economic rent created by the MPA – i.e. equation (5).

The total cost of policing effort is:

TC = cost per boat × number of police boats (10)

TC is drawn in Figure 17.3 as a simple increasing linear function. Equation 10 assumes that all policing costs are variable costs. Fixed policing cost – the cost of

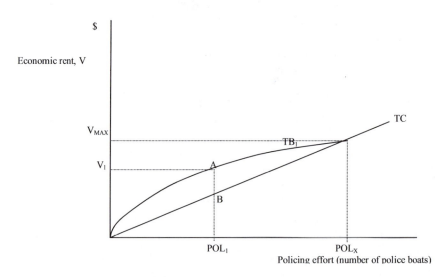

FIGURE 17.3 Optimal policing effort

headquarters, for example – is easily incorporated as a positive y-axis intercept in Figures 17.3 and 17.4. Several different compliance-monitoring methods exist, including shore-based or buoy-based radar, aerial surveillance, sub-surface "pop-up" buoys, the integrated seabed hydrophone array, and on-board vessel monitoring systems that signal the position of boats. As is discussed in NMFS (2003), the cost of operating these systems can vary significantly. It is assumed here that the policing authorities have selected the most cost-effective policing technology.

It is indicated in Figure 17.3 that the optimum number of police "boats" (the measure of policing effort) is POL_1, being determined where marginal benefit equals marginal cost. Other noteworthy features of the equilibrium solution are a) the distance AB measures the net benefit of policing effort; and b) $V_{MAX} - V_1$ measures the sustainable economic rent lost due to continuing illegal activities. In other words, given policing costs, it is not optimal to maximize economic rent along $f(x)$. This agrees with a widely held view in economics literature on crime and punishment that, in the presence of positive marginal policing cost, it is not necessarily optimal to eliminate all illegal activity (Becker, 1968).

6 The effect of some exogenous events on the equilibrium solution

The foregoing discussion can be used to show the effects of three exogenous shocks on, respectively, optimal policing effort, the net benefit of policing, and the amount of sustainable economic rent given up when policing effort is optimized. To begin with, notice in Figure 17.4 that an upward rotation of TB_1 to TB_2 increases net

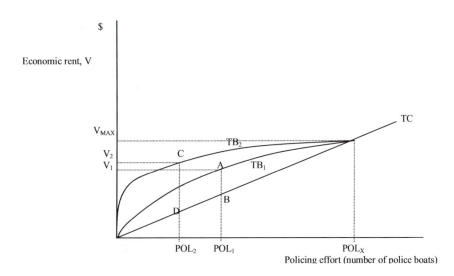

FIGURE 17.4 Effect of greater policing productivity

benefit from AB to CD, reduces lost economic rent due to continuing illegal activity from $V_{MAX} - V_1$ to $V_{MAX} - V_2$, and reduces the total cost of policing from its level at B to its level at D. Clearly, anything that causes the TB function to rotate upward creates several worthwhile benefits.

The factors than can cause an upward rotation of TB in Figure 17.4, implying an increase in rent saving per police boat, are as follows. First, better policing techniques, or the introduction of rules that make policing easier (e.g. requiring fishers constantly to report their positions), will raise policing productivity. Since in equilibrium there are fewer police boats at POL_2, but more economic rent is protected from degradation, $V_2 > V_1$, rent-saving per police boat must have increased. That is, each remaining police boat will be intercepting a larger amount of illegal rent extraction.[11]

Second, rent saved per police boat may be increased through better education of fishers and other human users of an MPA about the biological and economic damage that illegal activities can cause. Charles, Mazany and Cross (1999) and Sutinen and Kuperan (1999) discuss the effect of moral values to be a good citizen on reducing illegal activity. Education about the objectives of fisheries management, and the contributions that individual fishers and other users of an MPA can make to improve a marine ecosystem, can be thought of as bolstering moral awareness. Moreover, according to NMFS (2003), because illegal activity is sometimes inadvertent, education is valuable in simply informing potential visitors to an MPA about the existence of restrictions. Assuming that such education reduces illegal activity, it is reasonable to suppose that the remaining illegal fishing boats will be able to gather more illegal rent per boat due to the relief from the external diseconomy of overfishing by the other illegal fishing boats that have removed themselves.

The matter of the effect of a closed zone on aggregate harvests may be relevant to the issue of policing costs as acceptance of the rules of a closed zone is probably more likely if aggregate harvests increase. If harvests decrease – as is the case in many of the simulated bioeconomic models cited earlier – stakeholders may be less willing to go along with the rules, probably behaving in ways that raise policing costs. As Cooter and Ulen (1997) point out, efforts to create a social surplus – such as the adoption of laws relating to an MPA – need to be seen as being reasonable as well as rational if they are to be effective. They also argue that "social norms" (or "customs") can even take the place of enacted laws – and the policing of those laws, in coping with external costs – such as those incurred in over-fishing (or, in their example, northern Californian open range cattle ranching). Kuperan and Sutinen (1998) also acknowledge that fishing restrictions are more likely to be obeyed by fishers if they are perceived as being "fair". Similarly, fisheries co-management, by giving fishers a say in the design and operation of a fisheries regime, may increase compliance – see *inter alia*, Nielsen, Vedsman and Friis (1997); Holland and Ginter (2001); Eggert and Ellegard (2003); and Nielsen and Mathiesen (2003).

Third, tougher laws against illegal activities will rotate TB upward in Figure 17.4. The argument here is similar to the previous discussion in relation to the effect of better education. Thus, if tougher laws reduce illegal activity, rent saved per police boat will increase. The counterpart to this argument is the well-known proposition that, if penalties are increased, for any given probability of being caught, illegal activity will decline as expected marginal benefit declines. Indeed, Kuperan and Sutinen (1998) in their study of fishers' behavior find empirical support for this hypothesis.

7 Conclusions

This chapter has considered some of the main biological and economic consequences of marine protected areas (MPAs). It began by pointing out that MPAs have been widely adopted in order to protect marine environments in the face of overfishing. It was recognized that a key consideration in the establishment of an MPA is the use of the correct biological model – otherwise, it may not be sited to maximize the biological and economic payoffs. Assuming that this issue is resolved, the chapter went on to discuss the principles of optimal zoning: zones should be designed and policed so as to equalize the marginal social cost of human activity between them. It was further argued, given that the policing of an MPA involves positive marginal cost, that it is generally not optimal to aim for maximum economic yield. Rather, some sustainable economic rent may have to be given up because the cost of catching the last (hopefully few) illegal human users is too high.

Finally, the economic model offered in this chapter – which I have tried to base on what is known about the relevant marine biology – suggests that as economic rents are likely to be created through biological spillovers to adjacent areas, these rents too may be worthwhile protecting. Assuming that policing costs are not excessive, it would appear sensible to design MPAs with buffer zones up against the exclusion zones. Indeed, as discussed in Chapter 16, this design is used in the Great Barrier Reef Marine Park.

Notes

1 "Marine Protected Areas, Optimal Policing and Optimal Rent Dissipation", *Marine Resource Economics,* 9 (4), 481–93, 2004.
2 About 1,300 MPAs have already been established worldwide (Boersma and Parrish, 1999).
3 There may also be a case for buffer zones so that genuine mistakes by fishers and other human users of ocean space do not damage highly sensitive protected areas. See Chapter 16, where the Great Barrier Reef Marine Park is discussed.
4 Choice of a social welfare function is of course fraught with controversy – not least in the context of the governance of fisheries, where "stakeholder" interests are often to the fore. This chapter simply accepts the notion – that is widely, even if not universally, accepted in fisheries economics – that the attainment of a social optimum (such as maximum economic yield – Chapter 8) is desirable. An increase in aggregate harvests following the introduction of a no-take zone is helpful in that a Pareto improvement in stakeholders' welfare is at least possible. Based on the calibrated simulation model of Holland (2000), actual Pareto improvement is doubtful as fishers are likely to be differentially impacted by

area closures – those harboring near a closed area having further to travel to the remaining open fishing grounds.

5 The creation of property rights is not uncontroversial – see Macinko and Bromley (2002). Giving away property rights may be socially unfair when at least some fishers already have high levels of income or wealth. The creation of property rights might also preclude the introduction of more efficient or socially acceptable fisheries institutions at a later date.

6 The negative effect of the given human activity on sustainable rent could be modeled to occur only after some threshold level of activity has been surpassed.

7 Sanchirico and Wilen (1999) state that fishers will equate marginal rents between areas outside a closed zone. However, they were referring to private economic rents. The argument for zoning here is based on inequality between social values, and these will not necessarily be equalized by unregulated fishing activity.

8 This statement ignores the policing cost considerations discussed elsewhere in this chapter.

9 The required element of volume in Figure 17.1 is $dV = 2\pi dx f(x)$.

10 Such illegal activity could be in terms of use of illegal gear (e.g. trawling in a no trawling zone) or harvesting over a predefined total allowable catch (that could be set to zero). According to, *inter alia*, Charles, Mazany and Cross (1999), illegal activity is likely to occur when its marginal benefit exceeds marginal cost. Marginal cost includes the expected value of any fines – calculated as the probability of being caught and punished multiplied by the size of the fine.

11 Since productivity per police boat increases, this may create an incentive to use more police boats. However, net benefit of policing still increases, and economic rent lost due to continuing illegal activity still falls.

18

CONTRACTUAL DIFFICULTIES IN ENVIRONMENTAL MANAGEMENT

The case of United States wetland mitigation banking[1]

1   Introduction

This chapter offers a principal–agent model of private contracting in mitigation banking aimed at protection of wetland acreage and habitat, biodiversity and physical functions of US wetlands. While it is straightforward to design an incentive contract, such a contract may be incapable of achieving the federally mandated objective of no net loss of wetland functions through wetland mitigation; there may be failure of contract design or execution. Also considered are several institutional mechanisms that may promote the convergence of private contracting and attainment of mandated wetland protection. These include greater oversight by the government, payment of subsidies, greater accuracy in the identification of actual wetland quality by the principal, and use of several other incentive alignment mechanisms.

Wetlands perform valuable functions including shoreline anchoring and protection, nutrient and toxin filtering, and acting as reservoirs for flood control and as a wildlife habitat for plants, birds, fishes, mammals and other biota. However, over one-half of US wetland acreage has been lost to agricultural, urban and commercial uses – such as housing, highways, airports, harbors, marinas and industrial parks (Dahl, Johnson and Frayer, 1991). Very largely, these functions cannot be commercialized – and so protected – by landowners, but legislation exists (see below) aimed at mitigating "unavoidable" losses of wetlands through creation or restoration of wetland acreage elsewhere. However, loss of wetland acreage still occurs. This chapter investigates why these losses persist in the important case of mitigation banking – a for-profit private sector institutional arrangement run with some governmental oversight.

Mitigation of wetland functions lost to property development is through various avenues. Credits purchased by property developers from for-profit mitigation banks account for about one-third of total mitigated wetland acreage in the United States (ELI, 2006). Of the remainder, over one-half was mitigated by property developers themselves, and a small amount of mitigation was by "in-lieu fee", whereby a property developer pays a third party to restore wetland rather than using either of the other two methods. There are four types of mitigation: "creation", "restoration" (including of abandoned industrial land, lands dominated by invasive species, and areas of wetland cut off from a contiguous productive environment by linear developments such as roads, bridges and railways), "enhancement" of targeted functions of undisturbed wetland, and "preservation" of existing wetland through legal actions such as a land easement, or protection through the erection of fences (ELI, 2006).

As estuaries often include large areas of wetland, we offer a brief background.[2]

Estuaries

Estuaries provide a wide selection of habitats including sand banks, mud flats, lagoons and wetlands. Estuarine-dependent commercial fish species in the USA include Gulf shrimp, Pacific salmon, oysters (Pacific and Eastern), non-ocean clams, American lobster, stripers and blue crab. For some species these habitats are critical for just a part of their life cycle, for others they are permanent residents. Table 18.1 shows how dependent many fisheries are on estuaries in the USA.

Several studies of the value of coastal wetlands to commercial fisheries have been conducted. For example, Ellis and Fisher (1987) constructed a bio-economic model of fish stocks' dependency on US coastal wetland. They found in simulations that an increase in wetland acreage from 25,000 to 100,000 increased net social welfare (fishers' producers' surplus plus consumers' surplus) by about $400,000 (converted to 2013 dollars) per year. With a 3 percent discount rate over fifty years this gives a net present value of about $10 million; at 6 percent, $6.3 million.

Elsewhere in the world, Brander, Florax and Vermaat (2006) found that the worldwide annual value of wetlands is nearly $3,000 per hectare; and a study of the economic value of the Olango Island coral reef-mangrove swamp-wetland ecosystem in the Philippines, focusing on fisheries, seaweed farming, bird habitat and tourism, found that the wetland component alone added $389,000 annually to the

TABLE 18.1 Share of total landings by weight of top estuarine-dependent species in total harvest by state and region

Region	Share of top estuarine-dependent species in total catch, percent
Northeast Atlantic	40.5
Maryland	82.5
Virginia	88.9
Southeast Atlantic	69.7
Florida	30.9
Gulf of Mexico	95.6
California and the Pacific	2.1
Northwest Pacific	12.8

Based on Lipton and Kasperski (2008)

total valuation and that the annual cost of managing the ecosystem was only about $100,000 (White, Ross and Flores, 2000).

2   US legislation

The relevant US legislation is contained in section 404 of the *Clean Water Act* (1972),[3] section 10 of the *Rivers and Harbors Act* (1899)[4] and in the wetland conservation provisions of the *Food Security Act* (1985).[5] The practice of mitigation banking is systematized in the *Federal Guidance for the Establishment, Use and Operation of Mitigation Banks* (1995).[6] While US laws require mitigation of impacts, growth of private (or "entrepreneurial") mitigation banking initially developed without legislation of details (see Sheahan, 2001). These details had to be developed between private contractors. Some examples are the definition of the "mitigation credit" as the traded unit, the stage at which mitigation credits could be awarded to a mitigation bank, and just how the quality of wetland functions were to be measured.[7]

3   Mitigation banks

A typical mitigation bank is of a defined size, say, 70 acres, of which, perhaps, one-half is wetland acreage.[8] A mitigation contract is signed between a mitigation bank and a responsible government agent or agencies, the US Army Corps of Engineers, the US Environmental Protection Agency, the US Fish and Wildlife Service and, perhaps, a state agency such as California's Department of Fish and Game. These principals are responsible for setting targeted quality of wetland mitigation, and for awarding "credits" to a mitigation bank in lieu of the quality and acreage rehabilitated.[9]

Credits become available for sale by a mitigation bank to property developers once specified mitigation work has been verified by the principal as completed. The "service areas" of a mitigation bank are limited to nearby areas in order to mitigate like with like, and to maintain acreage in given localities.

Some estimates put the cost of wetland restoration at between $25,000 and $130,000 per acre, while credits have sold for as much as $250,000 per acre in New Jersey.[10] More recent cost estimates by the Army Corps of Engineers indicate that lowest restoration costs range from about $3,000 to $16,000 per acre, plus land acquisition costs. High-end restoration costs are much higher, ranging from $100,000 to $350,000 per acre (ELI, 2006, p. 28). Such is the array of these estimates that little can be inferred about the profitability of wetland mitigation banking. However, there is a suggestion that, as costs are by no means trivial in relation to revenues, mitigation bankers are likely to be cost-conscious investors in wetland restoration.

4 Social benefits

As property developers are unlikely to be specialists in wetland mitigation, their costs are likely to be higher than those of specialists in wetland creation or restoration. To some extent, therefore, the development of private sector mitigation banking over the last thirty years or so is a response to cost differences between property developers and specialist mitigation bankers, with a potential social surplus derived from trading mitigation credits. As such, the social value of mitigation banking is derived in much the same way as other private institutions trading in, say, pollution permits – that is, the equation of the marginal costs of abatement between polluters.[11] Other advantages of mitigation banking are consolidation of wetland restoration into large areas rather than them being dispersed as on-site mitigation by property developers; that mitigation occurs before impact; and that mitigation banks can become centers of expertise in wetland mitigation (Department of Fish and Game, 2003, pp. 3–5).

Thirty-one US states host mitigation banks, and, in 2005, there were 405 approved mitigation banks – a multiple of almost eight compared with 1992. A further 169 banks were seeking approval. In the case of approved banks, 70 percent were "private commercial", with mitigation credits for sale on the open market; 4 percent were "public commercial", sponsored by public agencies to mitigate for either public or private wetland development; and 25 percent were single client banks where the bank sponsor was the main purchaser of credits.[12]

5 Mitigation failures

As indicated earlier, mitigation efforts are often criticized for failing to protect US wetlands (see, for example, GAO, 2005; Sheahan, 2001; Smoktonowicz, 2005). Castelle et al. (1992, p. i) found that "follow-up studies indicate that the average rate of compliance with permit conditions was 50%. Common problems include inadequate design; failure to implement the design; lack of proper supervision; site infestation by exotic species; . . . failure to adequately maintain water levels; and failure to protect projects from on-site and off-site impacts such as sediments, toxics, and off-road vehicles." Harrison (1995) points out that mitigation banks often put little effort into restoration projects. Kukoy and Canter (1995) assert that non-compliance with Section 404 permit requirements was quite widespread. Redmond (1990) monitored 1,262 permits issued by the Florida Department of Environmental Regulation. The key finding was that only about one in four projects were ecologically successful in the sense that they had or would probably become serviceable wetlands of the type permitted as a mitigation wetland. Instead, mitigation banking has contributed to over-development by property developers of natural wetland habitats, without adequate replacement through restoration of physical, chemical, biological or hydrological functions of mitigated wetlands.[13] Moreover, Sheahan (2001, p. 22) offers evidence of a high failure rate of on-site mitigation by non-specialists.

6 Explaining mitigation failures

To explain mitigation failures we focus on mitigation contract design and execution in the presence of asymmetric information. The perspective of a principal–agent model would seem to be useful as a mitigation bank, the agent, works daily on a mitigation site, it will be more familiar than is the principal with key characteristics of the site – such as the condition of the many determinants of its hydrology that are critical in the health of re-engineered wetlands (e.g. Montalto et al., 2002). Moreover, as oversight by the principal is not continuous, the agent has some scope to cut corners on amounts of mitigation investment, so reducing its costs.[14]

The focus here is on the award of mitigation credits by a governmental regulatory agency – the "principal" – to a mitigation bank, "the agent", for the physical restoration work that it performs on a wetland site. For purposes of economic analysis the mitigation contract is characterized by: a) an agreed specification of inputs to be applied to improve the functioning of a defined acreage (examples of inputs include construction work to establish a viable hydrology, plantings of desirable species, and elimination of exotic species from the site. The vector X_N represents this set of pre-defined inputs); b) specification of the number of mitigation credits, F, that will be awarded for; c) creation of pre-defined wetland functions; and d) an understanding that if the target wetland functions are not achieved, wetland credits may not be released unless specified remedial work is performed – the additional input vector X_E.

Feasible contracts

A mitigation bank's net payoff for restoring a wetland depends on the number of credits awarded less the cost of creating those credits. Because it is difficult for the principal to observe investments being made, an agent, hoping that the principal will not notice, might reduce the level of investment below contractual limits – so lowering its costs.

A mitigation bank's expected payoff from "shirking" on the level of investment, $E(\Pi_S)$, measured in credits is:

$$E(\Pi_S) = F - [pWX_S + (1 - p)W(X_S + X_E)] \tag{1}$$

where F is the number of mitigation credits awarded for restoration work, p is the probability of under-investment in mitigation not being detected, and $(1 - p)$ is the probability of under-investment being detected. W is a vector of the costs measured in credits of physical inputs.[15] X_N is a vector of government-stipulated physical inputs, and X_S is a vector of a subset of government-stipulated physical inputs. That is, X_S is the "shirking" level of investment – chosen by a mitigation bank if, indeed, it chooses to shirk. Both the amount and cost of investment with shirking are lower than without shirking. The level of X_S would be determined by the minimum set of "gardening" inputs that an agent reasons must be seen to be done, and the less thorough is governmental oversight the lower is X_S. If the agent thought that oversight was so thorough that any shirking would be spotted by the principal, then $X_S = X_N$. X_E is the additional cost imposed on a mitigation bank if it is caught under-investing in mitigation.[16] Thus, equation (1) says that a mitigation bank's expected profit measured in net credits when shirking occurs equals the difference between the number of mitigation credits awarded and the probability weighted average production cost; the larger is p, the lower is probability weighted cost and the greater is $E(\Pi_S)$.

The expected payoff from not shirking, $E(\Pi_N)$, is:

$$E(\Pi_N) = F - [(1 - q)WX_N + qW(X_N + X_E)] \tag{2}$$

Here, q is the probability that the government thinks that low investment in mitigation has occurred when, in fact, a mitigation bank has met its contractual obligations. This would be an unfortunate situation for a mitigation bank, but it is possible since the government does not continuously observe investment, and the quality of rehabilitated wetland is subject to random variations in the state of nature. Thus, observed low quality of a completed restoration project might be taken as a signal that under-investment occurred, rather than, for example, that the site's hydrology turned out less favorable than anticipated. X_N is again a vector of government-stipulated physical inputs, and, even though X_N has been invested, extra investment, X_E, is required.

The incentive compatibility condition, whereby the mitigation bank chooses not to shirk and to invest in inputs as laid out in the mitigation contract, is found by equating equations (1) and (2). On rearrangement this yields

$$X_E \geq (X_N - X_S)/[1 - (p + q)] \qquad \equiv X_0 \tag{3}$$

where X_0 is the minimum X_E consistent with incentive compatibility.

If the principal wants an agent to invest in a mitigation project, it must set $E(\Pi_N) = U$, where U is reservation profit – the return on investment in a comparable risk class outside of mitigation banking. Subtracting U from the right-hand side of equation (2) and rearranging yields the participation constraint:

$$X_1 \equiv (F - WX_N - U)/(qW) \geq X_E \tag{4}$$

where X_1 is the maximum X_E that can be imposed by the government while still inducing a mitigation bank to invest in mitigation.

Assuming that the vectors X_E, X_N and X_S each contain only one input, Figure 18.1 can be drawn. Both the participation and incentive constraints are simultaneously fulfilled at X^*_N and X^*_E in Figure 18.1. If the contract between the principal and the agent states X^*_N and X^*_E, the agent will want both to participate and to aim to fulfill its contractual investment obligations.[17]

A problem with actual mitigation contracts becomes immediately apparent. In practice, if shirking is detected, the agent is required to invest just enough to put the problem in the field right. However, X^*_E in equation (3) implies a penalty for an agent caught shirking. For example, suppose that $(p + q) = 0.2$; from equation (3) this implies $X^*_E = 1.25(X_N - X_S)$. The implication is that the agent should make good the investment shortfall, $(X_N - X_S)$, *and* pay what amounts to a fine – in this case, equal in value to 25 percent of the investment shortfall. While, as is mentioned below, mitigation bank contracts can allow for administrative penalties, according to GAO (2005) they are not enforced.

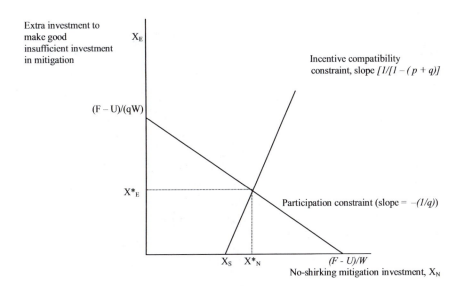

FIGURE 18.1 Feasible mitigation contracts

Another possible cause of contract failure

Given poor physical or biological conditions at a potential mitigation site, the government may have to stipulate a required level of investment X_{N1}. In Figure 18.2, as X_{N1} is to the right of X^*_N no feasible contract can be written that fulfills both the incentive and participation constraints at this level of investment.[18]

If the government were to set X_E consistent with the participation constraint (point B), X_E will be too low to fulfill the incentive alignment constraint. Recalling that X_E is a sort of "punishment" for not fulfilling contractual obligations, low X_E will induce the agent to "shirk" on the level of investment: to invest X_S rather than X_N. Alternatively, if the government reduces required investment to, say, X^*_N per mitigation credit awarded, knowing that X_{N1} is required, quality of restored wetland will be impaired.

Contractual difficulties also arise if X_S is low – shirking as a way of life, as it were – as this shifts the incentive compatibility constraint to the left, reducing the area of feasible contracting. There is no direct evidence on X_S but there is some indirect evidence. In an extensive study by the Government Accounting Office it was concluded that "because many projects that we reviewed did not receive oversight, the [Army Corps of Engineers] districts cannot definitively assess whether compensatory mitigation has been performed on thousands of acres" (GAO, 2005, p. 9). Thus, if a mitigation bank anticipates that a principal may not verify its work, the incentive to shirk, with a low level of X_S, is all the greater. An unenforced contract is not worth the paper it is written on.

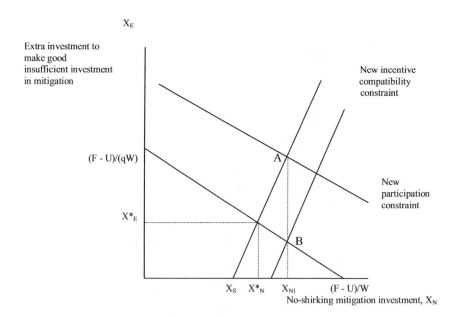

FIGURE 18.2 Creating a feasible mitigation contract

7   Improving contract design and execution

Given that wetland restoration costs may be high – X_{N1} in Figure 18.2 – the frequency of the undesirable outcome of poor quality restoration may be reduced by finding ways to shift the participation constraint outward so that it passes through point A, or to shift the incentive compatibility constraint downward so that it passes through point B.

Perhaps the most important action that principals can take is to enforce mitigation contracts through careful inspection of finished work. The effect would be to reduce the incentive to shirk, so shifting X_S and the incentive compatibility constraint to the right.

The matter of inspection has been the subject of a withering GAO investigation. According to the GAO,

> Overall, the Corps districts we visited have performed limited oversight to determine the status of required compensatory mitigation . . . we found little evidence that required monitoring reports were submitted or that the Corps conducted compliance inspections.
>
> (GAO, 2005, p. 5)

Reasons for this were found to be that:

> the Corps [had] conflicting guidance, which notes that compliance inspections are crucial yet makes them a low priority, as well as limited resources contribute to their low level of oversight of compensatory mitigation.
>
> (GAO, 2005, p. 5)

And,

> We found that, sometimes, district officials wanting to pursue enforcement actions after detecting instances of noncompliance may be unable to do so because they have limited their enforcement capabilities by not specifying the requirements for compensatory mitigation in permits.
>
> (GAO, 2005, p. 6)

Another method that principals can use to enforce compliance (effectively increasing X_S) is to report serious violators to the local US attorney to file civil or criminal actions – but the GAO (2005, p. 5) found no evidence that this had happened. Nor was it found that principals had used their powers to assess administrative penalties of up to \$27,500, nor to suspend or to revoke permits. Moreover, mitigation bank contracts usually include two other incentive alignment mechanisms: the posting of bonds that may be forfeited in the case of inadequate work, and the sequenced release of credits as quality in the field is verified. However, the effectiveness of these is greatly reduced if principals do not properly inspect finished work.

The participation constraint can be shifted outward from the origin through payment of a subsidy to a mitigation bank. The subsidy reduces costs, so lowering W. However, new legislation would be needed for this, and given that the system is already under-funded to the extent that money is not available for thorough inspections, one wonders whether the use of subsidies is likely. The area of feasible contracting can also be increased by reducing q, the possibility that the principal will incorrectly judge that work that was properly completed was not done so. Lower q swings the participation constraint outward from the origin.

8   Conclusions

This chapter has argued that widespread failure to mitigate wetland losses through the practice of private-sector mitigation banking is tied up with problems of contract design and execution. In the first place, it may not be possible to write an efficient incentive contract if investment in restoration is too expensive (i.e. X_{N1} is to the right of X^*_N in Figure 18.2). Nor is it likely that a contract will be efficient if it does not include penalties (over and above the cost of necessary extra investment in mitigation) for shirking, or, where it does, if it is known that they are almost never enforced. Moreover, even when an efficient mitigation contract can be written, the amount of money that the Federal government is willing to allocate to contract enforcement appears to be insufficient – at least this is the implication of the GAO (2005) study. Moreover, high costs of proper contract enforcement could be so great as to negate any social surplus created through trading in mitigation credits. At the very least, legislatures and principals have an urgent need to discover and apply low-cost methods of contract enforcement, and/or to look for places where mitigation is a relatively easy technical exercise and is, therefore, less costly.

Notes

1   "Contractual Difficulties in Environmental Management: The Case of Wetland Mitigation Banking", *Ecological Economics*, 63 (2–3), August 2007, 446–451, Ecological Economics of Coastal Disasters – Coastal Disasters Special Section.

2   Author's note: I was brought up on the estuary of the River Dee facing Wales, with the Hilbre Island bird sanctuary less than two miles offshore. You could walk there when the tide was out; with 32' spring tides it went out a long, long way. My parents' house was a stone's throw from the shore, which during summer weekends was wonderfully filled with visiting families and their little children, building sand castles and having donkey rides. In other seasons a trainer brought racehorses down to the sands – four or five of them at a time running hard into the wind with tails out, swinging like weathervanes. Wind-yachting on the sands was and still is popular and, particularly so, windsurfing on the Marine Lake, which was no more than 200 yards from our house. Up-river just a few miles are extensive wetlands that have taken over in recent decades. Indeed, Parkgate was once a thriving port, but now grasses grow right up against the seawall. No more are local shrimp being sold by aproned ladies from their front door steps. As a boy I made a bit of money fishing. Follow the tide out, set two stakes in the sand with line and hooks

between, dig like the devil for lugworm, bait the hooks, and leave ahead of the tide. Then follow the tide out and collect the fish – flounder mainly, sometimes sea bass and the odd weaver fish.

3 This act requires a permit for discharges of dredged or fill material into the waters, including wetlands, of the United States.

4 Specifically, "it shall not be lawful to excavate or fill, or in any manner to alter or modify the course, location, condition, or capacity of, any port, roadstead, haven, harbor, canal, lake, harbor of refuge, or inclosure within the limits of any breakwater, or of the channel of any navigable water of the United States, unless the work has been recommended by the Chief of Engineers and authorized by the Secretary of War prior to beginning the same" (33 USC paragraph 403: "Obstruction of Navigable Waters Generally: Wharves; Piers, etc; Excavation and Filling in", available online at http://riverfront.org/parks/riverside-park).

5 The "swampbusters" provision of this act (Title XII, subtitle C) denies farmers federal benefits if they convert wetlands for food production. However, they may be let back into Federal support programs if they mitigate wetland losses.

6 The latter was issued under the signatures of five assistant secretaries in the Departments of Agriculture, Interior and Commerce, the Army and the Environmental Protection Agency.

7 Institutional details of mitigation banking are described, *inter alia*, in Bonnie (1999); Castelle et al. (1992); ELI (2006); GAO (2005); Federal Register (1995); Sheahan (2001); Weems and Canter (1995); and Wheeler and Strock (1995).

8 For a description of several mitigation banks see Department of Fish and Game, 2003.

9 Quality of restored wetland functions can vary, as is implied in the following statement by three biologists: "There is no recipe for restoration that will work at all sites. The success of tidal marsh restoration efforts depends heavily on the extent to which the designer understands the site and the materials being utilized during construction. Projects need well-defined objectives and attention paid to detail. Site morphology, substrate transmissivity, and porosity all have the potential to make or break a project, and should therefore be considered carefully in design development" (Montalto, Steenhuis and Parlange, 2002, p. 46). Wetland habitat and biotic valuation by experts can use the Delphi method of scoring the many characteristics of a wetland on a scale of 0 to 1 and then combining the individual scores into a weighted average quality index. Mitsch and Gosselink (2000, pp. 591–96) point out that several quality assessment methods exist, including the Habitat Evaluation Procedure used by the US Fish and Wildlife Service, the Wetland Evaluation Technique used for a time by the US Army Corps of Engineers, and the recently developed hydrogeomorphic classification. These authors also observe that economic valuation of wetlands depends, inter alia, on the correct identification of habitat, biotic and other physical characteristics.

10 *The Economist*, August 10th, 2000.

11 See, for example, Baumol and Oates (1988); Bohringer (2002); and Stavins and Whitehead (1992).

12 Data in this paragraph is drawn from ELI (2006).

13 See also Choi (2004).

14 In the model of Fernandez and Karp (1998) a mitigation bank tries to maximize the option value of a wetland tract, assuming that finished quality is perfectly observable by the principal. However, this model does not take account of possible principal–agent problems.

15 The cost of investment in a tract measured in credits is simply the dollar cost divided by the market price of a credit.

16 In practice, the principal may require the agent to increase expenditure on inputs as work progresses. Hey and Philippe (1999) have a good description of this in the case of wetland mitigation in the Florida Keys.

17 If X_E is set lower than X^*_E down the incentive compatibility constraint, an agent's expected profit would increase above the minimum level required to engage in mitigation banking. This would be an unnecessary extra return to the agent, and it could be construed as government favoritism.

18 Evidence in the field comparing restored wetland with undisturbed control wetlands suggests that restoration outcomes are uncertain and may take between twenty and fifty years to recreate (Coats, Swanson and Williams, 1989; Pfadenhauer and Grootjans, 1999; Zedler, 1996). Cumulative investment cost would likely increase substantially if mitigation banks were required to continue investing in restoration projects for such extended periods.

PART VIII

Pollution

19

OCEANS AND NON-POINT SOURCE POLLUTION

1   Non-point source pollution – an intractable problem

In the Gulf of Mexico out from the Mississippi delta there is a "dead zone", an area about the size of New Hampshire. Marine life is mainly absent because of eutrophication (an excessive richness of nutrients) that causes hypoxia – much reduced oxygen levels in the seawater. The source of the nutrients, mainly nitrogen and phosphorus, is fertilizer runoff from the many farms in the huge Mississippi drainage basin.

Eutrophication causes large algae blooms in spring, which when they die sink to the bottom to be consumed by bacteria that in turn consume the oxygen. Fish in the area either move away or die. Other large marine areas similarly affected include western Long Island Sound, Chesapeake Bay, Narragansett Bay and Pensacola Bay. According to the Environmental Protection Agency (2002) over one-half of US estuaries are polluted enough to damage aquatic life and reduce recreational values. A later study concluded that US mainland coastal waters are in poor to only fair condition (EPA, 2004). Indeed, dead zones are a worldwide phenomenon, with large ones in the Black Sea, the Baltic Sea and in the Kattegat between Sweden and Denmark.

Teck et al. (2010) sought expert opinion on the vulnerability of US west coast marine ecosystems. Vulnerability is determined by the combination of exposure to a stressor, sensitivity to negative impact, and resilience – ability to recover from the impact of the stressor. They found that four intertidal ecosystems – mudflat, salt marsh, beach and rocky intertidal – were most vulnerable to human stressors. The worst stressors for US western coastal ecosystems did not in fact include hypoxia; instead, they were invasive species, ocean acidification, sea temperature change, sea level rise, and habitat alteration from coastal engineering. Offshore ecosystems were seen as being most vulnerable to ocean acidification, demersal destructive fishing and shipwrecks.

In a similar study Kappel et al. (2012) investigated pollution problems in off-shore New England. Expert opinion was sought on the vulnerability of 58 marine ecosystems to 14 anthropocentric-caused stressors. Examples of pollution stressors include nitrogen and sediment runoffs, invasive species and ocean dumping. According to the experts all of the pollution-related stressors listed in Table 19.1

TABLE 19.1 Vulnerability to anthropocentric-caused marine ecosystem stressors: New England

Stressor	*Significantly adversely affected marine ecosystem*
Nutrient input: causing harmful algal blooms	Tidal flats and hard bottom offshore shelf
Nutrient input: causing hypoxic[1] zones	Tidal flats and near-shore soft bottom
Nutrient input: into eutrophic[2] waters	Tidal flats, near-shore soft bottom, hard bottom shelf
Ocean mining (sand, minerals, etc.)	Hard bottom offshore shelf
Ocean dumping: marine debris (trash, etc.)	Beach, soft bottom shelf
Ocean dumping: toxic materials	Offshore soft bottom bathyal[3] zone, soft bottom shelf
Pollution input: atmospheric	Offshore soft and hard bottom shelf, near-shore hard bottom
Pollution input: inorganic	Offshore soft and hard bottom shelf
Ocean pollution (from ships, ports, etc.)	Near-shore and offshore soft bottom shelf
Sediment input: increase	Tidal flats and barrier beaches
Diseases and pathogens	Soft bottom shelf
Invasive species (from ballast, etc.)	Beach, rocky intertidal, salt marsh, near-shore hard bottom, near-shore soft bottom, hard bottom shelf, soft bottom shelf, soft bottom bathyal, shallow pelagic,[4] deep pelagic

Based on Kappel et al. (2012)

had above average adverse impact on one or more marine environments. Particularly vulnerable are beaches, tidal flats, near-shore hard bottom, near-shore soft bottom, hard bottom continental shelf, soft bottom continental shelf and soft bottom bathyal.

2   Social cost of eutrophication-hypoxia

The economic cost of eutrophication-hypoxia takes the form of an external diseconomy – see Figure 19.1. Here, marginal private cost of producing corn causes nutrient runoff and hypoxia downstream. Without action to correct this, external diseconomy output will be Q_1, but the socially optimal output is lower, at Q_2, with the consequent deadweight loss (the social loss) triangle as indicated. Also, notice that even at the socially optimal output some negative externality remains; but it would not be economic to remove it because the marginal benefit of the corn output exceeds the social cost of production.

3   Reducing the social cost of eutrophication-hypoxia

The question is: what steps might be taken to reduce the social cost of the negative externality caused by non-point source nutrient flow into coastal waters? The EPA (2010) suggested tax incentives to farmers that implement "best management practices" to reduce nutrient runoff; insurance programs for farmers that choose to reduce fertilizer use to below "recommended" levels, in case crops turn out smaller than "normal"; and, if states don't introduce programs, the Federal government could use the power of the purse – e.g. withhold federal funds for highway construction (highways being a non-point pollution source).

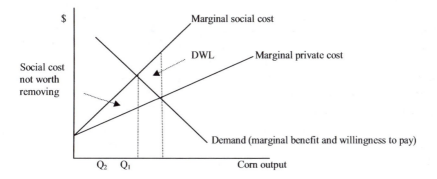

FIGURE 19.1 The deadweight loss of excessive corn output

4 Existing US legislation relating to non-point source pollution

At the present time some programs exist that are designed to cope with non-point source pollution:

1   The National Non-point Source Pollution Program under section 319 of the *Clean Water Act*. Under this program, matching Federal grants are available to states to develop programs to manage non-point source pollution.
2   The *Coastal Zone Management Act*, whereby states are required to develop plans that include enforceable management measures to control non-point source pollution.
3   The US Department of Agricultural Conservation Programs that make payments to farmers that implement wetland and grassland conservation programs.

The Ocean Commission (2004) summarized these programs thus: "the management of non-point source pollution in coastal areas includes a mix of planning requirements, state actions, direct funding incentives, and grant programs to encourage standard setting and implementations" (p. 167). Evidently, since eutrophication-hypoxia remains a problem in US waters, these programs are insufficient.

5 A market-based approach to reducing mitigation costs

There is some scope, but probably not much, for reducing the cost of limiting nitrogen and phosphorus runoff into the Gulf of Mexico using pollution permit trading. According to Ribaudo, Heimlich and Peters (2005), municipal and industrial point sources account for about 11 percent of runoff and agricultural nonpoint sources more than 65 percent. At the same time, it is more expensive per unit of nitrogen/phosphorus removed to reduce point source pollution through wastewater treatment plants than it is through non-point sources accomplished by, among other things, planting vegetation barriers or extending inland wetland. Cost reduction is achieved if the (high cost) point source polluters purchase pollution credits from farmers, allowing the former to reduce the constraint on their levels of pollution. This would be offset by reduced pollution flow from the non-point source polluters. All sides would win, given that the fee paid by point source polluters was less than the cost of their own mitigation efforts; and farmers would gain if the fee was greater than the cost of their expenditure on mitigation.

It is worth mentioning that not all of the gain in reducing mitigation costs would constitute a net social benefit because some agency would need to monitor whether the farmers were in fact mitigating by the contracted amounts. Another consideration is that, as corn production causes more fertilizer runoff per unit of output than other crops (such as alfalfa, which actually absorbs nitrogen), the amount of runoff could be reduced by ending corn production subsidies to farmers aimed at increasing both famers' incomes and production of ethanol (Bernell, 2013). It is somewhat odd, therefore, that a market-based solution – pollution permit trading with associated transaction costs – is reached for in the face of a government-orchestrated market distortion (agricultural subsidies). Although rather complex to work out, the first best policy may well be to end the market distortion, rather than to adopt a second best policy aimed at reducing its intractable damaging impact.

6   Benefit–cost analysis of investment to reduce coastal hypoxia

Perhaps surprisingly, benefits derived from reduced hypoxia in coastal waters may not be large. Thus, Diaz and Solow (1999) failed to uncover impacts caused by hypoxia. "Overall, fisheries landings statistics for at least the last few decades have been relatively constant." Why this was so was not known, but it could be that landings were maintained because of increased fishing effort, or that the fishers simply followed the fish as they moved out of hypoxic waters.

Doering et al. (1999) discuss the costs of efforts to reduce fertilizer runoff down the Mississippi River. They found that increasing the area of wetlands to absorb fertilizer runoff is not as cost-effective a fertilizer restriction; that fertilizer restrictions are better than a fertilizer tax because the latter is a cost borne by farmers; that vegetative buffers – grasses in particular – grown on farmland and along river banks are the least cost-effective; and that a five million-acre wetland restoration combined with a 20 percent reduction in fertilizer use is the most cost-effective and practicable strategy examined for meeting a 20 percent nitrogen loss-reduction goal. However, they also pointed to two adverse side effects of such a program: reducing fertilizer use would lower agricultural output and raises prices, and production would to some extent shift to areas not subjected to fertilizer-use restrictions and this could increase fertilizer runoff in other areas.

7   The general theory of second best and cleaning up hypoxia

The simple analysis in Figure 19.1 of the benefits of reducing fertilizer use implicitly assumes that there is only one distortion in corn production – the distortion being that the social cost of production is greater than the private cost of production, and that private producers ignore the external diseconomy caused by fertilizer runoff. In this simple case all that has to be done is to reduce corn output to its socially optimal level.

However, economic policy is by no means so straightforward in the presence of two or more distortions. Thus, according to the general theory of second best, there is no presumption that welfare must increase if just one distortion is removed leaving at least one other in place.[5]

The problem of hypoxia in an open access fishery relates to the fact that there are two distortions (more if we include subsidies for corn production, but here we restrict ourselves to just two). Thus, up-stream farmers cause an external diseconomy for downstream fishers because there are no property rights in hypoxic-free seawater; and the lack of property rights or effective management measures in a fishery means that fishers create deadweight losses through over-fishing. As we saw in Chapter 8, over-fishing removes achievable economic rent; reduces output per unit of effort, leading to an overly large fishing industry; reduces the weight of the catch; and reduces fish biomass to below the socially optimal level. At issue is what would be the social benefits of expensively investing in removing one distortion – the lack of property rights in clean seawater – while the distortion of an open access fishery remains in place.

If the cause of the hypoxia is removed, the carrying capacity of the fishery will increase. In Figure 19.2, with severe hypoxia the lower total revenue curve in the fishery is the relevant function. When hypoxia is reduced the fishery moves to a greater carrying capacity and the upper total revenue function is relevant.

However, the fishery is open assess, and, given the total fishing cost function, when the waters are cleaned up fishing effort increases from E_1 to E_2. In both equilibriums no economic rent is earned because the fishers compete it away. There will be more effort expended, but the fishers will continue to earn only their transfer earnings. In a flexible economy and in the long-run, extra workers in the fishery simply shift out of different employments.

The fish catch is larger though, as is signified on the vertical axis by the higher \$ value of the catch – we are assuming a fixed price of fish. The latter is not an objectionable assumption if the fish caught in a cleaned–up estuary or bay is only a small part of the total fish supply. Indeed, in their assessment of the effect of the Neuse River estuary and Pamlico Sound in North Carolina, Huang et al. (2012) estimated that hypoxia reduced the annual catch of brown shrimp by about 13 percent, but with no effect on price as the fishery is only a small part of the total shrimp supply in the area. If there is no effect on the price of fish there is no change in consumers' surplus following the reduction in hypoxia.

We can see therefore that in an open access fishery with economic rent competed away what is needed for a net benefit to occur is for the price of fish to fall,

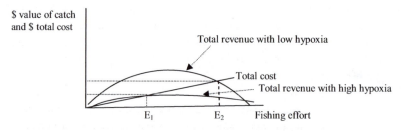

FIGURE 19.2 Comparison of a fishery with and without hypoxic seawater

because consumers' surplus would then increase. In turn, and still assuming an open access fishery, this suggests that for a policy of hypoxia-reduction to yield economic benefits it must have a significantly large impact on fish supply so as to reduce fish prices. This would probably be the case if the Gulf of Mexico dead zone was cleaned up. But the cost of this would be enormous given the size of the drainage area and the expense of the various mitigation policies – such as extending wet-lands, setting land aside for vegetation barriers and reducing fertilizer use. And there would likely be the two unintended consequences referred to earlier: food prices could rise, and, as agriculture at the margin shifts to other areas, fertilizer runoff could increase hypoxia in other waters.

However, there are some other benefits of reducing hypoxia that have not so far been mentioned. For example, in the Huang et al. (2012) study not only does the brown shrimp catch increase – so too does that of blue crab. Also, if people living in the locality put a positive value on having greater access to fresh, "local" fish, they will count this as a benefit. Finally, less hypoxic waters could increase other use values – sports fishing and swimming, for example; and non-use values will have to be counted if citizens put a value on ecosystem improvement.

Without knowing the value of these things – the impact on fish prices and other use and non-use values, as well as the unintended adverse consequences mentioned earlier – a complete benefit–cost study of investment in fertilizer runoff cannot be performed. But what can be said for sure is that benefits would be larger if the relevant fisheries were not open access. Moreover, it is an arguable point that in the presence of mild hypoxia it is not clear whether the net economic benefits of policy action are greater investing in reducing the hypoxia or in managing a fishery so as to maximize its economic rents – to end open access that is.

One final point is that while cleaning up small hypoxic areas – a single estuary or bay – may yield small or no net benefits, a larger program, by significantly increas-ing fish supply, could yield larger net benefits even in the face of an open access or otherwise poorly managed fishery. This point of view urges treating hypoxia reduction in US coastal waters as a long-term, incremental program – one body of water at a time.

8 Conclusions

This chapter has discussed the problem of "dead zones" caused by fertilizer runoff into areas of saltwater. While causes are well known, what to do about the problem is not so clear. The impact of hypoxia on fish catch may not be as great as feared, at least not in the Gulf of Mexico, because fishers can shift with the fish to outside the hypoxic zones. Also, it is argued that policy toward restoring clean ocean water has to consider at least three distortions: lack of property rights in hypoxic-free ocean water, lack of property rights in open access fisheries (or, at least, other-wise badly managed fisheries), and government subsidies increasing incentives to produce fertilizer-intensive crops. It is suggested that significant net benefits from reducing fertilizer runoff may only show up either if many sources are targeted at the same time – in the US context involving an enormous program – or if programs are incremental, requiring a long wait before significant benefits become noticeable.

Notes

1 Hypoxic – reduced oxygen content of water.
2 Eutrophic – water high in nutrients causing reduced oxygen and algae blooms.
3 Bathyal zone – marine ecologic realm lying between 200 and 2,000 meters (660 and 6,600 feet) below the surface.
4 Pelagic zone – the water column above the benthic or bottom zone.
5 The general theory of second best is due to Lipsey and Lancaster (1956).

20

OIL POLLUTION FROM SHIPS

1   Introduction

In 1979 ships spilled about 3,200,000 metric tons of oil into the sea, over three-quarters of it deliberately – mainly when de-ballasting, washing out oil tanks and during regular maintenance such as pumping out the bilges (Cuisine and Grant, 1980).

There are two international treaties that we are concerned with in this chapter: the *International Convention for the Prevention of Pollution of the Sea by Oil* (OILPOL, 1954), entering into force in 1958; and the *International Convention for the Prevention of Pollution from Ships* (MARPOL, 1972 and 1978), entering into force in 1983. The first of these was largely ineffective, while the second is effective, though not perfectly, in reducing deliberate oil pollution at sea.

Changing state behavior in a desired direction, or lack thereof, is a recurring theme in this book. We have seen that treaty observance can follow on from one of several situations:

1   A preponderant actor "leaning on" other countries to comply;
2   where the treaty simply reflects existing behaviors – as with customary international law; or

3   countries realize there is a coordination problem and that a treaty is a way to solve it.[1]

Point (1) in this list is the preponderant actor model discussed in Chapter 12. Point (2) was discussed extensively in Chapter 1 – countries agree only to treaties they find agreeable; and point (3) about resolution of a coordination game was discussed in Chapter 10.

In the case of a treaty to control deliberate oil pollution at sea, we argue in this chapter that point (1) is relevant. Thus, a forcing hegemon (a preponderant actor), the USA, was indeed needed to move an effective treaty. As we saw in Chapter 12, a preponderate actor encourages international acceptance of a treaty by setting a deadline, and threatening that, if the other actors do not agree on a set of effective rules, it will impose its own; the preponderant actor chooses last. Point (2) is not relevant as MARPOL did change behavior. We also argue that points (1) and (3) are not mutually exclusive because a preponderant actor was required to bring the oil pollution coordination game under MARPOL to the better of its two equilibriums.[2]

Even without the "push" of a preponderant actor, MARPOL has an important treaty characteristic that is much better than can be found in OILPOL. By setting equipment standards – the installation of equipment required to reduce oil pollution – compliance with MARPOL was easily verifiable through simple inspection.[3] OILPOL was ineffective because it set performance standards – "no more than so much pollution while at sea" – that were unenforceable because of the lack of an ocean-wide policing authority. Thus, countries that signed OILPOL were covered by point (2) above – signing meant that no change in behavior was necessary. As we saw in Chapter 14, countries that sign treaties that do not want them to change behavior make sure that policing authority is weak. In fact, in the case of deliberate oil pollution at sea, such is the vast scale of the oceans that policing could not help but be next to non-existent.

The search for an international convention on oil pollution at sea dates to the 1920s. In June 1926, at the invitation of the USA, a Preliminary Conference on Oil Pollution of Navigable Waters was held in Washington DC "to facilitate an exchange of views on technical matters and to consider the formulating of proposals for dealing with the problem of oil pollution of navigable waters through international agreement" – but nothing came of it (UN, 1958, p. 169). Then in July 1934 the UK sent a letter to the League of Nations drawing attention to the pollution of the sea coasts of the UK, damage to inshore fisheries, and destruction of sea birds caused by discharge of oil from vessels at sea. The next year the League supported an international convention limiting oil pollution, whereby oil-burning and oil-carrying ships would be prevented from discharging oil or oily mixtures in coastal areas. A Committee of Experts was convened and drew up a draft Convention based on the draft *Washington Convention* of 1926. However, World War II intervened and nothing was done. Afterward, in May 1954, a UN conference in London adopted OILPOL. The *Convention* came into force in 1957. Various standards were set, including a 50 mile/100 parts per million oil discharge standard, "large" ships being banned from polluting entirely; and from 1969 a 60 liter per mile discharge standard was set.

2   Coordination game

By replacing performance standards with equipment standards MARPOL created a coordination game in which it was advantageous for shippers to move to the new standards. MARPOL did this by creating a network effect – basically, a ship had to have installed the necessary equipment if it wanted to be allowed into the network of ports of the signatory countries.

In the coordination game of Figure 20.1 (where the numbers are shippers' profits in millions of dollars) there is no dominant strategy and there are two Nash equilibriums: abate, abate, and pollute, pollute. Thus, by abating a shipper is allowed into any port, and this is profitable. By polluting, shippers have to pay fines. If one shipper abates and the other pollutes we assume that the latter makes extra profits that are not entirely eliminated by any fines incurred.[4] The abate, abate combination is the best outcome (it's Pareto optimal). However, and this is most important, playing abate requires a player to trust the other player also to play abate. For example, starting from pollute, pollute, if the row player plays abate, but the column player continues to play pollute, the row player's payoff falls from 0 to –1. Thus, for the good outcome – abate, abate – to occur each player has to trust the other to play abate.

This is where equipment standards are important: whether a ship conforms to equipment standards is easily verified. For example, MARPOL 1973 required continuous monitoring of discharges of oily water, required governments to provide on-shore treatment facilities at ports and oil terminals, set stricter standards in the Mediterranean, Red Sea, Persian Gulf and Baltic Sea, and required that tankers over 70,000 dwt had segregated ballast tanks so ballast water never entered tanks used for carrying oil. MARPOL 1978 added further regulations, including lowering the segregated ballast tank requirement for all new tankers over 20,000 dwt.

	Abate	Pollute
Abate	2 \ 2	1 \ -1
Pollute	-1 \ 1	0 \ 0

FIGURE 20.1 Ocean dumping as a coordination game

Under MARPOL, trust in the other player also playing abate is not so much the issue; trust in effective policing is. The advantage of equipment standards is that policing occurs while a ship is in port and not out of sight on distant waters; MARPOL substantially reduced policing costs relative to OILPOL. The reason that enforcement on the high seas is not so effective, as we saw in Chapters 3 and 4 on maritime piracy, is not only that it is expensive; it is also because, as a mixed good (a good with private and public good characteristics), countries have incentives to under-invest in it.

3 Network effect

In reality there are a lot more countries involved in world shipping than just the two shown in Figure 20.1. Suppose that there are 70 of them. If just one country adopts the new equipment standards, requiring its own ships to abide by them and refusing entry to its ports by ships that do not meet the equipment standards, it will probably put it at a competitive disadvantage – its own ships will have higher operating costs, and goods delivered to its ports in equipment-compliant ships are probably going to cost more. There is, therefore, not much of an incentive for a signatory country actually to adopt and enforce the new equipment standards.

The situation is different if many of the 70 players are already enforcing the agreed equipment standards. The shipping of a country that has not yet adopted these standards will now be at a competitive disadvantage because it will be refused entry to the ports of the countries that have. As more countries refuse entry to tankers not complying with equipment standards, it becomes less and less beneficial not to comply with them.

4 Preponderant actor

We saw in Chapter 12 that under certain circumstances a single country can force compliance with an international agreement on other countries; such a country is called a preponderant actor, or a hegemon. At issue is this: beginning with just one country playing abate, how and why will all the other countries get drawn into playing abate when initially it is not in their interests to do so? Indeed, at the beginning ratification of MARPOL was slow; but then in stepped the preponderant actor, the USA.

In 1972, under the *Ports and Waterways Safety Act* the USA resolved in the follow-ing few years to replace performance standards with equipment standards for ships plying its EEZ, and in 1978 the USA threatened to ban non-complying tankers from US waters.[5] Not coincidentally, in the same year there was a second MARPOL conference that added tougher equipment standards. As the USA is prominent as a world importer, once it had threatened to impose equipment standards other countries followed with their own; being shut out of shipping goods to the USA would have been intolerable, so they hurriedly agreed to MARPOL, which became effective in 1983. In effect, the preponderant actor had set itself in the position of choosing last – the threat was either collectively agree to MARPOL or we will set the standards.

One last feature worth mentioning is that the leverage on world shipping exerted by the USA as a preponderant actor was enhanced by this network effect. Even if the shippers of a country did not directly trade with the USA, this country could still be drawn in to adopt the new equipment standards because its ships traded with countries that did, and these countries had adopted and were policing the new standards. It appears therefore that the US threat to impose its own equipment standards not only drew the attention of countries that traded with it but also took the world shipping industry as a whole past a tipping point – enough countries wanted to be part of the treaty that they all (or almost all) wanted to be.

5   Effectiveness of MARPOL

Equipment standards set under MARPOL were effective in reducing deliberate oil pollution at sea, which quickly dropped from over two million tons in 1973, to about 1.5 million tons in 1980, and to a little over 0.5 million tons in 1990 – a sustained downward trend despite a tripling of world trade (in value terms) over the same period.[6] Also, in a National Academy of Sciences workshop in 1990 it was said that MARPOL was responsible for a 60 percent reduction in oil pollution at sea, and that since 1979 there was a significant reduction in beach tar around the world.[7] However, as it is true that dumping oil at sea is less costly than disposing of it through port facilities, there still remains an incentive to pollute. In fact, Peet (1992) reports that in 1990 there were 125 cases of alleged oil dumping. He puts this down to both an inadequate level of enforcement (an old story in this book) and possibly an inadequate level of fines (also an old story).

6   Conclusions

Controlling oil pollution at sea by ships is a relative success story in oceans treaty formation. The path was not straightforward, however. Beginning as early as the 1920s, some major countries tried to reduce the amount of oil pollution by requiring shippers to control their rates of deliberate pollution – the so-called "performance" standards. However, as it proved next to impossible to enforce these standards shippers and their governments largely chose not to abide by them. The international treaty signed in the 1950s, OILPOL, failed because it was unenforceable. This situation changed following the passage of MARPOL in 1973/78, under which signatories had to abide by easily policed and enforced equipment standards. Yet, because it is expensive to install the necessary equipment, it was not obvious why all, or most, countries would install them. It was the USA, acting as a preponderant actor to close its ports to non-compliant shipping that encouraged enough countries to become equipment compliant.

Notes

1 This classification is nicely stated by Mitchell (1994).
2 Grolin (1988) implicitly makes this point.
3 See Curtis (1984) for agreement on this point.
4 Peet (1992) suggests that fines levied might have been on the low side.
5 The US Coast Guard was required to set equipment standards if, by 1976, internationally agreed equipment standards had not been established.
6 Trade data from the *Economist*, May 18th, 2013, p. 82. Pollution data from www.oceans-atlas.com/unatlas/issues/pollutiondegradation/oil_poll/oil_pollution.htm.
7 Quoted in Peet (1992), p. 277.

PART IX
Minerals

21

TAXING OFFSHORE OIL AND GAS

Many governments have well-developed arrangements governing oil company access to offshore oil and gas based on lease block systems. Entry is by no means "open access", the main cause of uneconomic exploitation of fisheries resources. Governments also have well-developed methods for sharing excess profits with oil companies, taking the form of lease block auctions, royalty payments and oil taxation; many governments do in fact collect a good deal of available economic rents. There is some irony in this as it is powerful "big oil" that is subjected to constraints imposed by governments aimed at rational resource exploitation and rent sharing, while much smaller fishing companies are able to fight off similar constraints with obvious negative results for the state of the world's fisheries.

1   Some background

Offshore hydrocarbons are big business. In 2010 offshore oil production was 23.6 million barrels per day – 30 percent of global production; and offshore gas production was 2.4 billion cubic meters per day – 27 percent of global production.

TABLE 21.1 Gulf of Mexico US Federal submerged lands oil production, average annual thousands of barrels per day

	Year 0	Year 1	Year 2	Year 3	Year 4	Year 5	Year 6	Year 7	Year 8	Year 9
1980s		719	786	876	956	941	960	892	818	764
1990s	739	799	822	825	860	943	1,021	1,129	1,228	1,354
2000s	1,430	1,536	1,555	1,537	1,462	1,279	1,293	1,282	1,156	1,562
2010s	1,551	1,317	1,266							

US Energy Information Administration, 2013, available online at www.eia.gov/dnav/pet/hist/ LeafHandler.ashx?n=PET&s=MCRFP3FM2&f=A

Offshore oil and gas reserves accounted for, respectively, 20 and 25 percent of the world total. Offshore production is widely spread, with the three largest producing areas being the Middle East (22 percent), Africa (20 percent) and the North Sea (17 percent); North America is the 6th largest producing area, with 8 percent. Annually, about 3,500 offshore wells are drilled by a world fleet of 1,350 drilling rigs, and there are about 17,000 offshore production platforms (Energies Nouvelles, 2012).

The US 1953 *Outer Continental Shelf Lands Act* gives federal jurisdiction over the US outer continental shelf – i.e. beyond state-waters for purposes of minerals leasing. The Secretary of the Interior is authorized to apply the public trust doctrine to balance the interests of the oil industry, the fishing industry and environmentalists.

As Table 21.1 shows, offshore oil and gas production in the main US producing area, the Gulf of Mexico, increased from about 700,000 barrels per day in 1981 to 1.55 million barrels per day in 2010, declining somewhat thereafter due to a ban on drilling following the massive Deepwater Horizon oil spill. Even so, US offshore production amounts to about 30 percent of domestic oil production and 25 percent of domestic gas production.

While large reserves of oil and gas are thought to exist offshore at the present time, offshore activity is restricted to only two areas: western and central Gulf of Mexico and Alaska. That offshore oil and gas production is so geographically restricted in the USA owes to the 1969 Santa Barbara blowout that led to a slew of environmentally conscious legislation. By the 1980s about 98 percent of US outer continental shelf was off limits. The Clinton Administration extended the ban on leasing in new areas to 2012; and although in March 2010 the Obama Administration proposed opening new areas mainly from Delaware southward to central Florida,[1] it quickly changed its mind following the Deepwater Horizon spill. The ban now extends through 2017.[2]

In 1964, under the *Continental Shelf Act*, the UK claimed its continental shelf and drew up the Petroleum Production Regulations for licensing and control of offshore hydrocarbons. It also issued the first round of licenses under a lease block system that is similar to the Americans'. The UK continental shelf is divided into rectangles with perimeters of one degree of latitude by one degree of longitude. Each rectangle is further divided into thirty blocks of approximately 250 km². Companies are invited to apply for the right to explore blocks selected by the government in licensing rounds held every two years.

Offshore oil and gas production can yield extraordinarily high profits for oil companies, in which the owners of the resource – the people of a nation – want to share. For example, the US *Outer Continental Shelf Act* requires the Department of the Interior to ensure that the United States receives the fair market value of US oil and gas resources.[3] Oil companies are to be allowed to make a "fair" rate of return. Any rate of return above this is a windfall gain collected by the oil company rather than by the owners of the resource.

At issue is how to transfer economic rents from oil companies to government. There are three broad methods of extracting natural resource rents: through auctions whereby oil companies make up-front payments to obtain the rights to develop offshore lease blocks; through royalty payments whereby an oil company "hands over" (pays in kind) a percentage of the physical oil or gas produced, or, as is more often the case, a percentage of the cash value of the oil and gas produced; and, third, through taxation of profits.

2   Economic rent defined

The concept of economic rent is accredited to David Ricardo: it is a surplus due to the "original and indestructible powers of the soil". In other words, it is value that has been created by nature and not by the creative efforts of workers – their creative work is in extracting the oil. Most importantly, economic rent can be taxed away without altering supply, as that resource already exists. Annual economic rent is calculated as:

$$\text{Annual economic rent} = \text{annual total revenue} - \text{annual economic cost} \quad (1)$$

where in the case of offshore oil

$$\text{Annual total revenue} = \text{price per barrel} \times \text{number of barrels produced}$$

$$\text{Annual total economic cost} = \text{quantity of inputs} \times \text{respective supply prices}$$

In the latter equation, the inputs are labor and capital but not the *in situ* oil, as it is a "gift of nature". By "supply prices" is meant the minimum price a factor of production, say, labor, will work for a firm. That is, "supply price" is the same as an input's transfer earnings. For example, a down-hole tools supplier has a minimum supply price of its equipment, which, as we will see, oil companies try to reveal through a closed-bid competitive auction. Economic rent and "economic profit"

TABLE 21.2 Annual economic rents of six hypothetical oil fields

Field no.	Oil price per barrel $	Economic cost per barrel $	Economic rent per barrel $	Number of barrels recoverable per year (millions)	Annual economic rent ($ billions)
1	100	24	76	100	7.60
2	100	40	60	10	0.60
3	100	48	52	300	15.60
4	100	80	20	120	2.40
5	100	100	0	40	0
6	100	120	–20	20	Field not developed

are equal if the factor supply curves are perfectly elastic (horizontal), otherwise oil companies and their suppliers share in the economic rent. Of interest is how to extract economic rent from oil companies.

A fundamental principle of taxation is that a tax should be non-distortionary. If taxes have to be collected then they should as far as possible not interfere with the allocation of resources that would otherwise prevail. This principle is based on the idea that (under certain assumptions) unhindered markets achieve the most efficient allocation of resources.

As equation (1) indicates, economic rent generated by an oil field is determined by the difference between total revenue and total economic cost. Table 21.2 shows the economic rents of six hypothetical oil fields assuming an oil price of $100 per barrel.

Looking at field number 1, with a $100 per barrel oil price and a recovery cost of $24 per barrel, *per* barrel economic rent is $76. As it is expected that 100 million barrels of oil per year will be recovered from field 1, annual economic rent is $7.6 billion. Similar calculations are performed for the other five fields and their annual economic rents are recorded in the final column of Table 21.2.

Field 5 is the marginal field: it is in production but earns no economic rent. Its revenues are just enough to cover costs with a "fair" rate of return on capital. Notice that a rise in the price of oil to $120 per barrel would bring field number 6 into production as the marginal field and the economic rents on all the other fields would increase.

Figure 21.1 is based on the data in Table 21.2 with the oil fields aligned in order of increasing production cost.

Economic rent in the short- and long-run

Offshore oil production has three stages – exploration, development and production. Each of these has its own sunk (or non-recurring) costs – for example, seismic

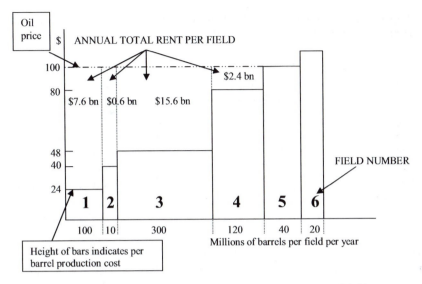

FIGURE 21.1 Production costs, oil price and economic rents of six oil fields

surveys in the exploration stage, and the use of drilling companies in the development phase. Since sunk cost at the third and final stage of production includes the sunk costs of the earlier stages, once production has begun short-run economic rent, as calculated by equation (1) using annual revenues and costs, may appear to be large. It might be tempting therefore for a government to tax this economic rent at a high rate, since an oil company will remain in production as long as taxes don't reduce after-tax revenues below current total variable cost.

However, looking to the long-run it would be a mistake to set offshore oil taxation at a level that removes all, or even most, of this short-run economic rent. At such a high tax rate oil companies would reason that the rate of return is too low to encourage them to invest in the sunk costs incurred in the exploration or development of *new* oil fields. Thus, supposing that the normal rate of profit on investment for the class of risks incurred by oil companies is 12 percent, the rate of tax on them should leave them earning a net rate of return of at least 12 percent in the long-run – when all costs are counted, including the sunk costs of the earlier stages of oil production.[4]

We now discuss the three main methods of collecting economic rents: auctions, royalties and taxes.

3   Auctions

The US outer-continental shelf (OCS) leasing mechanism works like this: the Bureau of Ocean Energy Management, Regulation and Enforcement (which used to be called the Minerals Management Service) selects a tract of submerged land

and divides it into approximately nine square mile blocks. Interested oil companies then perform seismic surveys (but no drilling) on their chosen block(s) and decide whether and how much to bid for what's on offer – a fixed term (usually five-year) lease with a small annual rental.

The government announces a closing date for a first-price sealed bid auction and on the chosen day the "envelopes" are opened and the winning bidder announced. The winning bidder pays its so-called "bonus" bid and then has the right to explore and develop the lease block it has acquired. If it finds oil the lease is automatically renewed; if not, the oil company has the option of renewing it. In the event that a block is productive, royalties are paid to the US government. For existing leases this rate is typically $16\frac{2}{3}$ percent with, from June 2007, the rate on new leases raised to $18\frac{3}{4}$ percent.

Thus, with auctions oil companies make up-front payments to the government. There are four main advantages of up-front payments:

1   The government obtains income early in the life of a field.
2   As the winning bidder must value the lease block most highly of all bidders it is possible that it is the low-cost producer – otherwise it could not have bid so high. This is a clear advantage of an auction system over administrative allocation of lease blocks; government is unlikely to have a good idea as to respective oil company costs.
3   If there were no other payments to be made, distortions to resource allocation would be minimal. To illustrate, a tax on your income may cause you to work fewer hours – so causing a misallocation of time. However, if you paid a lump sum tax at the beginning of the year how many hours you worked during the year is unaffected by the tax which is now a bygone – a "sunk cost".
4   The amount of a bid will be related to the net present value (calculated as the expected discounted value of the annual economic rents) of a lease block. In principle, in a competitive auction, with all bidders having complete information, the bid price will approach the expected value of the discounted annual rents because firms are competing for the right to collect those economic rents. As rational bidding requires knowledge of the likely expected net profits, knowledge of a lease block's geology is crucial.

Thus, if the six oil fields in Table 21.2 and Figure 21.1 were the only fields on each of six different lease blocks, the present value of each block can be calculated. To do this some additional assumptions are needed. First, assume that each field has a ten-year commercial life and, second, that oil companies apply a 12 percent discount rate to the annual economic rents. That is, they require a 12 percent rate of return. If they think that they cannot get this rate of return they will not be interested in bidding in the first place. With a 12 percent discount rate the corresponding economic rents over the ten-year life of the fields is as shown in the right-hand column of Table 21.3.

TABLE 21.3 Expected discounted economic rents

Field number	Annual economic rent ($ billions)	Expected economic rent ($ billions); ten-year life, 12% discount rate
1	7.6	42.9
2	0.6	3.4
3	15.6	88.1
4	2.4	13.6
5	0	0
6	Field not developed	Field not developed

The present value of the annual economic rent generated by field number 1 is $42.9 billion. The present values of the economic rents of the other five fields are also shown.

As indicated earlier, since oil companies are willing to compete to obtain these economic rents their maximum bid prices in principle would approach these values. If this happens the government would collect the expected value of the economic rent, leaving the oil companies only with a "fair rate of return" equal to their 12 percent rate of normal profit.

According to a 1976 US Department of the Interior task force, government receives fair market value for a lease block when the lessee receives no more than a "normal" rate of return. Under this criterion, if the "normal" rate of return is 12 percent, lessees should be left with no economic rent as their bid prices or other methods of extracting economic rents – royalties and taxes – would transfer it to the government. Such an extraction of rents would not discourage production because the oil companies are still left making a "normal" rate of return.

However, in 1982 a Department of the Interior task force set a new "fairness" criterion. "The task force indicated that fair market value was not the value of the oil and gas eventually discovered and produced; instead it is the value of 'the right' to explore and, if there is a discovery, to develop and produce the energy resource" (GAO, 2008, p. 3).

In the foregoing discussion, as an oil company bids the discounted expected value of rents, it doesn't matter which of the two Department of Interior criteria are used – the outcome is one and the same because the discount rate is a fixed rate at 12 percent. However, if the discount rate applied by oil companies was higher than the assumed "normal" 12 percent rate of return, they would bid lesser amounts for the lease blocks; and if government could not make this difference up with higher royalty or tax rates, oil company gains would be "the people's loss".

There are indeed problems with the lease block auction arrangement that speak directly to this issue. Moreover, any increases in oil prices would produce windfall gains only for the oil companies.

Problems with up-front rent collection

As nice as the theory of up-front rent collection through lease block auctions sounds, there are several problems with it:

1   The efficiency of a competitive auction depends on the bidders having equally good knowledge of the geology of the lease blocks up for sale. In practice this may not be the case – especially on "drainage" leases, where a company is already producing oil or gas on an adjacent block. In fact, it is known that winners in offshore lease block auctions are often oil companies that lease an adjoining block (Porter, 1992). This appears to be because the company next door has a better idea of the geology of an adjoining block. This company knows that other companies will on average place low bids because of their higher risks caused by their lack of knowledge. Therefore, it too places a low bid. Porter (1992, p. 34) indeed finds that economic rents earned by winning bidders on drainage leases are higher than on "wild cat" leases (where no bidder has an informational advantage), and suggests that winners of drainage leases should pay higher royalty rates than winners of wildcat leases.

2   The private rate of discount is likely to be higher than the social rate of discount because oil companies are less well diversified than are governments. A government is more diversified because it owns all of the lease blocks, while an individual oil company leases only a few of them. Because oil companies are less well diversified their risks are greater and they will apply higher discount rates to the expected profit stream. Accordingly, bids will be lower – for example if a 20 percent rather than a 12 percent discount rate is applied to field 1 in Table 21.3 expected economic rent falls from $42.9 to $31.9 billion.

3   Winning a lease block in a competitive auction may be subject to the "winner's curse". In other words, the winning bidder may be the one that most over-values it and subsequently incurs losses. Knowing this risk, bidders may increase their rates of discount and place lower bids.

4   Oil companies could collude to reduce their bids. According to Haile, Hendricks and Porter (2010), there is tentative evidence for this on drainage leases at least prior to 1973.

5   If there is political risk that a lease block could be nationalized without fair compensation oil companies will include a risk-premium in their bids and correspondingly reduce their bids.[5]

6   Economic rents also depend on the level of oil prices. A sharp rise in oil prices (as occurred in 1973–74, 1979–80, 1990–91, 2000, 2003–2006, 2008 and 2011) creates large windfall economic rents that a government cannot share in if it is using only an up-front rent-collection system – a point raised in GAO (2008, p. 7), where the rigidity of the US oil rent-extraction system is emphasized. Moreover, with an auction system it is the oil companies that bear the risk of

lower oil prices. The relative rigidity of the American system in the face of sometimes sharply fluctuating oil prices therefore raises oil company risks. In turn this is likely to be reflected in higher discount rates and reduced profit sharing with government.

7   Up-front rent collection leaves oil companies bearing all of the risks that a lease block will not in fact yield any oil or gas in commercial quantities. The greater is the risk of this the larger will be the discount rate applied to expected economic rents and, therefore, the lower will be bid prices and rent collected by the government.

A superior approach to rent collection is for the government to share in the risk of a "dry" block. Such a risk sharing system would not rely solely on up-front payments but would collect rents on an annual basis if and when they appear. We return to this argument below when we discuss the Brown tax.

Before going on to discuss royalties and oil taxation we digress to discuss some features of the global offshore oil supply industry. We will see that while governments use the lease block auction to extract rents from oil companies, the latter also use auctions aimed at ensuring that they pay only competitive prices for the many inputs they purchase.

4   Offshore oil supply industry

A fuller description of the offshore oil gathering industry is contained in Hallwood (1990, 1991a, 1991b); here, only a few stylized facts are listed. First, the international offshore oil supply industry is made up of two quite distinct groups of firms – the oil companies and the multinational offshore oil supply firms. The oil companies create "pools" of demand in geographically wide-spread offshore oil provinces and the multinational suppliers supply these markets, almost always through affiliates they establish for this purpose. The dynamics of this internationalization process belongs largely to the theory of the multinational corporation. More descriptively, the international offshore oil supply industry can be likened to a Silk Road caravan that many centuries ago moved goods out of China: many firms traveled together and were serviced along the route by "locationally" fixed firms – in the context of the offshore oil supply industry, like hotel services.

Second, the operational focus of offshore oil production is the oil production platform with its associated topside and seabed fixed structures. An oil company will own (often in a consortium) the production platform and its fixtures – but it will have had other companies complete the design and construction work.

Third, a large expense is the use of an offshore drilling rig. Unlike the production platform, however, an oil company will usually *not* own the rigs that it uses, preferring to hire on a time-contract basis the services of specialist offshore drilling companies. There are many other service inputs into offshore oil gathering and it is a striking fact that oil companies also usually purchase these on a time-contract basis.[6] As an oil company executive put it to me: apart from the platform, "an oil company aims to own as little as possible".

Invited tender-bid auction

As already mentioned, potential suppliers are required to compete through a procurement auction for the right to supply an oil company with inputs. Such a system benefits the purchaser by affecting a carryover of pre-contract award price-competition into the contract execution period. Like bonus bidding for offshore lease blocks in the USA, this market-arrangement is a variety of first-price sealed bid procurement auction with bidders being individually invited to bid. By using the invitation, oil companies are able to keep the costs of assessing bids down. The sealed bid element can be explained with reference to Robinson (1985), who argued that sealed bidding is preferable to open bidding when bidders have a propensity to collude because less information is (legally) passed between bidders.

5 Royalties

Royalties are paid by oil companies as a percentage of oil output, thereby raising the marginal costs of production. This is a well-established result in the literature (e.g. Reece, 1979). For example, if the royalty rate is 18 percent an oil company has to incur the cost of producing 118 barrels of oil in order to add 100 barrels of oil to the output it can sell. By raising the marginal cost of production a royalty system is distortionary. Thus, in Table 21.2 and Figure 21.1, because of its increased production costs from $100 to $118 per barrel, the marginal field, field number 5, is no longer economic and will not therefore be developed. Moreover, if the royalty rate was a little over 25 percent field number 4 would be uneconomic as well.

Distortions occur in another dimension. It is usually the case that as an oil field ages its marginal cost of production rises – for example, gas may have to be pumped back into it in order to maintain pressure and its rate of oil flow. At some point marginal cost becomes so high that the field will be abandoned. As the effect of royalty payments is that marginal costs rise further, abandonment will occur sooner.

Sliding scale royalty systems are used around the world, but not in the USA, the aim being to collect more of the rent generated by the more productive fields – fields 1 and 2 in Figure 21.1, for example. The sliding scale may be constructed using various methods. For example, the royalty rate is increased when a field's aggregate oil production passes a certain trigger point. The underlying assumption is that, as fixed costs between fields are likely to be similar, fields that produce more oil are more profitable. Another sliding scale method is to increase the royalty rate as the ratio of cumulative total revenues to cumulative total costs increases.

6 Taxing offshore oil: General tax principles

Choice of a tax regime should correspond to certain criteria:

1   Neutrality of impact on effort. A petroleum tax regime should extract only economic rent and not bias resource allocation; in particular, it should not reduce levels of exploration, development or production. Just as much oil should be produced over the same time period with a tax regime as without one. As we have just seen, this is not the case with a royalty regime.
2   Taxation should only be of long term-rents so that full cost recovery by oil companies is allowed. Profits tax rates, therefore, should not be punitive.
3   Risk sharing. The prospective profitability of an offshore lease block is not known with certainty. At issue is how risks are to be shared between the resource owners and, what in effect are their agents, the oil companies. The more risk that is transferred to an oil company, the greater will be its desired rate of return. As future expected profits would then be discounted at a higher discount rate there is again the danger that marginal fields will not be developed.
4   Return on marginal (no rent) projects should not be affected by the tax regime – otherwise they may not be implemented.
5   Horizontal equity. Projects with similar costs – and, therefore, economic rents – should be treated equally.
6   Vertical equity. The proportion of rent taken through taxes should be equal between fields. There is, though, a case for a progressive tax rate whereby a higher proportion of the profits of more profitable fields is taken.

Thus, again with reference to Figure 21.1, what a tax regime should aim for is to skim off only the economic rent of each oil field. If it does this and nothing more, all five oil fields will remain in production, the resource owner will be rewarded a fair return on its property and the producers will have earned a fair return on the risks taken and effort expended.

7 An ideal tax – the Brown tax

The Brown tax is an "ideal" tax. It is paid as a percentage of revenues net of costs, at, say, a 50 percent rate. If net revenue is positive, an oil company pays taxes to the government. If net revenue is negative, the government pays a 50 percent subsidy to an oil company. The advantage of this system is that risks are shared between government and oil companies. This contrasts with auction, royalty and other tax systems. As the government makes no contribution to production costs, all of these leave the oil companies bearing up-front risks before production begins – if it begins. As a Brown tax would lower risks, oil company discount rates should be lower, with the result that more oil exploration, development and production would be done.

However, a disadvantage of the Brown tax is that while it improves tax efficiency it introduces a principal–agent problem. An oil company (the agent), knowing that losses are featherbedded by subsidies, may not strive to minimize costs. With the principal (the government) bearing a proportion of losses, the agent has reduced incentives to contain costs. If so, effort would become less cost-efficient than if oil companies, at least initially, bear all of the costs. To cope with this principal–agent problem a government would need to collect detailed information on oil company operations. In effect, it would need to get into the offshore oil business. In fact, although a Brown tax has attractive properties, one has never been put into operation.

8 Resource rent taxes

A resource rent tax (RRT) is a tax on a project's net cash flow once it has become profitable.[7] Expense incurred prior to production beginning is carried forward to be set against tax liabilities. The tax code will specify a threshold level of profits (allowing an oil company a fair rate of return). A positive tax rate on profits above this threshold is set. The latter may escalate as rates of profit above the threshold rise.

With an RRT the government shares in risks only if a project becomes profitable – as it is only then that accumulated costs are set against net cash flows. Because of this, an RRT is not exactly the same as a Brown tax. However, the RRT concept has been written into many offshore oil taxation regimes around the world. Zhang (1997) finds that PRT if applied properly is non-distortionary.

In practice, details of oil tax regimes differ between countries. Kemp (1990) examined the petroleum tax systems in ten countries, finding that they all introduced distortions at the margin. His main conclusion was that "a combination of bonus bids with a resource rent tax offers the best hope for the accurate collection of economic rents without introducing distortions" (p. 324). Combinations of rent-extraction devices that include a significant component of fixed rate royalties – as in the USA's bonus bidding and royalty system – were found to introduce the most severe distortions. In a later study he examined the oil tax systems of the UK, Norway, Denmark and the Netherlands, finding that all of them had the desirable property of being progressive with respect to levels of profits – the larger were profits, the larger the government take. This flexibility allows governments to share in windfall profits of higher oil prices, yet does not unduly penalize oil companies when oil prices fall. However, in all four cases he found a distortionary component in that the tax regimes tended to discourage the development of new fields (Kemp, 1992).

9 Size of rents collected

No study has ever definitively measured economic rents, as this would require knowing the opportunity costs of all inputs into offshore oil gathering – the production costs in Table 21.2 are known for sure. The best that can be done is to make rough estimates.

One rough estimate is that of the "government-take", which is defined as annual:

[royalties + rents + other taxes + other fees]/oil company revenues

where "other fees" includes bonus bid payments.[8]

GAO (2008, p. 11) refers to a comprehensive study of government-takes in 104 countries. These vary widely from 18 to 98 percent. The USA's Gulf of Mexico's ranking was only 93rd lowest – 92 countries had larger government takes – and that take was 44 percent, a figure confirmed by three other studies. Taking a single year, in 2005, of sales revenue of $15.4 billion, $6.33 billion, or 41 percent, was collected by the Federal government.[9] The GAO does not think that this low government-take is "fair" because Gulf of Mexico oil reserves are plentiful (due to relatively low exploration and development costs) and the USA is a good country in which to do business (because of the low political risk). However, these are only loose indicators of opportunity costs of operating in the Gulf of Mexico; the GAO thinks these costs to be low and, by implication, that oil companies are retaining a large proportion of the economic rents.

By comparison, according to the UK Offshore Operators Association, of the price of a barrel of oil about 71 percent pays for production costs (exploration, development and production costs taken together), 16 percent goes to taxes, and 13 percent is left for the producer (UKOOA website *circa* 2009). UKOOA also estimates that marginal government tax-take from North Sea fields ranges from 40 percent to 70 percent. That is, for each extra £1 of profits, up to 70 percent is paid to the government in extra taxes. In an earlier study at the height of the British sector North Sea oil boom, Kemp and Hallwood (1983) estimated that for 26 North Sea oil fields taken together, the UK government's tax share of profits was 81 percent.

Notes

1 Congressional Research Service (2010).
2 Committee on Natural Resources, http://naturalresources.house.gov/news/documents-ingle.aspx?DocumentID = 267985.
3 Stated in US Government Accountability Office, *Oil and Gas Royalties*, GAO-08-691, September 2008.
4 Here is an example of excessive short-run rent taxation. In December 2005 the British government doubled corporation tax on North Sea producers and Shell, a major oil company, immediately announced that it was cutting its North Sea exploration drilling programs by one-third – from three to two drilling rigs, potentially leaving billions of barrels of oil in the ground (*The Scotsman*, December 16th, 2005).
5 An interesting point is that the jump in oil prices in 1973–74 followed quite quickly on from the nationalization of foreign oil companies by the host governments. If the latter applied lower discount rates to expected profit steams, they would want to leave the oil in the ground for longer. Hence, rates of production were expected to fall and oil prices jumped.
6 Examples of specific inputs to oil gathering include mud engineering and logging, well site geology, core analysis, electrical logging services, wireline services, workover services,

reservoir engineering and production engineering. Geophysical and geological services, while not entirely specific to the oil industry, do require a large industry-specific body of knowledge. Many types of equipment are also specific to – but mobile within – the oil industry: drill rods, downhole tools and many other types of tools are examples.

7 Since 1984 *Australia* has used a resource rent tax whereby, on a project-by-project basis, positive net cash flows are taxed (with allowance for accumulated costs) after a specified rate of return – calculated as a premium on the government bond rate – has been reached. The tax system of the *Canadian Federal government* also approximates an RRT regime. Federal taxes are paid on a project basis with allowance for accumulated costs. The regime combines a low royalty on gross revenues, and a net profit tax. In the *United Kingdom*'s oil tax regime, each offshore oil field is fiscally "ring-fenced" – meaning that corporate income tax is on a profits-per-field basis, and a petroleum revenue tax (PRT) is also levied on a project's net cash flows. However, there is no allowance for accumulated costs. Even so, the UK tax regime is aimed at taxing economic rents, as the rate of PRT is quite frequently altered as oil prices fluctuate. Popular in some *developing countries* is a volume percentage tax that is stated as a percentage of oil volume produced. If an oil company buys back this oil, the system amounts to a tax on gross revenue. Volume percentages are similar, therefore, to a tax system of gross revenue percentages. In a production sharing agreement a country actually takes possession of some oil from the oil company and markets it itself through a national oil company.

8 In the USA a winning bidder has to pay one-fifth of the bonus bid immediately, and the remainder along with the annual rental at the end of the first year (GAO, 2008, p, 8).

9 Minerals Management Service.

22

US ROYALTY RELIEF, RENT SHARING AND OFFSHORE OIL PRODUCTION[1]

1   The issue
2   Economic analysis
3   Conclusions

1   The issue

Under the *Deepwater Royalty Relief Act* (1995), royalty relief is given as an incentive to increase offshore oil exploration, development and production; relief was given on leases awarded between 1996 and 2000 for drilling in water in the Gulf of Mexico deeper than 200 meters. When the program expired in November 2000, the responsible authority, the Minerals Management Service, continued with a similar relief arrangement. In August 2005 the *Energy Policy Act* came into force; section 344 extended royalty relief to gas production in US waters of more than 200 meters deep, and section 345 provided for additional mandatory royalty relief for deepwater oil drilling.[2] However, the 2008 federal budget proposed repeal of sections 344 and 345 of the 2005 *Act*.[3] This short chapter discusses why repeal of royalty relief is justified in terms of fairer sharing of economic rents between oil companies and the owners of US submerged lands – American citizens. Admittedly, repeal of royalty relief could reintroduce a small tax distortion to offshore oil activity to the extent that royalty payments render some deepwater offshore oil production uneconomic. However, as the calculations by Ashton, Upton and Rothkopf (2005) discussed below imply, the distortionary effect of royalties on US deepwater offshore oil activity is slight, while their effect on lost government revenue is very great. A fair-minded observer might conclude therefore that the distortion–fair shares trade-off offered by the ending of royalty relief was worthwhile accepting.[4]

Ashton, Upton and Rothkopf (2005) calculate that royalty relief offered to oil companies for wells drilled in marginal, deepwater fields has little effect on oil production, but could cost the government a great deal in forgone royalty revenues. Projected total oil production was expected to increase by only 0.9 percent, gas production by 0.6 percent, and offshore oil reserves by only 1.1 percent. The cost of these small increases in reserves and output is estimated to be about $48 billion in present value (2003 constant dollar) terms, or 7 percent of projected offshore oil and gas royalty revenues.

The reason for the cost ineffectiveness of Federal government's royalty relief program is caused by the behavior of marginal production costs, which are known to increase sharply as oil production moves into deeper waters – beyond 5,000 feet in the case of the Gulf of Mexico. Indeed, the Federal government justifies royalty relief for marginal fields on the basis that their exploration, development and production costs are high, and need to be subsidized.

2 Economic analysis

Economic analysis of the foregoing findings is straightforward. We can begin by writing oil company operating profit net of corporation taxes and royalties as

$$\Pi = [PQ(1 - r) - C](1 - t)$$

where Π is profit net of corporation tax, t, and royalty rate, r. P is the market price of a barrel of oil, Q is the level of oil production per period of time, and C is the cost of producing a barrel of oil.

Multiplying through and rearranging gives

$$\Pi = PQ(1 - r - t + rt) - C(1 - t)$$

And dividing through by Q yields

$$\Pi/Q = P(1 - r - t + rt) - C(1 - t)/Q$$

which states that net operating profit per barrel = net price minus net per barrel cost of production.

The effect of royalty payments and corporation taxes on net price, production and the combined tax-royalty take is shown in Figure 22.1, which uses a stylized function reflecting the government's assumption of sharply rising marginal costs as oil production moves into deep waters.

P_1 is price before corporation tax and royalties. At P_1 production per year would be Q_1. As corporation tax and royalty are levied, net price is NP_1, and production

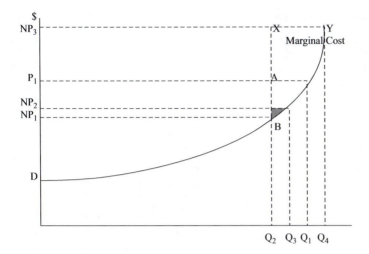

FIGURE 22.1 Oil production under rising marginal cost

is Q_2. Government revenues are P_1ABNP_1, equal to about 40 percent of economic rent (area P_1ABD) – the approximate government-take in the US case. Oil company net revenue is NP_1BD, equal to about 60 percent of economic rent.

Waiving royalties on marginal fields raises net price received by oil companies on production from these fields by between 12 and 16 percent (equal to the royalty rates). Thus,

$$NP_2 = P_1(1 - t) > NP_1 = P_1(1 - r - t + rt)$$

As a result, oil production rises from Q_2 to Q_3. Corporation tax and royalty-receipts on the pre-existing fields (i.e. those producing up to Q_2 barrels of oil) remains unchanged.

Net operating profit on the marginal fields is:

$$\Pi = [P_1(Q_3 - Q_2)(1 - t)] - C(1 - t)$$

Forgone royalty revenue on the marginal fields is $P_1(Q_3 - Q_2)r$, which is equal to a portion of the shaded area in Figure 22.1. It is not the whole area as corporation tax is collected on profits generated by this marginal deepwater production.

It is observed that royalty relief has only a small effect on offshore oil production but the cost is not great in terms of forgone royalty revenue. However, royalty relief is much more costly if market prices of oil skyrocket, as they did between 1999 and 2006 – from less than $20 per barrel to almost $80 per barrel. Suppose that at the much higher market prices, net price with royalty relief would rise to NP_3. Forgone royalty revenue is now much greater than at lower market prices (proxied by P_1)

when the royalty relief incentives scheme was put into effect. At NP_3 forgone royalty revenue is now a portion of the much larger area XYB.

It follows therefore that a sensible royalty relief program would phase royalty relief out – i.e. companies would pay royalties once oil prices had reached a critical level high enough to cover production costs, so as not to leave oil companies with "too much" economic rent. This level would be where market price net of corporation tax and royalties is equal to cost of production net of corporation taxes. That is, where $P(1 - r - t + rt) = C(1 - t)/Q$. Given estimated costs of producing in deepwater, this critical market price might be between \$40 and \$50 per barrel.

However, the Department of the Interior argued that "The continued use of royalty relief in the deep waters of the Gulf provides the needed economic incentive to keep industry moving forward on new technologies and exploring deeper water frontiers" (2007). Accordingly forgone royalty relief might be worthwhile if, by creating an incentive to operate in deepwater, oil companies were given an incentive to create the technology to make this possible. However, as the foregoing economic analysis indicates, it is the steep increase in oil prices (by a multiple of four) rather than royalty relief (only 12–16 percent of revenue) that is clearly proving critical in inducing oil companies to move into deeper offshore waters. The effect of higher prices on offshore oil activity has been frequently analyzed. For example, Kemp and Stephen (2006) estimate that the number of exploration wells drilled in the British sector of the North Sea would almost double from 20 to 38 per year as oil prices increased from \$25 to \$40 per barrel. Kemp and Kasim (2000) calculate that oil sector investment depends positively on oil prices, and a similar finding is found for investment in the US oil sector (Farzin, 2001).

3   Conclusions

Given sharply rising production costs in deepwater oil fields, royalty relief of, at most, 12–16 percent is an incentive of marginal significance in either stimulating exploration activity or in spurring technological change. Indeed, royalty relief, by raising net price, could have the reverse of the intended effect on technological change, as oil companies' incentive to be cost-efficient is somewhat reduced. Besides, it is the sharply higher oil prices of recent years that have created much stronger incentives to move into deeper waters. The main effect of royalty relief therefore has been to reduce the government's share of offshore oil rents.

Notes

1 First appeared as "A Note on US Royalty Relief, Rent Sharing and Offshore Oil Production", *Energy Policy*, 35, 5077–5079, 2007.
2 Energy Information Administration, Office of Oil and Gas (2006) *Overview of the Federal Offshore Royalty Relief Program*, June 2006, p. 1, available online at http://tonto.eia.doe.gov/FTPROOT/features/ngoffshore.pdf.

3 Minerals Management Service, US Department of the Interior, *Budget Justifications and Performance Information for FY 2008*, p. 9, available online at www.doi.gov/budget/2008/ data/greenbook/FY2008_MMS_Greenbook.pdf.
4 Besides, in practice completely non-distortionary taxes can hardly be the standard set for the establishment of any rent-sharing tax regime.

23

DEEP SEA MINING: RETROSPECT AND PROSPECT

1   Introduction

In a 5 million km^2 area of the eastern Pacific Ocean more than 27 billion tonnes of polymetallic nodules could be laying on or just under the seabed; they could yield perhaps 7 billion tonnes of manganese, 340 million tonnes of nickel, 290 million tonnes of copper and 78 million tonnes of cobalt.[1] Though not insignificant, this area is only about 3 percent of the total area of the Pacific Ocean. Another report claims that mineral deposits on or just under the sea floor could contain ten times the amount of commercially valuable minerals as those on land.[2]

International public law governing deep sea mining (DSM) for minerals is moving toward a system similar to that governing offshore oil industries operating in the EEZs.[3] As discussed in Chapter 21, to govern their offshore oil provinces countries have taken the powers to introduce regulatory regimes that divide their ocean spaces into lease blocks, restricting access through licensing, promoting economically efficient resource extraction, and aiming for the "fair" sharing of economic rents between oil companies and governments. However, the path toward a similar and internationally acceptable DSM regime has not been straightforward, and nor is it complete. The rules relating to DSM originally set out in UNCLOS 1982 have had to be substantially revised and although ratified in 1996 they are still incomplete, particularly with respect to the governance of rent sharing between mining companies and the International Seabed Authority (ISA).

2   Common heritage of mankind

Despite its shortcomings the existing deep sea mining regime can be counted as a singular achievement of international diplomacy regarding the exploitation of high seas ocean resources. It is the only regime so far to be based on the *common heritage of mankind* doctrine (see Chapter 1 for a discussion of the *common heritage of mankind*). Specifically, the Preamble of UNCLOS 1982 says, referring to UN resolution 2429, December 1970, that "the General Assembly of the United Nations solemnly declared *inter alia* that the area of the seabed and ocean floor and the subsoil thereof, beyond the limits of national jurisdiction, as well as its resources, are the common heritage of mankind, the exploration and exploitation of which shall be carried out for the benefit of mankind as a whole, irrespective of the geographical location of States". In other words, economic rents are to be shared globally. There is to be no "gold rush" where corporations or countries that get there first scoop available economic rents – this of course being very different to high seas fisheries.

Part XI of UNCLOS 1982 defined three critical components of a future DSM regime: the "*Area*", the "*Authority*" and the "*Enterprise*".

The "*Area*" is the high seas beyond any country's EEZ. "All rights in the resources of the Area are vested in mankind as a whole" (Article 137).

The "*Authority*" became the International Seabed Authority (ISA), headquartered in Kingston, Jamaica. A report to the ISB in 2013 describes the Authority as the "Mining Ministry of the Area", having responsibility for administrative and fiscal affairs relating to DSM.[4] The Authority has three organs: an Assembly, Council and Secretariat. The Assembly of all members of the ISA sets general policies; the Council, a sub-set of Assembly members, sets specific policies consistent with those general policies;[5] and the Secretariat performs administrative functions for the Authority, the Assembly and the Council.

As to the sharing of economic rents, Article 140 says that "The Authority shall provide for the equitable sharing of financial and other economic benefits" between countries. Moreover, Article 160 (f)(i) says that the Assembly will "consider and approve, upon the recommendation of the Council, the rules, regulations and procedures on the equitable sharing of financial and other economic benefits derived from activities in the Area and the payments and contributions made . . . taking into particular consideration the interests and needs of developing States and peoples who have not attained full independence or other self-governing status".

This latter Article is very interesting because, in emphasizing the interests of developing countries, UNCLOS 1982, in its DSM Articles, was helping in the promotion of a "new international economic order" (NIEO). The latter had been of intense but controversial interest in the 1970s in academic circles, and in the UN and some of its organs such as the General Assembly and the United Nations Conference on Trade and Development (UNCTAD). As is argued in the next section, it was this promotion of an NIEO that delayed ratification of the UNCLOS and required the articles relevant to the DSM regime to be re-written.

The function of the *"Enterprise"* is much like that of a national oil company (an oil company controlled by a government rather than private shareholders), except the Enterprise acts as the agent of the "Authority", itself charged with managing the common interests of mankind in DSM. Thus, "The Enterprise shall be the organ of the Authority which shall carry out [DSM] activities in the Area directly . . . as well as the transporting, processing and marketing of minerals recovered from the Area" (Article 170). While private DSM ventures would be allowed into the Area they would operate only as contractors to the Enterprise; "the plan of work shall, in accordance with Annex III, article 3, be in the form of a contract" (Article 153).

3 A new international economic order

The immediate origin of the initiative to establish a new international economic order (NIEO) was in the UN General Assembly's Sixth Special Session (1974), when the *Program of Action on the Establishment of a New International Economic Order* was adopted. The countries leading this initiative were the Group of 77 developing countries (G77) that stood to benefit. Its fundamental objective was to alter the distribution of world income in favor of poor countries. The principal sphere of action to achieve this objective was in the production and marketing of primary commodities – including metals – through an Integrated Program for Commodities, especially with the aim of raising prices and reducing price volatility. The latter was to be achieved through commodity stockpiling financed by a Common Fund. As the second Secretary General of UNCTAD, itself devoted to promoting G77 interests, remarked, "I am not interested in the mere stabilization of prices but in an overhaul of a system which still largely reflects a colonial or neocolonial relationship in terms of ownership, processing, marketing and distribution [of primary commodities]."[6,7]

It is against this political background – the promotion of developing country interests – that certain features of the DSM regime contained in Part XI of UNCLOS 1982 can be understood. Hence the reference in Article 140 to the development of the Area "taking into particular consideration the interests and needs of developing States and peoples", and in Article 143 to "ensuring that programs are developed through the Authority . . . for the benefit of developing States and technologically less developed States with a view to: (i) strengthening their research capabilities; (ii) training their personnel and the personnel of the Authority in the techniques and applications of research; [and] (iii) fostering the employment of their qualified personnel in research in the Area".

Moreover, Article 144 aimed "to promote and encourage the transfer to developing States of DSM technology and scientific knowledge". Similarly, in Article 144 the Authority "shall initiate and promote: (a) programs for the transfer of technology to the Enterprise", and directly relating to the issue of the management of international commodity markets, Article 151 states that "The Authority shall have the right to participate in any commodity conference dealing with those commodities and in which all interested parties including both producers and consumers participate. The Authority shall have the right to become a party to any arrangement or agreement resulting from such conferences. Participation of the Authority in any organs established under those arrangements or agreements shall be in respect of production in the Area."

What these articles boil down to is that the Area was to be developed for the particular benefit of developing countries; that multinational mining companies involved in DSM would be required to transfer their proprietary technologies to the Enterprise; and that the Authority would have the right to determine production schedules through its right to participate in international commodity conferences that aimed to manage the prices of primary commodities, including minerals obtained through DSM.

However, developed countries would have none of this. As Brauninger and Konig (2000) observe, developing countries had much more reason to support the proposed UNCLOS 1982 DSM regime than did developed countries. In particular, they found that the more a country expected to benefit from changing the *status quo* in the international mining and commodity regimes the more likely it was to support UNCLOS Articles 133–183 of Section XI; conversely, the less a country expected to benefit from changing the *status quo* the less likely it was to support these articles.

4   The 1990–1994 negotiations

Based as it was on the notion of an NIEO, industrialized countries did not support the provisions of UNCLOS 1982 Part XI. Failure to ratify led, in July 1990, to the Secretary General of the UN convening the first of 15 meetings of States Parties. These discussions significantly modified Part XI, and a new agreement, known as *Agreement on Part XI*, or as the *1994 Implementing Agreement*, was signed in July 1994, entering into force two years later. The Preamble reaffirmed the *common heritage of mankind* doctrine in application to DSM, but there were significant modifications: the relationship between the Enterprise and commercial mining companies was changed so that the latter would no longer be mere contractors to the former and, if at all, the Enterprise would now work in joint ventures with commercial companies – otherwise, the latter would operate independently. Second, States Parties were no longer under obligation to fund mining by the Enterprise and the Authority was to be financed by assessments of State Party members according to the UN scale – implying that developed countries would not pay more than their "fair share". Third, mining companies would no longer have to transfer proprietary DSM technologies to the Enterprise. Essentially, the *Implementing Agreement* allowed for the commercial exploitation of deep sea minerals. Moreover, with the demise of the NIEO's ideas on commodity price stabilization, the idea that the Authority would manage levels of DSM production and prices was also dropped.

However, the standard exploration contract does require commercial companies to send "confidential" Annual Reports to the ISA including those on matters that, if it were the offshore oil industry, commercial companies would rather keep to themselves.[8] For example, a statement of the quantity of polymetallic nodules recovered as samples or for the purpose of testing has to be reported. Information of this kind could be valuable to rival mining companies if it ever got out. Thus, as discussed in Chapter 21, if and when a lease block comes up for auction an oil company operating an adjacent lease block is known to have an advantage because of its superior geological knowledge of the area. Moreover, while offshore oil companies purchase most of their inputs – they are vertically disintegrated – they do almost all of their own reservoir engineering consultancy and production engineering consultancy in-house (Hallwood, 1990, pp. 36–37). The reason for this is that the information gathered in these two activities is commercially sensitive and they want to keep it to themselves.

However, it should be emphasized that the most important conception in the 1994 *Implementing Agreement* is that DSM would *not* be open access. Access is governed by the Authority. Furthermore, the "world community" is to share in economic rents if and when they materialize.

5 Rent sharing

Mining companies have to pay a $250,000 license fee for an exploration contract that is good for fifteen years, and will pay annual fixed fees to the Authority – at similar levels to what is normal for on-land mining ventures – once commercial production has started. However, while what amount to "lease blocks" are familiar from the offshore oil industry, there is no conception of open bidding for them; rather, an "exploration area" is exclusively "allocated" for exploration purposes.[9] Thus, a DSM company may apply for "a tenured mining license" and if it obtains one will operate in the "area under contract". To obtain a tenured mining license a company has to provide detailed information to the Authority on its technical, fiscal and environmental qualifications and a record of approved funding for the operation (ISA, 2013a, p. 5). Thus, DSM tenure licenses are allocated administratively and so might not gain possible efficiency advantages associated with lease block bonus bidding (such as winning bidders likely being low-cost producers) familiar in the offshore oil industry; and nor would the economic rent sharing aspect of bonus bidding be available.

However, the 1994 *Implementing Agreement* did allow that "consideration should be given to the adoption of a royalty system or a combination of a royalty and profit-sharing system".[10] As of summer 2013 consideration is still being given to the matters of royalties and profit-sharing. A consultancy report to the ISA and published as ISA Technical Study 11 said that "whatever resource rent process is employed [it should be] . . . simple, equitable, transparent, defensible and responsive to change", and that "monitoring should be carried out to ensure that the Authority receives its fair share of resource rents after deductions and that host country commercial policies do not give an unfair advantage to the commercial exploiter of the resources".

The report also detailed some technical aspects of resource rent taxation, pointing out that "in terms of decreasing administrative efficiency, the most common royalties would be ranked as follows: (a) Unit-based royalties based on units of volume or weight; (b) *Ad valorem* royalties based on value of sales; (c) Hybrid royalties; (d) Profit-based royalties" (ISA, 2013b, p. 6) – but that in terms of economic efficiency the order should be reversed. For example, royalties paid on a residual, i.e. profits, do not introduce distortions to decision-making, while unit-based royalties are treated as a cost of production by operators and will, therefore, introduce such distortions, e.g. abandonment of a "tenure" earlier than otherwise. On these latter two matters see Chapter 21 on production distortions and fiscal aspects of offshore oil taxation. However, these detailed fiscal matters are in a state of flux and nothing is as yet definitive.

6   A high-grading issue

An interesting rule adopted by the ISA concerns performance guarantees, and one in particular is that a DSM company is discouraged on the pain of financial penalties from "high-grading" recovered mineral deposits – just taking the easiest to get, lowest-cost, recoverable reserves. While no such performance guarantees exist in the offshore oil industry, in DSM the requirement has merit. This is because, with offshore oil production, equipment such as a production platform and pipelines remain as fixtures. An oil company operates to maximize the financial return on these fixtures and abandonment will only occur when oil reserves or well pressures have fallen so low as to turn financial returns negative. However, in the DSM business major production equipment – e.g. mining ships and ROVs – are easily moved. In this case the best way to maximize the rate of return on such expensive moveable assets is to operate them over the highest-density mineral deposits, moving on when these are worked out and leaving behind medium- or lower-grade deposits.

7   Negative externalities

Two other interesting features of the standard operating contract concerns dealing with possible negative externalities of DSM. First, contractors have a contractual obligation to minimize environmental damage – a requirement consistent with international agreements regulating pollution at sea by ships (see

Chapter 20). Second, if any objects of an archaeological or historical nature are discovered they are not to be disturbed. This latter requirement is consistent with UNESCO's *Convention on the Protection of the Underwater Cultural Heritage*, 2001, that calls for the *in situ* protection of historical wrecks, structures and artifacts – see Chapter 2.

8   Tenured mining licenses

The ISA issued regulations governing DSM – the Mining Code, which is periodi- cally added to – in 2000, and by 2013 had approved exploration contracts ("work plans") for a total of 17 commercial or state-sponsored enterprises. At this date there were four areas where DSM exploration was in progress: two areas in the Indian Ocean, one between Mauritius and the Cocos Islands, the other south of Madagascar; on the mid-Atlantic ridge northeast of Surinam; and in the Clarion- Clipperton Fracture Zone in the Pacific Ocean. Altogether these amount to a very small proportion of the world's oceans.

The largest single area is the Clarion-Clipperton Fracture Zone – a narrow, irregular, rectangular slice of Pacific Ocean lying between, to its west, Kiribati's and Hawaii's EEZs, and to its east, Mexico's EEZ (see Figure 23.1). The size of a con- tractor operating zone is not standardized but several companies have been granted zones of about 75,000 km^2, and a British company one about twice that.

9   Conclusions

Deep sea mining outside of any country's EEZ is not open access and so the rent dissipation experienced by badly managed high seas fisheries is not inevitable. The 1994 *Implementing Agreement* requires the International Sea Bed Authority to vet applicants and to issue licenses to companies with the requisite technology, skills and funding. Looking at the details of the standard exploration contract there is some doubt that maximization of economic rent is attainable because the allocation of areas under contract is done administratively rather than competi- tively, so that the ISB is in the business of "picking winners" rather than allowing competition in the market to determine which companies win what contracts. However, on the face of it, even if there is some inefficiency and rent dissipation this is surely a far cry from what it would have been had seabed mineral resources been open access.

Looking at rent sharing (equity), the *common heritage of mankind* doctrine is an influence on the DSM codes. However, it appears that current rules allow for little of it. Companies, commercial or state sponsored, with areas under contract pay minimal fees and if they become profitable DSM ventures would pay no royalties or taxes to the ISB – but this is not to say that this will always be the case.

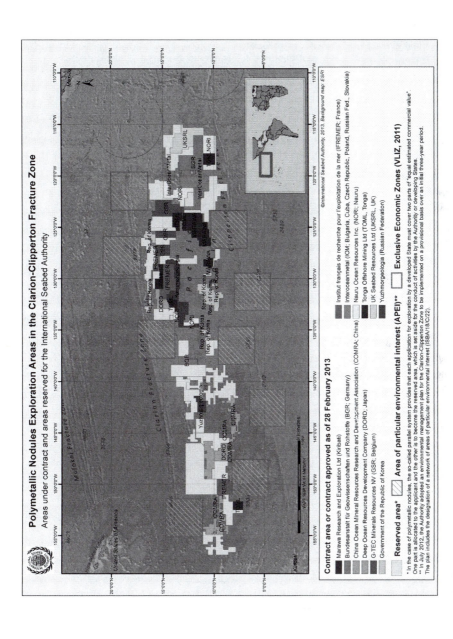

FIGURE 23.1 Areas under contract in the Clarion-Clipperton Zone

Source: Image courtesy of International Seabed Authority, available online at www.isa.org.jm/files/images/maps/CCZ-Sep2012-Official.jpg

Note

1 David Shukman (Science editor, BBC News), "Deep sea mining 'gold rush' moves closer", May 17th, 2013.
2 Marine Science Today, March 26th, 2013, available online at http://marinesciencetoday. com/2013/03/26/a-summary-of-deep-sea-mining/.
3 These minerals are grouped as polymetallic nodules, polymetallic sulphides, and cobalt-rich crusts. According to the International Seabed Authority polymetallic nodules contain manganese, nickel, cobalt and copper; "polymetallic sulphides" are hydro-thermally formed deposits of sulphides and some other minerals; and cobalt crusts are cobalt-rich iron/manganese (ferromanganese) hydroxide/oxide deposits formed from direct precipitation of minerals from seawater onto hard substrates containing minor but significant concentrations of cobalt, titanium, nickel, platinum, molybdenum, tellurium, cerium, and other metallic and rare earth elements.
4 Toward the development of a regulatory framework for polymetallic nodule exploitation in the Area International Seabed Authority ISBA/19/C/5.
5 Article 160 says that "The Assembly consists of all country members of the Authority and each member has one vote. The Assembly shall have the power to establish general policies in conformity with the relevant provisions of this [LOS] Convention on any question or matter within the competence of the Authority" (Article 160). That is, mat-ters relating to DSM policy are ultimately sanctioned by the Assembly, a place where developed countries would be a minority.
6 Quoted in Wassermann (1976), p. 22.
7 See Hallwood (1979) for an analysis of UNCTAD's commodity stockpiling objectives. See Hallwood and Sinclair (1981) for an analysis of how manipulation of oil prices by the Organization of Petroleum Exporting Countries destroyed any notion of developing country solidarity on commodity prices.
8 See the "Standard Clauses for Exploration Contract" on the ISA web site: www.isa.org. jm/files/documents/EN/Regs/Code-Annex4.pdf.
9 ISA Standard Clauses for Exploration Contract, section 1.
10 Agreement on Part XI, section 8 (1c).

APPENDIX

Benefit–cost analysis

At several points in this book the benefits of a "project" have been compared with its costs, and we have asked, "is it worth it?" For example, is it worth reducing nitrogen runoff into coastal waters, or limiting human activity around a coral reef or a wetland, or saving the blue whale from extinction? Similarly, is it worth taking action to reduce fishing effort and catches today, in order to have larger catches in the future (with less fishing effort)?

In the private sector, firms perform benefit–cost analysis (BCA) every day. For any suggested project, benefits are calculated as revenue inflows and costs as cash outflows. Given an appropriate rate of interest for borrowing costs, if revenue exceeds cost there is a net benefit, called profit, and a project may be proceeded with.

In the public sector, where a government has to choose which projects to pursue, calculation of net benefits is not so straightforward. Cash flows may not be the whole story, and what is the appropriate rate of interest to use?

The use of BCA is illustrated with the following simple example. It is determined that the annual cost of reducing nitrogen runoff from farms in a certain state, say, North Carolina, would cost $C, and scientists inquire into the prospective benefits. Suppose that benefit is limited only to an increased annual shrimp harvest.

1   Consumers' surplus as a measure of benefits

Market demand and supply curves for shrimp in the relevant locality are shown in Figure A.1. Initially we are at point A on the demand curve with supply curve S_1. Supply is assumed to be produced at a constant cost, hence S_1 is horizontal. The area below the demand curve and above the price line measures consumers' surplus. The monetary value of consumers' surplus indicates the net benefit derived from consuming the good.

If nitrogen runoff is reduced, more shrimp can be harvested and at point B the price of shrimp has fallen to P_2. There is also an increase in consumers' surplus, which is the measure of the reduced-nitrogen project's benefit. If the supply curves were upward-sloping, lower costs would also increase producers' surplus, and this too should be counted toward a project's benefits.

It is worthwhile thinking about what is the maximum amount consumers would be willing to pay for a project that increased the shrimp catch. The answer must be "an amount of money approaching the increased consumers' surplus", which we'll call $B. If they paid a sum any less than this they would still be better off.

2   The measuring rod of money

A complication in this BCA has to be faced. The scientists said that benefit is in terms of a larger shrimp catch, but the BCA has measured benefit in terms of money. There is a need to make this conversion from physical to monetary units so as to be able to compare like with like. The cost of less nitrogen use on farms might be smaller corn and wheat harvests. It is through conversion to monetary units that these costs and benefits can be directly compared.

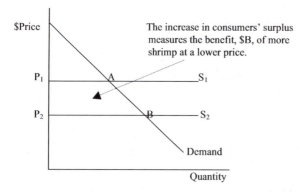

FIGURE A.1 Benefits measured as an increase in consumers' surplus

However, the measuring rod of money is not like other measuring rods. An extra $100 in the pay packet may well have a higher value measured in terms of satisfaction (or utility) gained to a poor person than to a rich person. This is not true of course with, say, measuring length – 36 inches is 36 inches whatever your income level. What we have to face is the declining marginal utility of money; as income increases, the utility (or satisfaction) that an extra $100 yields declines, or, at least, is likely to.

To understand the following discussion, recall that a price change has a substitution effect and an income effect. With the substitution effect, when the relative price of a good falls, consumers are encouraged at the margin to substitute consumption of it for that of some other good. With the income effect, when the price of a good falls, consumers experience a gain in real income – a given nominal income can now buy more goods in general. Here we are interested in the income effect.

If a good is not inconsequential in consumers' expenditure patterns, as price falls real income increases down the demand curve as shown in Figure A.2. However, we have just observed that the marginal utility of money declines as real income increases.

3   Adjusting measured benefits for the non-constancy of the marginal utility of money

The conundrum we have to face is that benefits and costs are measured in terms of money but that the value of money changes as those benefits come on stream. The solution to this conundrum is to measure benefits at a constant *real* income because the value of an extra $100 (the marginal utility of money) would then be constant.

Looking back at Figure A.1, what we did was to measure benefit at a constant *money* income. Money income was only in the background but the implicit assumption was that it was constant while the price of shrimp fell. Thus, if shrimp consumption is not an inconsequential fraction of consumer spending, real income must have been increasing down the demand curve. Now we see that this approach led us into the trap of using a stretchable measuring rod – and this is inadmissible.

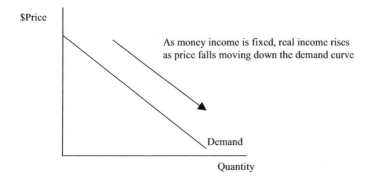

FIGURE A.2 Real income increases as price falls

4 Varying money income to stabilize real income

When price changes between P_1 and P_2 in Figure A.3, *real* income changes and this causes problems for the measurement of benefits. The solution is to stabilize *real* income by (theoretically) altering *money* income.

It is equally valid to stabilize real income at that level commensurate with P_1 or at the higher real income commensurate with P_2. Considering a price fall, if real income is stabilized on P_1 a *compensating variation* (a reduction) in *money* income is (theoretically) performed. However, if real income is stabilized at the level commensurate with the lower price, P_2, as price is increased to P_1 an *equivalent variation* (an increase) in money income is made.

5 Compensating variation and willingness to pay (WTP)

In Figure A.3 we begin at P_1 and price then falls to P_2. Real income would increase unless money income was taken away through a *compensating variation*. Hence, the compensated demand curve through point A is steeper than the uncompensated demand curve. Along the latter, also known as the Marshallian demand curve (in honor of Alfred Marshall, who was the first to recognize its limitations), real income increases, but real income is constant along the compensated demand curve. That is why, for any given price change, demand increases less along the compensated demand curve.

The increase in the monetary value of consumers' surplus under the compensated demand curve is measured as area X. Crucially, as this is measured at a constant real income the measuring rod of money is stable – the marginal utility of money does not change at a constant real income.

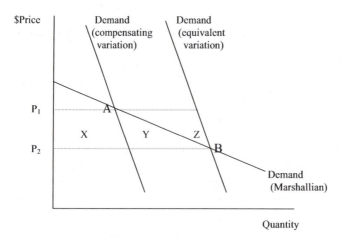

FIGURE A.3 Three ways to measure a project's benefits

Area X measures consumers' *willingness to pay (WTP)* for the project under consideration. Consumers would pay up to this amount because the project, if initiated, makes them this much better off.

6   Equivalent variation and the willingness to accept (WTA)

It is equally valid to measure a project's benefit at the higher real income commensurate with the lower price, P_2, in Figure A.3. The thought experiment now begins from a situation where the project has been executed, nitrogen runoff has been reduced and the shrimp catch has increased. What now would be the value of the project if we were to take it away?

If price increased from P_2 to P_1 consumers' real income would fall and an *equivalent variation* in *money* income would be necessary – it would have to be increased.

The equivalent demand curve runs through point B in Figure A.3 and it is steeper than the Marshallian demand curve. Being steeper indicates that demand falls off less as price rises. This is unsurprising, as we have again stabilized real income, but this time at a higher level.

The area X+Y+Z under the equivalent variation demand curve is also a valid measure of the benefits derived from a project of reduced nitrogen runoff. It is valid because with real income fixed the measuring rod of money is itself fixed. In this case the area under the demand curve measures *willingness to accept (WTA)* – meaning how much consumers would have to be paid to give up the benefits of reduced nitrogen runoff – price was at P_2.

7   Comparing the three measures of benefit

We have ended up with three different measures of the benefits of a project of reduced nitrogen runoff:

1   The area X under the compensated demand curve – a measure of WTP for the benefits of a project;
2   the area X+Y under the Marshallian demand curve;
3   the area X+Y+Z under the equivalent demand curve – a measure of WTA forgoing the benefits of a project.

In practical BCA it may not be possible to obtain estimates of all three measures of benefit. However, it might be possible to estimate the Marshallian demand curve from available data on prices, quantities and other relevant data. Estimates of both WTP and WTA may also be obtained, for example, through the technique of *contingent valuation* – which uses cunningly designed questionnaires to elicit these values from people.

A problem with both WTP and WTA is that both make extreme estimates of benefits – "the benefit is only area X", or "it is as much as areas X+Y+Z". Moreover, the difference between these estimates is greater the larger is a project's effect on real income, because the value of money will change by more. Fortunately, in many situations, a project, while increasing real income, may not do so by much – in which case all three measures will be close in value.

8 Property rights

In terms of our nitrogen runoff story, if farmers have the right to pollute – by default, they have a (property) right to use coastal waters to dispose of their nitrogen – the amount of money they demand under WTA to give up this property right may be very large, for example a farmer might say, "My farming method is part of my identity; back to the *Mayflower* my family have done it this way, and I won't change it at any price." On the other hand, if the shrimpers had the right to non-polluted coastal waters, then the farmers would have to consider how much they would be WTP the shrimpers to let their nitrogen pollute those waters. This WTP would probably not amount to that much, as it would approximate the difference between the level of profits with and without nitrogen runoff.

9 Choice of discount rate

The choice of a discount rate to use in a BCA can have a major bearing on whether net present value (NPV) is positive or negative, and so whether a project is viable. This is especially true when costs are incurred early and benefits occur later. NPV is the difference between the present value of benefits and the present value of costs.

Consider that the present value of a project yielding a real value of $1,000,000 per year for fifty years is $50 million, but at a 12 percent discount rate it is only $8.3 million – or that the present value today of the $1 million benefit in the fiftieth year is only $3,460. Today nobody would pay more than this for that $1 million benefit in fifty years time. But at a 2 percent discount rate that 50th payment today is worth $372,000, or 107 times more.

So, the discount rate is a rate of interest and a cursory glance in the financial pages of a newspaper shows that there are many different rates of interest. The question is: which one to use? Theoretically, the correct rate of interest, or discount rate, is the *social rate of discount*. This is the discount rate if all relevant information is taken into account. There are two views on the choice of social discount rate for a public sector project:

1   *The social time preference rate view.* The STPR reflects households' preference for present consumption over future consumption. It is the STPR that determines how much households wish to save at different rates of interest – the rate of interest being the reward for waiting.
2   *The marginal productivity of capital view.* As public projects divert funds from private sector investment projects the correct interest rate to use is the rate of return on private sector investment – i.e. the marginal productivity of capital (MPK).

When capital markets are in long-run equilibrium the MPK and STPR are equal, so it would not matter which approach was used to determine the discount rate. However, there are grounds for supposing that market-determined rates of interest will exceed the social rate of interest (or discount). Here are some reasons:

> Households may have a "defective telescopic vision" – to use the terminology of the famous British economist A. C. Pigou. That is, they may irrationally prefer present consumption to future consumption because they are short-sighted. They don't save enough.
>
> Future generations yet to be born are obviously not active in present-day capital markets. If they were, they would be able to state their preferences on the preservation of environmental goods. If they want these goods to be preserved, in effect they are asking for a low discount rate to be used – most probably lower than present generations would choose.
>
> Calculated rates of return on private investment are on the high side. Risks in the private sector are high because an individual firm can practice only a limited amount of portfolio diversification. As the scope for project diversification in the public sector is much greater, the risk premium in the latter sector should be lower.
>
> All private sector interest rates include a premium for inflation expectations and only an inflation adjusted real rate should be used.

In practice, a BCA study has to choose a discount rate. In the US public sector until about two decades ago a 10 percent rate was used; more recently this has been reduced to 7 percent.

10 BCA – general discussion

BCA is sometimes accused of:[1]

1   *Ignoring equity issues.* Because of the declining marginal utility of money, other things equal, high-income people are WTP more for projects than are poor people. This suggests that public sector projects are likely to favor the preferences of higher-income people. Against this, it is society, through the political system, that allows income inequality with its associated allocation of resources. So why should allocation on non-market goods be any different?

2   *Causing possible adverse income distribution consequences.* If the gainers do not compensate the losers from a project, income distribution may be worsened. To ignore this is to accept whatever income distribution consequences arise from a proposed project. Economic theory is aware of income distribution consequences yet seems to be wedded to the Kaldor-Hicks compensation principle – that a project is worthwhile if net present value is positive and gainers *could* compensate losers, but there is no requirement that such compensation takes

place. In other words, in BCA if a project's net present value is positive there is a case to proceed with it even if it creates harm to the environment and/or some people.

3   *Using incorrect market prices.* In the presence of market failures market prices are not equal to true marginal costs. If so, shadow prices, not market prices, should be used; but exactly how accurately can the latter be ascertained?

4   *Public choice issues.* In public choice theory, bureaucrats are viewed as attempting to maximize their own utility rather than that of society at large. This could warp project selection. The Army Corps of Engineers has been accused of favoring "big" projects, as has the World Bank.

5   *WTP is often based on ignorance of the environment.* Ecosystems can be very complex and not properly understood even by scientists, yet decisions on their disposition in BCA are left to the WTP of ordinary people.

6   *Inadequate treatment of risk.* A low-probability catastrophic event in BCA is accorded a low expected value – i.e. a small cost. Yet risk aversion might suggest that a project carrying this risk should *not* be proceeded with. This idea stands behind the long moratorium on the building of nuclear power stations in the USA.

7   *Problems in choosing the discount rate.* As we have seen, this choice can be critical, yet the theoretical basis of choice is questionable.

8   *WTP versus WTA.* We know that these can diverge a lot, and that which one is relevant in a BCA depends on the disposition of property rights. Using WTP to calculate environmental values recognizes that property rights are *not* invested in those that want an environmental good (such as the blue whale) protected.

Note

1 Hanley and Spash (1994, Chapter 14) have a rather good discussion of these issues.

BIBLIOGRAPHY

Acheson, J. E. (1979) "Variations in Traditional Inshore Rights in Maine Lobstering Communities," in R. Anderson (ed.), *North Atlantic Maritime Cultures*, Mouton, NY, 253–76.

Acheson, J. E. (1988) *The Lobster Gangs of Maine*, University of New England, Hanover and London.

Adam, P. B. (1980) "Life History Patterns in Marine Fishes and their Consequences for Fisheries Management," *Fisheries Bulletin*, 78 (1), 1–7.

Ahmed, M., Chiew Kieok Chong, Cesar, H. (eds) (2005) *Economic Valuation and Policy Priorities for Sustainable Management of Coral Reefs*, World Fish Center, Penang, Malaysia.

Alderton, T. and Winchester, N. (2002) "Globalisation and De-regulation in the Maritime Industry," *Marine Policy*, 26, 35–43.

Amacost, R. L. (1995) "Cost Reimbursement for USCG International Ice Patrol Activities," US Coast Guard Report Number CG-D-23-95.

Anderson, J. L. (1995) "Piracy and World History: An Economic Perspective on Maritime Predation," *Journal of World History*, 6 (2), 175–199.

Arin, T. and Kramer, R. A (2002) "Divers' Willingness to Pay to Visit Marine Sanctuaries: An Exploratory Study," *Ocean and Coastal Management*, 45, 171–183.

Asgeirsdottir, A. (2008) *Who Gets What?* State University of New York Press, Albany, NY.

Ashton, P. K., Upton, L. O. and Rothkopf, M. H. (2005) *Effects of Royalty Incentives for Gulf of Mexico Oil and Gas Leases, Volume 1: Summary*, OCS Study, MMS 2004-077, US Department of the Interior, Minerals Management Service, Economic Division, Herndon, VA.

Auster, P. J. and Shackell, N. L. (2000) "Marine Protected Areas for the Temperate and Boreal Northwest Atlantic: The Potential for Sustainable Fisheries and Conservation of Biodiversity," *Northeastern Naturalist*, 7 (4), 419–34.

Bahadur, J. (2009) "'I'm not a pirate, I'm the saviour of the sea'," *The Times*, April 16th.

Bahadur, J. (2011) *The Pirates of Somalia: Inside Their Hidden World*, Pantheon, New York.

Bailey, M., Sumaila, U. R. and Lindroos, M. (2010) "Application of Game Theory to Fisheries Over Three Decades," *Fisheries Research*, 102, 1–8.

Baker, M. and Miceli, T. (2005) "Credible Criminal Enforcement," *European Journal of Law and Economics*, 20, 5–15.

Balton, D. A. (1996) "Strengthening the Law of the Sea: The New Agreement on Straddling Fish Stocks and Highly Migratory Fish Stocks," *Ocean Development and International Law*, 27, 125–140.

Balton, D. A. (2001) "The Bering Sea Doughnut Hole: Regional Solution, Global Implications," in O. S. Stokke, *Governing High Seas Fisheries*, Oxford University Press, Oxford, Chapter 5.

Barrett, S. (2003) *Environment and Statecraft: The Strategy of Environmental Treaty-Making*, Oxford University Press, Oxford.

Bateman, S. (1998) "Economic Growth, Marine Resources and Naval Arms in East Asia – A Deadly Triangle?," *Marine Policy*, 23 (4–5), 297–306.

Baumol, W. J. and Oates, W. (1988) *The Theory of Environmental Management*, Cambridge University Press, New York.

Beattie, A., Sumaila, U. R., Christensen, V. and Pauly, D. (2002) "A Model for the Bioeconomic Evaluation of Marine Protected Area Size and Placement in the North Sea," *Natural Resource Modeling*, 15 (4), 413–437.

Becker, G. (1968) "Crime and Punishment: An Economic Approach," *Journal of Political Economy*, 76 (2), 169–217.

Becker, G. and Mulligan, C. (1997) "Endogenous Determination of Time Preference," *Quarterly Journal of Economics*, 112, August, 729–758.

Bekryaev, R. V., Polyakov, I. V. and Alexeev, V. A. (2010) "Role of Polar Amplification in Long-Term Surface Air Temperature Variations and Modern Arctic Warming," *J. Climate*, 23, 3888–3906.

Bellish, J. (2013) "The Economic Cost of Somali Piracy: 2012," Oceans Beyond Piracy, One Earth Future Foundation.

Bellwood, D. R. and Hughes, T. P. (2001) "Regional-Scale Assembly Rules and Biodiversity of Coral Reefs," *Science*, 292 (5521), 1532–1535.

Bellwood, D. R., Hughes, T. P., Folke, C. and Nystrom, M. (2004) "Confronting the Coral Reef Crisis," *Nature*, 429, June, 827–833.

Benvenisti, E. (2008) "The Conception of International Law as a Legal System," *Tel Aviv University Law Faculty Papers*, paper 83.

Bernell, D. (2013) "Ethanol: Politics, Policy and Impacts," paper presented at the Western Political Science Association Annual Meetings, Hollywood, March.

Bjorndal, T. and Munro, G. (2002) "The Management of High Seas Fisheries Resources and the Implementation of the UN Fish Stocks Agreement of 1995," Discussion Paper 2/2002, Centre for Fisheries Economics.

Blake, G. H. and Swarbrick, R. E. (1998) "Hydrocarbons and International Boundaries: A Global Overview," in Blake et al., *Boundaries and Energy: Problems and Prospects*, Kluwer Law International, London.

Blake, G. H., Pratt, M. A., Schofield, C. H. and Allison Brown, J. (eds) (1998) *Boundaries and Energy: Problems and Prospects*, Kluwer Law International, London.

Boadway, R., Marceau, N. and Marchand, M. (1996) "Time Consistent Criminal Sanctions," *Public Finance/Finances Publiques*, 51, 149–165.

Boersma, P. D. and Parrish, J. K. (1999) "Limiting Abuse: Marine Protected Areas, a Limited Solution," *Ecological Economics*, 31, 287–304.

Bohringer, C. (2002) "Industry Level Emission Trading Between Power Producers in the EU," *Applied Economics*, 34, 523–33.

Boncoeur, J., Alban, F., Guyader, O. and Thebaud, J. (2002) "Fish, Fishers, Seals and Tourism: Economic Consequences of Creating a Marine Reserve in a Multi-Species, Multi-Activity Context," *Natural Resource Modeling*, 15 (4), 387–411.

Bonnie, R. (1999) "Endangered Species Mitigation Banking: Promoting Recovery Through Habitat Conservation Planning Under the Endangered Species Act," *The Science of the Total Environment*, 240 (1–3), 11–19.

Bowden, A. (2010) "The Economic Cost of Maritime Piracy," working paper, One Earth Future Foundation.

Brander, L. M., Florax, R. J. G. M. and Vermaat, J. E. (2006) "The Empirics of Wetland Valuation: A Comprehensive Summary and a Meta-analysis of the Literature," *Environmental and Resource Economics*, 33, 223–250.

Brauninger, T. and Konig, T. (2000) "Making Rules for Governing Global Commons: The Case of Deep-Sea Mining," *Journal of Conflict Resolution*, 44 (5), 604–629.

Breach Marine Protection UK (1998) "Norwegian Minke Whaling: Killing Methods," available online at http://whales7.tripod.com/policies/methods.html.

Brewster, R. (2009) "The Limits of Reputation on Compliance," *International Theory*, 1 (2), 323–333.

Brown, K., Adger, W. N., Tompkins, E., Bacon, P., Shim, D. and Young, K. (2001) "Trade-off Analysis for Marine Protected Area Management," *Ecological Economics*, 37 (3), 417–434.

Brunnee, J. and Troope, S. J. (2011) "Interactional International Law: An Introduction," *International Theory*, 3 (2), 307–318.

Bryant, C. R. (2001) "The Archaeological Duty of Care: The Legal, Professional and Cultural Struggle over Salvaging Historic Shipwrecks," *Albany Law Review*, 65, 97–145.

Bulte, E. and Van Kooten, C. (1999) "Marginal Valuation of Charismatic Species: Implications for Conservation," *Environmental Resource Economics*, 14, 119–130.

Burke, L. (2011) "Reefs at Risk Revisited," World Resources Institute, UN conference "Keeping the Green Economy Blue," April.

Carr, L. and Mendelsohn, R. (2003) "Valuing Coral Reefs: A Travel Cost Analysis of the Great Barrier Reef," *Ambio*, 32 (5), 353–357.

Carson, R. T., Mitchell, R. C. and Conaway, M. B. (2002) "Economic Benefits to Foreigners Visiting Morocco Accruing from the Rehabilitation of the Fes Medina," in Navrud and Ready, *Valuing Cultural Heritage: Applying Environmental Valuation Techniques to Historic Buildings, Monuments and Artifacts*, Edward Elgar Publishing, Northampton, MA, 118–141.

Castelle, A. J., Conolly, C., Emers, M., Metz, E. D., Meyer, S., Witter, M., Mauermann, S., Bentley, M., Sheldon, D. and Dole, D. (1992) *Wetland Mitigation Replacement Ratios: Defining Equivalency*, Adolfson Associates Inc., for Shorelands and Coastal Zone Management Program, Washing Department of Ecology, Olympia, WA. Publication number 92-08.

Cesar, H. and Chiew Kieok Chong (2005) "Economic Valuation and Socioeconomics of Coral Reefs: Methodological Issues and Three Case Studies," in Ahmed, Chiew Kieok Chong, and Cesar (eds), *Economic Valuation and Policy Priorities for Sustainable Management of Coral Reefs*, World Fish Center, Penang, Malaysia, 14–40.

Cesar, H., Burke, L. and Pet-Soede, L. (2003) *The Economics of Worldwide Coral Reef Degradation*, Cesar Environmental Economics Consulting, Arnhem, and WWF-Netherlands, Zeist, The Netherlands.

Cesar, H., van Beukering, P., Pintz, S. and Dierking, J. (2004) "Economic Valuation of the Coral Reefs of Hawaii," *Pacific Science*, 58 (2), 231–242.

Charles, A. T., Mazany, R. L. and Cross, M. L. (1999) "The Economics of Illegal Fishing: A Behavioral Approach," *Marine Resource Economics*, 14, 95–110.

Choi, Y. D. (2004) "Theories for Ecological Restoration in Changing Environment: Toward 'Futuristic' Restoration," *Ecological Research*, 19 (1), January, 75–83.

Christie, D. R. and Hildreth, R. G. (1999) *Coastal and Ocean Management Law*, West Group, n.p., 156–70 especially.

Churchill, R. R. (2001) "Managing Straddling Fish Stocks in the North-East Atlantic: A Multiplicity of Instruments and Regime Linkages – but How Effective a Management?," in O. S. Stokke, *Governing High Seas Fisheries*, Oxford University Press, Oxford, 235–272.

Clark, C. W. and Lamberson, R. (1982) "An Economic History and Analysis of Pelagic Whaling," *Marine Policy*, 6 (2), 103–120.

Clark, W. G. and Hare, S. R. (2006) "International Pacific Halibut Commission Established by a Convention between Canada and the USA: Assessment and Management of Pacific Halibut – Data, Methods and Policy," Scientific Report 83.

Coase, R. (1960) "The Problem of Social Coast," *Journal of Law and Economics*, 3, October, 1–44.

Coats, R., Swanson, M. and Williams, P. (1989) "Hydrologic Analysis for Coastal Wetland Restoration, *Environmental Management*, 13 (6), 715–27.

Collins, S. (1999) "Overview of the Law of Long-Lost Shipwrecks," available online at www.nwrain.net/~newtsuit/legal/111sr/111s00.htm.

Comiso, J. C. (2003) "Warming Trends in the Arctic from Clear Sky Satellite Observations," *Journal of Climate*, 16, 3498–3510.

Commission of the European Communities (2009) "Reform of the Common Fisheries Policy," Green Paper, Brussels, 22.04.2009 COM(2009)163 final.

Congressional Research Service (2010) "U.S. Offshore Oil and Gas Resources: Prospects and Processes," April 26th, 7-5700, R40645, available online at www.crs.gov.

Cooke, J. G., Leaper, R. and Papastavrou, V. (2012) "Whaling: Ways to Agree on Quotas," *Nature*, February 16th, 308.

Cooter, R. and Ulen, T. (1997) *Law and Economics*, second edition, Addison-Wesley, New York.

Costello, C., Gaines, S. and Gerber, L. R. (2012) "A Market Approach to Saving the Whales: The Future of the International Whaling Commission is Tenuous. A 'whale conservation market' Might Rescue It," *Nature*, January 12th, 139–144.

Cotton, J. (2003) "From 'Timor Gap' to 'Timor Sea'," *Australian Quarterly*, 75 (2), March–April, 27–32.

Cuisine, D. J. and Grant, J. P. (1980) *The Impact of Marine Pollution*, Croom Helm, London.

Cullis-Suzuki, S. and Pauly, D. (2010) "Failing the High Seas: A Global Evaluation of Regional Fisheries Management Organizations," *Marine Policy*, 34 (5), 1036–1042.

Curtis, J. B. (1984) "Vessel-source Oil Pollution and MARPOL 73/78: An International Success Story," *Indiana Journal of Global Legal Studies*, 1 (2), 489–513.

Dahl, T. E. (1990) "Wetlands Losses in the United States, 1780's to 1980's. Report to the Congress," Technical Report PB-91-169284/XAB.

Dahl, T. E., Johnson, C. E. and Frayer, W. E. (1991) "Wetlands, Status and Trends in the Conterminous United States mid-1970's to mid-1980's," Technical Report, US Fish and Wildlife Service.

Darrington, G. P. (2002) "England and Wales: Recent Issues in Maritime Archaeology," in Ruppe and Barstad, *International Handbook of Underwater Archaeology*, Kluwer, Dordrecht, 367–379.

Day, J. C. (2002) "Zoning – Lessons from the Great Barrier Reef Marine Park," *Ocean and Coastal Management*, 45 (2), 139–156.

de Groot, O. J., Rablen, M. D. and Shortland, A. (2011) "Gov-aargh-nance – 'even criminals need law and order'," CEDI Discussion Paper Series 11-01, Centre for Economic Development and Institutions (CEDI), Brunel University.

Demsetz, H. (1967) "Towards a Theory of Property Rights," *American Economic Review Papers & Proceedings*, 56 (2), 347–359.

Department of Fish and Game (2003) *Report to the Legislature: California, Wetland Mitigation Banking*, Resources Agency, State of California.

Department of the Interior (2007) "Economic Incentives to Promote Offshore Energy Development," available online at www.doi.gov/initiatives/economic.html.

Diaz, R. J. and Solow, A. (1999) "Ecological and Economic Consequences of Hypoxia," NOAA Coastal Ocean Program Decision Analysis Series No. 16, US Department of Commerce, National Oceanic and Atmospheric Administration.

Doering, O. C., Howard, C., Heimlich, R. and Diaz-Hermelo, F. (1999) "Evaluation of the Economic Costs and Benefits of Methods for Reducing Nutrient Loads to the Gulf of Mexico," NOAA Coastal Ocean Program Decision Analysis Series No. 20, US Department of Commerce, National Oceanic and Atmospheric Administration.

Dromgoole, S. (2003) "UNESCO Convention on the Protection of the Underwater Cultural Heritage 2001: Implications for Commercial Treasure Salvors," *Lloyd's Maritime and Commercial Law Quarterly*, 3, 7–340.

Dromgoole, S. (2004) "Murky Waters for Government Policy: The Case of a 17th Century British Warship and 10 tonnes of Gold Coins," *Marine Policy*, 28, 189–198.

Dutton, Y. (2010) "Bringing Pirates to Justice: A Case for Including Piracy within the Jurisdiction of the International Criminal Court," discussion paper, One Earth Future Foundation, February, available online at www.oneearthfuture.org/siteadmin/images/files/file_52.pdf.

Dutton, Y. (2011a) "Maritime Piracy and the Impunity Gap: Insufficient National Laws or a Lack of Political Will?," *Tulane Law Review*, 86, 1111–1151.

Dutton, Y. (2011b) "Pirates and Impunity: Is the Threat of Asylum Claims a Reason to Allow Pirates to Escape Justice?," *Fordham International Law Journal*, 34, September 18th, 236–256.

Dyson, J. (1986) "Captain Hatcher's Richest Find," *Reader's Digest*, 129 (10), 111–115.

Eckert, R. D (1979) *The Enclosure of Ocean Resources*, Hoover Institution, Stanford, CA.

Economist (2000a) "The Politics of Whaling," *Economist*, September 9th, p. 42.

Economist (2000b) "Timor's Troubled Waters," *Economist*, December 2nd, p. 44.

Economist (2000c) "What Price Coral?," *Economist*, November 2nd.

Economist (2004) "Australia and East Timor: Beggar Thy Neighbor," *Economist*, June 5th, p. 40.

Economist (2006) "Trouble at the Mill," *Economist*, January 28th, p. 42.

Eggert, H. and Ellegard, A. (2003) "Fishery Control and Regulation Compliance: A Case for Co-Management in Swedish Commercial Fisheries," *Marine Policy*, 27, 525–533.

Elferink, A. G. O. (2001) "The Sea of Okhotsk Peanut Hole de facto Extension of Coastal State Control," in Stokke, *Governing High Seas Fisheries*, Oxford University Press, Oxford, Chapter 6.

ELI (2006) "2005 Status Report on Compensatory Mitigation in the US," Environmental Law Institute Report, April.

Ellis, G. M. and Fisher, A. C. (1987) "Valuing the Environment as Input," *Journal of Environmental Management*, 25, 149–156.

Encyclopedia of Earth (2013) "United Nations Convention on Law of the Sea (UNCLOS), 1982," available online at www.eoearth.org/article/United_Nations_Convention_on_Law_of_the_Sea_(UNCLOS),_1982.

Energies Nouvelles (2012) "Offshore Hydrocarbons," available online at www.ifpenergie nouvelles.com.

Energy Information Administration, Office of Oil and Gas (2006) "Overview of the Federal Offshore Royalty Relief Program," June, p. 1, available online at http://tonto.eia.doe.gov/FTPROOT/features/ngoffshore.pdf.

EPA (Environmental Protection Agency) (1995) "Federal Guidance for the Establishment, Use and Operation of Mitigation Banks," 60 (228), November 28th, 58, 605–58, 614.

EPA (2002) "National Water Quality Inventory: 2000 Report," EPA-841-R-02-001, Washington DC, August.

EPA (2004) "National Coastal Condition Report II," EPA-620/R-03/002, Washington DC, February.

EPA (2010) "Scientific Assessment of Hypoxia: In US Coastal Waters," Inter-Agency Working Group on Harmful Algal Blooms, Hypoxia and Human Health, September.

Erceg, D. (2006) "Detering IUU Fishing Through State Control Over Nationals," *Marine Policy*, 30, 173–179.

FAO (Food and Agricultural Organization) (1997a) *Review of the State of World Fishery Resources: Marine Fisheries*, FAO, Rome.

FAO (1997b) *Review of the State of World Fishery Resources: Marine Fisheries: Regional Reviews: Northwest Atlantic*, FAO, Rome.

Farrow, S. (1996) "Marine Protected Areas: Emerging Economics," *Marine Policy*, 20 (6), 439–446.

Farzin, Y. H. (2001) "The Impact of Oil Price on Additions to US Proven Reserves," *Resources and Energy Economics*, 23, 271–291.

Fernandez, L. and Karp, L. (1998) "Restoring Wetlands Through Wetlands Mitigation Banks," *Environmental and Resource Economics*, 12, 323–344.

Field, B. (1989) "The Evolution of Property Rights," *Kyklos*, 47 (3), 319–345.

Fitzpatrick, J. (1996) "Technology and Fisheries Legislation," in *Precautionary Approach to Fisheries*, Part 2: Scientific Papers, FAO Fisheries Technical Paper 350, FAO, Rome.

Fletcher-Tomenius, P. and Forrest, C. (2000) "Historic Wreck in International Waters: Conflict or Consensus?," *Marine Policy*, 24, 1–10.

Freeman, A.M. (1991) "Valuing Environmental Resources under Alternative Management Regimes," *Ecological Economics*, 3 (3), 247–256.

Fu, Xiaowen, Ng, A. K. Y. and Yui-Yip Lau (2010) "The Impacts of Maritime Piracy on Global Economic Development: The Case of Somalia," *Maritime Policy and Management*, 37 (7), 677–697.

Gallic, L. B. and Cox, A. (2006) "An Economic Analysis of Illegal, Unreported and Unregulated (IUU) Fishing: Key Drivers and Possible Solutions," *Marine Policy*, 30, 689–695.

GAO (Government Accounting Office) (2005) "Corps of Engineers Does Not Have an Effective Oversight Approach to Ensure that Compensatory Mitigation is Occurring," GAO-05-898, September.

GAO (2008) "Oil And Gas Royalties: The Federal System for Collecting Oil and Gas Revenues Needs Comprehensive Reassessment," GAO-08-691.

Gislason, H., Sinclair, M., Sainsbury, K. and O'Boyle, R. (2000) "Symposium Overview: Incorporating Ecosystem Objectives within Fisheries Management," *ICES Journal of Marine Science*, 57, 468–475.

Goldsmith, J. L. and Posner, E. A. (1999) "A Theory of Customary International Law," *The University of Chicago Law Review*, 66 (4), Autumn, 1133–1177.

Goldsmith, J. L. and Posner, E. A. (2005) *The Limits of International Law*, Oxford University Press, Oxford.

Gordon, H. G. (1954) "The Economic Theory of a Common Property Resource: The Fishery," *Journal of Political Economy*, 62 (2), April, 124–142.

Gould, H. (2011) "Categorical Obligation in International Law," *International Theory*, 3 (2), 254–285.

Grolin, J. (1988) "Environmental Hegemony, Maritime Community and the Problem of Oil Tanker Pollution," in Morris, M. A. (ed.), *North–South Perspectives on Marine Policy*, Westview Press, Boulder CO.

Guha, B. and Guha, A.S. (2011) "Pirates and Traders: Some Economics of Pirate-Infested Seas," *Economics Letters*, 111, 147–150.

Gutiérrez, N. L., Hilborn, R. and Defeo, O. (2011) "Leadership, Social Capital and Incentives Promote Successful Fisheries," *Nature*, 470, February 17th, 386–389.

Guzman, A. J. (2009) "How International Law Works: Introduction," *International Theory*, 1 (2), 285–293.

Gylfason, T. and Weitzman, M.L. (2002) "Icelandic Fisheries Management: Fees versus Quotas," paper presented at the Center for International Development, Harvard University, May 20th.

Hagemann, F. (2010) "Strategic Planning for Comprehensive Security in the European Union's Military Operations: EUFOR RD Congo, EUFOR TCHAD/RCA and EUNAVFOR for Somalia," Monterey Naval Post Graduate School, June.

Haile, P., Hendricks, K. and Porter, R. (2010) "Recent U.S. Offshore Oil and Gas Lease Bidding: A Progress Report," paper presented at the 36th Annual EARIE Conference in Ljubljana and the 7th Annual IIOC in Boston, February 17th.

Hall, D.C., Hall, J. V. and Murray, S. N. (2002) "Contingent Valuation of Marine Protected Areas: Southern California Rocky Intertidal Ecosystems," *Natural Resource Modeling*, 15 (3).

Hallwood, P. (1979) *Stabilization of International Commodity Markets*, JAI Press, Greenwich, CT.

Hallwood, P. (1990) *Transaction Costs and Trade Between Multinational Corporations: A Study of Off Shore Oil Production*, Unwin-Hyman, London.

Hallwood, P. (1991a) "On Choosing Organizational Arrangements: The Examples of Offshore Oil Gathering," *Scottish Journal of Political Economy*, 38 (3), August, 227–241.

Hallwood, P. (1991b) "Foreign Ownership and Industrial Organization in the Scottish Offshore Oil Supply Industry," *Journal of Energy and Development*, 14 (2), 221–236.

Hallwood, P. and Edwards, R. (1980) "The Determination of Optimum Buffer Stock Rules," *The Quarterly Journal of Economics*, February, 94 (1), 151–166.

Hallwood, P. and Sinclair, S. W. (1981) *Oil, Debt and Development: Open in the Third World*, George Allen and Unwin, London.

Hallwood, P. and Miceli, T. (2006) "Murky Waters: The Law and Economics of Salvaging Historic Wrecks," *Journal of Legal Studies*, 35 (2), 285–302.

Hallwood, P. and Miceli, T. (2011) "'Keystone Cops' Meet 'Pirates of the Somali Coast': The Failure of International Efforts to Control Maritime Piracy," Department of Economics Working Paper, University of Connecticut.

Hanley, N. and Spash, C. (1994) "Environmental Limits to CBA?," in Hanley, N. and Spash, C., *Cost–Benefit Analysis*, Elgar, Cheltenham.

Hannesson, R. (1998) "Marine Reserves: What Will They Accomplish?," *Marine Resource Economics*, 13, 159–170.

Hannesson, R. (2002) "The Economics of Marine Reserves," *Natural Resource Modeling*, 15 (3).

Harrison, W. (1995) "Can You Bank on Wetland Mitigation? New Developments in Wetland Mitigation Banks," University of Mississippi Law Center, *Water Log*, 15 (1), 10–11.

Hart, D. R and Rago, P. J. (2006) "Long-Term Dynamics of U.S. Atlantic Sea Scallop *Placopecten magellanicus* Populations," *North American Journal of Fisheries Management*, 26 (2), 490–501.

Hatcher, M., de Rham, M. and Thorncroft, A. (1987) *Geldermalsen, The Nanking Cargo*, Hamish Hamilton, London.

Helfand, G. E. and Rubin, J. (1994) "Spreading versus Concentrating Damages: Environmental Policy in the Presence of Nonconvexities," *Journal of Environmental Economics and Management*, 27, 84–91.

Herrick, S. F., Rader, B. and Squires, D. (1997) "Access Fees and Economic Benefits in the Western Pacific United States Purse Seine Tuna Fishery," *Marine Policy*, 21 (1) 83–96.

Hey, D. and Philippe, N. S. (1999) *A Case for Wetland Restoration*, John Wiley and Sons Inc., New York.

Heyward, A., Pinceratto, E. and Smith, L. (1997) *Big Bank Shoals of the Timor Sea: An Environmental Resource Atlas*, Australian Institute of Marine Science and BHP Petroleum, Melbourne.

Hjort, J., Jahn, G. and Ottestad, P. (1933) "The Optimum Catch," *Hvalradets Skrifter*, 7, 92–107.

Holland, D. S. (2000) "A Bioeconomic Model of Marine Sanctuaries on Georges Bank," *Canadian Journal of Fisheries and Aquatic Sciences*, 57, 1307–1319.

Holland, D. S. and Brazee, R. J. (1996) "Marine Reserves for Fisheries Management," *Marine Resource Economics*, 11, 157–71.

Holland, D. S. and Ginter, J. J. C. (2001) "Common Property Institutions in the Alaskan Ground Fisheries," *Marine Policy*, 25, 33–42.

Homans, F. R. and Wilen, J. E. (1997) "A Model of Regulated Open Access Resource Use," *Journal of Environmental Economics and Management*, 32, 1–21.

Honneland, G. (2001) "Recent Global Agreements on High Seas Fisheries: Potential Effects on Fisherman Compliance," in Stokke, *Governing High Seas Fisheries*, Oxford University Press, Oxford, 121–39.

Huang, L., Nichols, L. A., Craig, J. K. and Smith, M. D. (2012) "Measuring Welfare Losses from Hypoxia: The Case of North Carolina Brown Shrimp," *Marine Resource Economics*, 27 (1), 3–23.

Hurd, I. (2012) "Almost Saving Whales: The Ambiguity of Success at the International Whaling Commission," *Ethics and International Affairs*, 26 (1), 103–113.

Hutchings, J. A. (2000) "Collapse and Recovery of Marine Fishes," *Nature*, 406, August 24th, 882–885.

Hutter, M. and Rizzo, I. (1997) *Economic Perspectives on Cultural Heritage*, St. Martin's Press, New York.

IMO (International Maritime Organization) (2009) "Djibouti Meeting," IMO website, available online at www.imo.org/OurWork/Security/PIU/Pages/DCCMeeting.aspx.

ISA (International Seabed Authority) (2013a) "Towards the Development of a Regulatory Framework for Polymetallic Nodule Exploitation in the Area," published as *International Seabed Authority Technical Study 11*, ISA, Kingston, Jamaica.

ISA (2013b) "Executive Summary of 'Towards the Development of a Regulatory Framework for Polymetallic Nodule Exploitation in the Area'," ISBA/19/C/5, March 25th.

Jensen, C. L. (2002) "Reduction of the Fishing Capacity in 'Common Pool' Fisheries," *Marine Policy*, 26, 155–158.

Joint Standing Committee on Treaties (2002) "Report 49: The Timor Sea Treaty," Canberra, available online at www.aph.gov.au/house/committee/jsct/timor/report/fullreport.pdf.

Juda, L. (1997) "The 1995 United Nations Agreement on Straddling Fish Stocks and Highly Migratory Fish Stocks: A Critique," *Ocean Development and International Law*, 28, 147–166.

Kappel, C. V., Halpern, B. S., Selkoe, K. A. and Cooke, R. M. (2012) "Eliciting Expert Knowledge of Ecosystem Vulnerability to Human Stressors to Support Comprehensive Ocean Management," in Perera, A. H., Ashton, D. C. and Johnson, C. J. (eds), *Expert Knowledge and Its Application in Landscape Ecology*, Springer, New York, 253–277.

Kemp, A. G. (1990) *Petroleum Rent Collection Around the World*, The Institute for Research on Public Policy, Halifax, Nova Scotia.

Kemp, A. G. (1992) "Development Risks and Petroleum Fiscal Systems: A Comparative Study of the UK, Norway, Denmark and the Netherlands," *The Energy Journal*, 13 (3), 15–32.

Kemp, A. G. and Hallwood, P. (1983) "The Benefits of North Sea Oil," *Energy Policy*, June, 119–130.

Kemp, A. G. and Stephen, L. (1998) "Exploration and Development Prospects in the UKCS: The 1998 Perspective," University of Aberdeen, Department of Economics, North Sea Study Occasional Paper no. 68, September.

Kemp, A. G. and Kasim, S. (2000) "An Econometric Model of Oil and Gas Exploration Development and Production in the UK Continental Shelf: A Systems Approach," Aberdeen University, North Sea Oil Occasional Paper no. 79, December.

Kemp, A. G. and Stephen, L. (2006) "Prospects for Activity Levels in the UKCS to 2035 after the 2006 Budget," Aberdeen University, North Sea Study Occasional Paper no. 101, April.

Kenchington, R. A. (1990) *Managing Marine Environments*, Taylor and Francis, New York.

Keyuan, Z. (2005) "The Sino–Vietnamese Agreement on Maritime Boundary Delimitation in the Gulf of Tonkin," *Ocean Development and International Law*, 36, 13–24.

Kilpatrick, R. L. (2011) "Borrowing from Civil Aviation Security: Does International Law Governing Airline Hijacking Offer Solutions to the Modern Maritime Piracy Epidemic off the Coast of Somalia?," Oceans Beyond Piracy Working Paper, August.

Kindleberger, C. P. (1986) "International Public Goods without International Government," *American Economic Review*, 76 (1), 1–13.

King, R. J. (2002) "The Timor Gap, 1972–2002," available online at www.aph.gov.au/house/committee/jsct/timor/subs/sub43.pdf of Justice.

Knowlton, N. (2001) "Coral Reef Biodiversity – Habitat Size Matters," *Science*, 292, May 25th, 1493–1495.

Kontorovich, E. (2009) "Piracy and International Law," paper presented at the Global Law Forum, Jerusalem Center for Public Affairs, February.

Koskenniemi, M. (2011) "The Mystery of Legal Obligation," *International Theory*, 3 (2), 319–325.

Kukoy, S. J. and Canter, L. W. (1995) "Mitigation Banking as a Tool for Improving Wetland Preservation via Section 404 of the Clean Water Act," *Environmental Protection*, 17 (4), 301–308.

Kuperan, K. and Sutinen, J. G. (1998) "Blue Water Crime: Deterrence, Legitimacy, and Compliance in Fisheries," *Law and Society Review*, 32 (2), 309–337.

Kuronuma, Y. and Tisdell, C. A. (1994) "Economics of Antarctic Minke Whale Catches: Sustainability and Welfare Considerations," *Marine Resource Economics*, 9, 141–158.

Kydd, A. (2009) "Reputation and Cooperation: Guzman on International Law," *International Theory*, 1 (2), 295–305.

Laist, D. W., Knowlton, A. R., Mead, J. G., Collet, A. S. and Podesta, M. (2001) "Collisions between Ships and Whales," *Marine Mammal Science*, 17 (1), 35–75.

Lake Champlain Maritime Museum (1994) "JASON Curriculum," Working Draft, March.

Lal, P. (2005) "Coral Reef Use and Management – The Need, Role, and Prospects of Economic Valuation in the Pacific," in Ahmed, Chiew Kieok Chong and Cesar, *Economic Valuation and Policy Priorities for Sustainable Management of Coral Reefs*, World Fish Center, Penang, Malaysia, 59–78.

Lawrence, E. (1991) "Poverty and the Rate of Time Preference: Evidence from Panel Data," *Journal of Political Economy*, 99 (1), 54–77.

Leeson, P. (2007) "An-arrgh-chy: The Law and Economics of Pirate Organization," *Journal of Political Economy*, 115: 1049–1094.

Lipsey, R. G. and Lancaster, K. (1956) "The General Theory of Second Best," *The Review of Economic Studies*, 24 (1), 11–32.

Lipton, D. and Kasperski, S. (2008) "Estuarine Restoration and Commercial Fisheries," in Pendleton, L. H. (ed.), *The Economic and Market Value of America's Coasts and Estuaries: What's at Stake*, Arlington, VA, Chapter 4: Restore America's Estuaries.

Lodge, M. W., Anderson, D., Lobach, T., Munro, E., Sainsbury, K. and Willock, A. (2007) *Recommended Best Practices for Regional Fisheries Management Organizations: Report of an Independent Panel to Develop a Model for Improved Governance by Regional Fisheries Management Organizations*, Chatham House, London.

Macinko, S. and Bromley, D. (2002) *Who Owns America's Fisheries?*, Pew Ocean Science Series, Island Press, Washington DC.

Mantzouni, I., Sørensen, H., O'Hara, R. B. and MacKenzie, B. R.(2010) "Hierarchical Modelling of Temperature and Habitat Size Effects on Population Dynamics of North Atlantic Cod," *ICES Journal of Marine Science*, 67 (5), 833–855.

Mary Rose Annual Report (2002) available online at www.cix.co.uk/~mary-rose/2002.pdf.

Masson, R. C. (2010) "Piracy: A Legal Definition," US Congressional Research Service, December 13th.

Mazzanti, M. (2001) "The Role of Economics in Global Management of Whales: Reforming or Refounding IWC?," *Ecological Economics*, 36, 205–221.

McClanahan, T. R., Graham, N. A. J., Calnan, J. M. and MacNeil, M. A. (2007) "Toward Pristine Biomass: Reef Fish Recovery in Coral Reef Marine Protected Areas in Kenya," *Ecological Applications*, 17, 1055–1067.

McCook, L. J. et al (2010) "Adaptive Management of the Great Barrier Reef: A Globally Significant Demonstration of the Benefits of Networks of Marine Reserves," *Proceedings of the National Academy of Sciences, USA* (Proc. Natl. Acad. Sci. USA), 107 (43), 18278–18285.

McDorman, T. L. (2005) "Implementing Existing Tools: Turning Words into Actions – Decision-Making Processes of Regional Fisheries Management Organizations," *International Journal of Marine and Coastal Law*, 20 (3–4), 423–457.

McLaughlin, S. L. (1995) "Roots, Relics and Recovery: What Went Wrong with the Abandoned Shipwreck Act of 1987?," *Columbia-VLA Journal of Law and the Arts*, 19, 149–198.

Miller, G. (1987) "The Second Destruction of the Geldermalsen," *American Neptune*, 47 (4), 275–281.

Milon, J. W. (2000) "Pastures, Fences, Tragedies and Marine Reserves," *Bulletin of Marine Science*, 66 (3), 901–916.

Minerals Management Service, US Department of the Interior (2008) "Budget Justifications and Performance Information for FY 2008," p. 9, available online at www.doi.gov/budget/2008/data/greenbook/FY2008_MMS_Greenbook.pdf.

Minney, T. (2010) "Somali Pirates Stock Exchange Finances Sea Ventures," *African Capital Markets News*, April 28th, available online at www.africancapitalmarketsnews.com/402/somali-pirates-stock-exchange-finances-sea-ventures/.

Minns, C. K., Randall, R. G., Smokorowski, K. E., Clarke, K. D., Vélez-Espino, A., Gregory. R. S., Courtenay, S. and LeBlanc, P. (2011) "Direct and Indirect Estimates of the Productive Capacity of Fish Habitat under Canada's Policy for the Management of Fish Habitat: Where Have We Been, Where Are We Now, and Where Are We Going?," *Canadian Journal of Fisheries and Aquatic Sciences*, 68 (12), 2204–2227.

Mirovitskaya, N. S., Clark, M. and Purver, R. G. (1993) "North Pacific Fur Seals: Regime Formation as a Means of Resolving Conflict," in Young, O. R. and Osherenko, G. (eds), *Creating International Environmental Regimes*, Cornell University Press, Cornell, NY.

Mitchell, R. B. (1994) "Regime Design Matters: Intentional Oil Pollution and Treaty Compliance," *International Organization*, 48, 425–458.

Mitsch, W. J. and Gosselink, J. G. (2000) *Wetlands*, John Wiley and Sons Inc., New York.

Moberg, F. and Folk, C. (1999) "Ecological Goods and Services of Coral Reef Ecosystems," *Ecological Economics*, 29, 215–233.

Montalto, F. A., Steenhuis, T. and Parlange, J. Y. (2002) "The Restoration of Tidal Marsh Hydrology," in Brebbia, C. A. (ed.), *Coastal Environment: Environmental Problems in Coastal Regions IV*, WIT Press, Boston.

Morgan, L. E., Chih-Fan Tsao and Guinotte, J. M. (2007) "Ecosystem-Based Management as a Tool for Protecting Deep-Sea Corals in the USA," in George, R. Y. and Cairns, S. D. (eds), *Conservation and Adaptive Management of Seamount and Deep-Sea Coral Ecosystems*, Rosenstiel School of Marine and Atmospheric Science, University of Miami.

Murphy, S. D. (2006) *Principles of International Law: A Concise Handbook*, Thomson–West, n.p.

Myers, R. A. and Worm, B. (2003) "Rapid Worldwide Depletion of Predatory Fish Communities," *Nature*, 423, May 15th, 280–283.

Naranjo, A. (2010) "Spillover Effects of Domestic Law Enforcement Policies," *International Review of Law and Economics*, 30, 265–275.

National Research Council (2001) *Marine Protected Areas: Tools for Sustaining Ocean Ecosystems*, National Academy Press, Washington DC.

Natural Resources Defense Council (2008) "Lethal Sounds," October 6th, available online at www.nrdc.org/wildlife/marine/sonar.asp.

Navrud, S. and Ready, R. (2002) *Valuing Cultural Heritage: Applying Environmental Valuation Techniques to Historic Buildings, Monuments and Artifacts*, Edward Elgar Publishing, Northampton, MA.

Nielsen, J. R. (2003) "An Analytical Framework for Studying Compliance and Legitimacy in Fisheries Management," *Marine Policy*, 27, 425–423.

Nielsen, J. R. and Mathiesen, C. (2003) "Important Factors Influencing Rule Compliance in Fisheries: Lessons from Denmark," *Marine Policy*, 27, 409–416.

Nielsen, J. R., Vedsmand, T. and Friis, P. (1997) "Danish Fisheries Co-management Decision Making and Alternative Management Systems," *Ocean and Coastal Management*, 35 (2–3), 201–216.

NMFS (National Marine Fisheries Service) (2003) "Enforcement/Compliance Roundtable: Discussion Summary – Madison-Swanson and Steamboat Lumps Marine Protected Areas," available online at www.nmfs.noaa/habitat/ecosystem/habitatdocs/enforcement-summary.pdf.

NMFS (2010) *Recovery Plan for the Sperm Whale* (Physetermacrocephalus), National Marine Fisheries Service, Silver Spring, MD.

Noakes, G. (2009) "Statement on International Piracy" before the US House of Representatives Committee on Transportation and Infrastructure subcommittee on Coast Guard and Maritime Transportation, February.

North, D. (1981) *Structure and Change in Economic History*, W. W. Norton, New York.

O'Connell, R. and Descovich, C. (2010) "Decreasing Variance in Response Time to Singular Incidents of Piracy in the Horn of Africa Area of Operation," Naval Post-graduate School, Monterey, CA, June, available online at http://edocs.nps.edu/npspubs/scholarly/theses/2010/Jun/10Jun_O_Connell.pdf.

O'Keefe, P. J. and Nafziger, J. A. R. (1994) "The Draft Convention on the Protection of the Underwater Cultural Heritage," *Ocean Development and International Law*, 25 (4), 391–418.

Oberthur, S. (1999) "The International Convention for the Regulation of Whaling: From Over-Exploitation to Total Prohibition," in *Yearbook of International Cooperation on Environment and Development, 1998/99*, Earthscan Publications, London.

Ocean Commission (2004) "Addressing Coastal Water Pollution," in *An Ocean Blue Print for the 21st Century*, Chapter 14, available online at www.oceancommission.gov/.

OECD (Organization for Economic Co-operation and Development) (1997) *Towards Sustainable Fisheries: Economic Aspects of the Management of Living Marine Resources*, OECD, Paris.

Parliament of Canada (2003) "A Report of the Standing Senate Committee on Fisheries and Oceans Straddling Fish Stocks in the Northwest Atlantic," June, available online at www.parl.gc.ca/Content/SEN/Committee/372/fish/rep/rep05jun03-e.htm.

Peacock, A. (1997) "Towards a Workable Heritage Policy," in Hutter and Rizzo, *Economic Perspectives on Cultural Heritage*, St. Martin's Press, New York, 225–235.

Pearce, W., Mourato, S., Navrud, S. and Ready, R. C. (2002) "Review of Existing Studies, their Policy Use and Future Research Needs," in Navrud and Ready, *Valuing Cultural Heritage: Applying Environmental Valuation Techniques to Historic Buildings, Monuments and Artifacts*, Edward Elgar Publishing, Northampton, MA.

Peet, G. (1992) "MARPOL Convention: Implementation and Effectiveness," *International Journal of Estuarine and Coastal Law*, 7, 277–299.

Pelkofer, P. (1999) "The Decision of the Supreme Court in the Brother Jonathan Case," available online at www.acuaonline.org/legalupdates/SupCtBroJon1.pdf.

Pew Oceans Commission (2003) "America's Living Oceans: Charting a Course for Sea Change," available online at www.pewtrusts.org/uploadedFiles/wwwpewtrustsorg/Reports/Protecting_ocean_life/env_pew_oceans_final_report.pdf.

Pezzey, J. C. V., Roberts, C. M. and Urdal, B. T. (2000) "A Simple Bioeconomic Model of Marine Reserve," *Ecological Economics*, 33 (1), 77–91.

Pfadenhauer, J. and Grootjans, A. (1999) "Wetland Restoration in Central Europe: Aims and Methods," *Applied Vegetation Science*, 2 (1), May, 95–106.

Pham Khanh Nam and Tran Vo Hung Son (2005) "Recreational Value of the Coral Surrounding the Hon Mun Islands in Vietnam: A Travel Cost and Contingent Valuation Study," in Ahmed and Chiew Kieok Chong (eds), *Economic Valuation and Policy Priorities for Sustainable Management of Coral Reefs*, World Fish Center, Penang, Malaysia, 84–107.

Pintassilgo, P. (2003) "A Coalition Approach to the Management of High Seas Fisheries in the Presence of Externalities," *Natural Resource Modeling*, 16 (2), 175–197.

Polacheck, T. (1990) "Year Round Closed Areas as a Management Tool," *Natural Resource Economics*, 4 (3), 327–354.

Polinsky, A. M. and Shavell, S. (2000) "The Economic Theory of Public Enforcement of Law," *Journal of Economic Literature*, 38, 45–76.

Pollicino, M. and Maddison, D. (2002) "Valuing the Impacts of Air Pollution on Lincoln Cathedral," in Navrud and Ready, *Valuing Cultural Heritage: Applying Environmental Valuation Techniques to Historic Buildings, Monuments and Artifacts*, Edward Elgar Publishing, Northampton, MA, 53–67.

Polunin, N. V. C. and Roberts, C. M. (1993) "Greater Biomass and Value of Target Coral-reef Fishes in Two Small Caribbean Marine Reserves," *Marine Ecology Progress Series*, 100, 167–176.

Pomeroy, R. S. and Berkes, F. (1997) "Two to Tango: the Role of Government in Fisheries Co-management," *Marine Policy*, 21 (5), 465–480.

Pomeroy, R. S., Katon, B. M. and Harkes, I. (2001) "Conditions Affecting the Success of Fisheries Co-management: Lessons from Asia," *Marine Policy*, 25, 197–208.

Poret, S. (2003) "Paradoxical Effects of Law Enforcement Policies: The Case of the Illicit Drug Market," *International Review of Law and Economics*, 22, 465–493.

Porter, R. H. (1992) "The Role of Information in US Offshore Oil and Gas Lease Auctions," National Bureau of Economic Research, w4185.

Post, J. R, et al. (2002) "Canada's Recreational Fisheries: The Invisible Collapse?," *Fisheries*, 27 (1), 6–17.

Randall, K. (1988) "Universal Jurisdiction Under International Law," *Texas Law Journal*, 66, March, 785–822.

Rayfuse, R. (2003) "Canada and Regional Fisheries Organizations: Implementing the UN Fish Stocks Agreement," *Ocean Development and International Law*, 34, 209–228.

Redmond, A. (1990) *Report on Mitigation in Florida State Permitting Efforts*, Florida Department of Environmental Regulation, Tallahassee, FL.

Reece, D. K. (1979) "An Analysis of Alternative Bidding Systems for Leasing Offshore Oil," *The Bell Journal of Economics*, 10 (2), 659–669.

Reef Research (1999) "Three Year Crackdown on Illegal Activity," *Reef Research*, 9 (1) March, available online at www.gbrmp.gov.au/corp_site/info/services/publications/reef_reasearch/issue…/1rmn1.htm.

Repetto, R. (2001) "A Natural Experiment in Fisheries Management," *Marine Policy*, 25 (4), July, 251–264.

Report of the Standing Senate Committee on Fisheries and Oceans (2003) "Straddling Fish Stocks in the Northwest Atlantic," Chair: Gerald J. Comeau, available online at www.parl.gc.ca/37/2/parlbus/commbus/senate/Com-e/fish-e/rep-e/rep05jun03-e.htm#A.%20%20The%201982%20United.

Research Program on Aquatic Agricultural Systems (2012) "Coral Reef Economic Value and Incentives for Coral Farming in Solomon Islands," Policy Brief, CGIAR Research Program on Aquatic Agricultural Systems, AAS-2012-14, World Fish Center, Penang, Malaysia.

Ribaudo, M., Heimlich, R. and Peters, M. A. (2005) "Nitrogen Sources and Gulf Hypoxia: Potential for Environmental Credit Trading," *Ecological Economics*, 52, 159–168.

Richards, L. J. and Maguire, J.-J. (1998) "Recent International Agreements and the Precautionary Approach: New Directions for Fisheries Management Science," *Canadian Journal of Fisheries and Aquatic Sciences*, 55 (6), 1545–1552.

Riesenfeld, R. (1942) *Protection of Coastal Fisheries Under International Law*, republished by William S. Hein & Co, Buffalo, NY (2000).

Roach, J. A. (1998) ""Shipwrecks' Reconciling Salvage and Underwater Archaeology," 22nd Annual Conference, Center for Oceans Law and Policy, University of Virginia School of Law.

Roberts, P. and Trow, S. (2002) *Taking to the Water: English Heritage's Initial Policy for the Management of Maritime Archaeology in England*, English Heritage, London, available online at www.english-heritage.org.uk/filestore/archaeology/maritime/pdf/maritime.pdf.

Robinson, M. S. (1985) "Collusion and the Choice of Auction," *The RAND Journal of Economics*, 16 (1), 141–145.

Rodwell, L. D., Barbier, E. B., Roberts, C. M. and McClanahan, M. (2002) "A Model of Tropical Marine Reserve-Fishery Linkages," *Natural Resource Modeling*, 15 (4), 453–486.

Romano, C. and Ingadottir, T. (2000) "The Financing of the International Criminal Court: A Discussion Paper," Center for International Cooperation, Project on International Courts and Tribunals, NYU and School of Oriental and African Studies, University of London, June.

Ruppe, C. V. and Barstad, J. F. (eds) (2002) *International Handbook of Underwater Archaeology*, Kluwer, Dordrecht.

Russ, G. R. and Alcala, A. C. (1996) "Marine Reserves: Rates and Patterns of Recovery and Decline of Large Predatory Fish," *Ecological Applications*, 6 (3), 947–961.

Russ, R. and Alcala, A. C. (2004) "Marine Reserves: Long-Term Protection is Required for Full Recovery of Predatory Fish Populations," *Oecologia*, 138 (4), March, 622–627.

Sanchirico, J. N. and Wilen, J. E. (1999) "Bioeconomics of Spatial Exploitation in a Patchy Environment," *Journal of Environmental Economics and Management*, 37, 129–150.

Sanchirico, J. N. and Wilen, J. E. (2001) "A Bioeconomic Model of Marine Reserve Creation," *Journal of Environmental Economics and Management*, 42, 257–276.

Sanchirico, J. N. and Wilen, J. E. (2002) "The Impacts of Marine Reserves on Limited-Entry Fisheries," *Natural Resource Modeling*, 15 (3), 280–302.

Scott, A. (1988) "Development of Property in the Fishery," *Marine Resource Economics*, 5, 289–311.

Seeney, J. C. (1999) "An Overview of Commercial Salvage Principles in the Context of Marine Archaeology," *Journal of Maritime Law and Commerce*, 30 (2), 185–203.

Sheahan, M. (2001) "Credit for Conservation: A Report on Conservation Banking and Mitigation Banking in the USA, and its Applicability to New South Wales," Volume I: Report, The Winston Churchill Memorial Trust of Australia.

Shepherd, J. (2002) "Fear of the First Strike: The Full Deterrence Effect of California's Two- and Three-Strike Legislation," *Journal of Legal Studies*, 31, 159–201.

Smith, J. D. and Wilen, J. E. (2003) "Economic Impacts of Marine Reserves: The Importance of Spatial Behavior," *Journal of Economics and Environmental Management*, 46, 183–206.

Smoktonowicz, A. B. (2005) "Federal Conservation of Wetlands Runs Amuck with Wetland Mitigation Banking," *Ohio Northern University Law Review*, 31 (1), 177–195.

Stavins, R. N. and Whitehead, B. W. (1992) "Dealing with Pollution: Market Based Incentives for Environmental Protection," *Environment*, 34, September, 6–11, 29–42.

Stejneger, L. (1925) "Fur-Seal Industry of the Commander Islands, 1897 to 1922," *Bulletin of the Bureau of Fisheries*, 41.

Stokke, O. S. (2001) *Governing High Seas Fisheries: The Interplay of Global and Regional Regimes*, Oxford University Press, Oxford.

Sumaila, U. (2002) "Marine Protected Area Performance in a Model of the Fishery," *Natural Resource Modeling*, 15 (4), 439–451.

Sumaila, U. R., Alder, J. and Keith, H. (2006) "Global Scope and Economics of Illegal Fishing," *Marine Policy*, 30, 696–703.

Sutinen, J. G. and K. Kuperan (1999) "A Socio-Economic Theory of Regulatory Compliance," *International Journal of Social Economics*, 26, 174–193.

Swanson, T. M. (1991) "The Regulation of Oceanic Resources: An Examination of the International Community's Record in the Regulation of One Global Resource," in Helm, D. (ed.), *Economic Policy Towards the Environment*, Blackwell, Oxford.

Sweeney, J. C. (1999) "An Overview of Commercial Salvage Principles in the Context of Marine Archaeology," *Journal of Maritime Law and Commerce*, 30, 185–203.

Sydnes, A. K. (2001) "Regional Fishery Organizations: How and Why Organizational Diversity Matters," *Ocean Development and International Law*, 32, 349–372.

Taylor, M. and Ward, H. (1982) "Chickens, Whales and Lumpy Goods: Alternate Models of Public-Goods Provision," *Political Studies*, 30 (3), 350–370.

Teck, S. J. et al. (2010) "Using Expert Judgment to Estimate Marine Ecosystem Vulnerability in the California Current," *Ecological Applications*, 20 (5), 1402–1416.

Thomson, A. (2009) "The Rational Enforcement of International Law: Solving the Sanctioners' Dilemma," *International Theory*, 1 (2), 307–321.

Thorson, J. T., Cope, J. M., Branch, T. A. and Jensen, O. P. (2012) "Spawning Biomass Reference Points for Exploited Marine Fishes, Incorporating Taxonomic and Body Size Information," *Canadian Journal of Fisheries Aquatic Science*, 69, 1556–1568.

Throckmorton, P. (1990) "The World's Worst Investment: The Economics of Treasure Hunting with Real Life Comparisons," Proceedings of the Conference on Historical and Underwater Archaeology, published by the Society for Historical and Underwater Archaeology, Germantown, MD, 6–10.

Tinch, R. and Phang, Z. (2009) "Sink or Swim: The Economics of Whaling Today," WWF and WDCS, available online at www.wdcs.org/submissions_bin/economics_whaling_report.pdf.

Turack, D.C. (2002) "The Concept of the Common Heritage of Mankind in International Law," *Journal of Third World Studies*, 19 (2), 339–340.

UN (1958) "United Nations Conference on the Law of the Sea," Geneva, Switzerland, February 24th to April 27th, A/CONF.13/8.

UNESCO (1999) *Background Materials on the Protection of the Underwater Cultural Heritage*, Vol. 1, UNESCO, Paris.

Ungoed-Thomas, J. and Woolf, M. (2009) "Navy Releases Somali Pirates Caught Red-handed: A Legal Loophole has Helped Scores of Somali Gunmen Escape Justice," *The Sunday Times*, November 29th.

United Nations Security Council (2011) "Report of the Special Adviser to the Secretary-General on Legal Issues Related to Piracy off the Coast of Somalia. A plan in 25 proposals," January, S/2011/30.

United States Geological Survey (2008) "Circum-Arctic Resource Appraisal: Estimates of Undiscovered Oil and Gas North of the Arctic Circle," Fact Sheet 2008-3049.

US Central Command (2009) "Pirate Attacks on the Rise off Somali Coast," September 29th, available online at www.centcom.mil/press-releases/pirate-attacks-on-rise-off-somalia-coast.

US Commission on Ocean Policy (2004) "Coordinating Management in Federal Waters," in *Preliminary Report of the US Commission on Ocean Policy – Governor's Draft*, US Government, Washington DC, Chapter 6.

US Ocean Commission (2004) "An Ocean Blueprint for the 21st Century Final Report of the U.S. Commission on Ocean Policy," Washington DC, available online at www.oceancommission.gov/documents/full_color_rpt/welcome.html.

Van Dyke, J. M. (2007) "Legal Issues Related to Sovereignty over Dokdo and Its Maritime Boundary," *Ocean Development and International Law*, 38 (1 and 2), 157–224.

Verissimo, D. and Metcalfe, K. (2009) "Whaling: Quota Trading Won't Work," *Nature*, 482, 162.

Vicuna, F.O. (1999) *The Changing International Law of High Seas Fisheries (Cambridge Studies in International and Comparative Law)*, Cambridge University Press, Cambridge.

Ward, T., Heinemann, D. and Evans, N. (2001) "The Role of Marine Reserves as Fisheries Management Tools," Department of Agriculture, Forestry and Fisheries, Bureau of Rural Services, Australia, available online at www.affa.gov.au.

Waring, G.T., Gerrior, P., Payne, P.M., Parry, B.L. and Nicolas, J.R. (1990) "Incidental Take of Marine Mammals in Foreign Fishery Activities off the Northeast United States, 1977–88," *Fishery Bulletin*, 88 (2), 347–360.

Wassermann, U. (1976) "Key Issues in Development: Interview with UNCTAD's Secretary General," *Journal of World Trade Law*, 10, 17–20.

Watling, L. and Norse, E.A. (1998) "Disturbance of the Seabed by Mobile Fishing Gear: A Comparison with Forest Clear-Cutting," *Conservation Biology*, 12 (6), 1180–1197.

Weems, W.A. and Canter, L.W. (1995) "Planning and Operation Guidelines for Mitigation Banking for Wetland Impacts," *Environmental Impact Assessment Review*, 15, 197–218.

Wheeler, D.P. and Strock, J.M. (1995) "Official Policy on Conservation Banks," California Environmental Protection Agency, April.

White, A.T., Ross, M. and Flores, M. (2000) "Benefits and Costs of Coral Reef and Wetland Management, Olango Island, Philippines," CRMP Document Number: 04-CRM/2000.

Wiswall, F.L. (1983) "Uniformity in Maritime Law: The Domestic Impact of International Maritime Regulation," *Tulane Law Journal*, 57, 1208–1237.

World Bank (1999) *Issues in Coral Reef Biodiversity Valuation: Results for Montego Bay*, principal authors: J. Ruitenbeek and C. Cartier, World Bank Research Committee Project RPO #682-22, Final Report, March.

World Bank (2009) *The Sunken Billions: The Economic Justification for Fisheries Reform*, World Bank and FAO, Washington DC.

Wright, R. (2008) "Piracy Set to Escalate Shipping Costs," *Financial Times*, November 20th.

Xue, G. (2005) "Bilateral Fisheries Agreements for the Cooperative Management of the Shared Resources of the China Seas: A Note," *Ocean Development and International Law*, 36, 363–374.

Young, O. (1989) "The Politics of International Regime Formation: Managing Natural Resources and the Environment," *International Organization*, 43 (3), 349–375.

Zacharchuk, W. and Waddell, P. (1986) "The Excavation of the *Machault*, An Eighteenth Century Frigate," Environment Canada, Parks, Ottawa.

Zedler, J.B. (1996) "Ecological Issues in Wetland Mitigation: An Introduction to the Forum," *Ecological Applications*, 6 (1), February, 33–37.

Zhang, L. (1997) "Neutrality and Efficiency of Petroleum Revenue Tax: A Theoretical Assessment," *The Economic Journal*, 107 (443), 1106–1120.

Zielger, D. (2007) "Smile Diplomacy: Working Magic along China's Periphery," in "Reaching for a Renaissance," *The Economist*, Special Report, March 31st.

INDEX